Praise for *Brazil's Dance with the Devil*

"People think speaking truth to power is easy, but if it was easy everyone would do it. This book does it. . . . It speaks truth to the powers that be, from Brazil to the US to FIFA to the IOC. It hits you like an uppercut that rattles your brain and sets it straight. I cannot recommend this book highly enough."

—John Carlos, 1968 Olympic medalist

"Dave Zirin has long stood on the edge of the sports writing world, exploding topics many of his colleagues are scared to approach. With *Brazil's Dance with the Devil*, he puts to bed any notion that the IOC and FIFA have the best interests of their host countries at heart. Brazil is a special country and Dave Zirin honors its people and history while mercilessly going after those who would undermine its people. This book is a remarkable mix of investigative sports journalism and insightful social history."

—Glenn Greenwald, author of *No Place to Hide*

"In a sports journalism landscape where it sometimes seems there are only those who fawn and those who pander, where curiosity about the world at large is in short supply, Zirin is an altogether different kind of presence. He does care, until it hurts, and consistently delivers unique takes on the nexus of sports and race, globalization, politics, and human rights. In *Brazil's Dance with the Devil*, Zirin's at his best, on familiar and fertile ground. Like so much of his work, it's incisive, heartbreaking, important, and even funny."

—Jeremy Schaap, ESPN, author of *New York Times* bestseller *Cinderella Man*

"For years, FIFA and the Brazilian government have failed to understand the complexity of the Brazilian populace, that it's possible both to love soccer and to be outraged over the organization of the World Cup at the expense of the people. Dave Zirin, one of our great chroniclers of sports and society, spent time on the ground in Brazil interviewing those most affected by the Brazilian World Cup and Olympics, and he comes away with the truth of it all: that the brutal expense of these mega-events isn't worth the investment of so much public money and historical memory. Everyone who watches the World Cup should read this book."

—Grant Wahl, senior writer, *Sports Illustrated*

"A vision from abroad about our Brazil from inside. It's a vision at once critical, smart, truthful, and free of prejudices, and does not spare any criticisms of his own country, the United States. Additionally, it's a generous vision that uplifts the great Brazilian people. Enthusiastically recommended!"

—Juca Kfouri, columnist, *UOL Esporte*, Brazil

"Dave Zirin offers a great, fast-paced primer for those who want to get up to speed with what is happening on the ground in Brazil as it prepares for the World Cup and Olympics. Zirin brings the reader through years of history in order to contextualize the tumult on the streets during the 2013 Confederations Cup and offers perspective on what the world can expect during the World Cup and Olympics. *Brazil's Dance with the Devil* gives insight into the linkages between corruption, massive public spending, and the folly of mega-event planning in a country with huge wealth inequalities and major infrastructure challenges. Zirin has done his homework and fieldwork, consulting the classics and experts to bring together a fast-paced, focused read for an international audience."

—Juliana Barbassa, former Rio de Janeiro correspondent, Associated Press

"Dave Zirin fans, of which I count myself as one, will relish his new book, *Brazil's Dance with the Devil*. With his unique sports-politics lens and artful storytelling, this book focuses on Rio's upcoming World Cup and Olympics. Readers will never again allow their love of sports to blind them to the repurposed political ends of big international sporting events."

—Nancy Hogshead-Makar, civil rights attorney, senior director of advocacy at Women's Sports Foundation, and Olympic gold medalist

"Dave Zirin does it again. In the way only he knows, he takes the political and makes it extremely personal and inserts us all into the heart of soccer in Brazil. You don't have to have ever watched a soccer match to be caught up in this epic story. Sports needs Dave Zirin more than it even knows—although after this book he probably won't be invited to carry the Olympic torch anytime soon."

—W. Kamau Bell, comedian

"Like everything Dave Zirin writes, this book is impassioned, deeply informed, and very readable. It's also a necessary book, because Brazil is a poorly understood country entering a crucial period. Zirin backs up his opinions with good, honest reporting. Brazil has a good friend in him."

—Simon Kuper, author of *Soccernomics*

Brazil's Dance with the Devil

The World Cup, the Olympics,
and the Fight for Democracy

By Dave Zirin

Haymarket Books
Chicago, Illinois

© 2014 Dave Zirin

First published in 2014 by
Haymarket Books
P.O. Box 180165
Chicago, IL 60618
773-583-7884
www.haymarketbooks.org
info@haymarketbooks.org

ISBN: 978-1-60846-360-2

Trade distribution:
In the US, Consortium Book Sales and Distribution, www.cbsd.com
In Canada, Publishers Group Canada, www.pgcbooks.ca
In the UK, Turnaround Publisher Services, www.turnaround-uk.com
In Australia, Palgrave Macmillan, www.palgravemacmillan.com.au
All other countries, Publishers Group Worldwide, www.pgw.com

Cover design by Ragina Johnson. Cover photo of graffiti depicting
Brazilian soccer player Ronaldinho in Vila Autódromo slum in
Rio de Janeiro by Ricardo Moraes, Reuters.

This book was published with the generous support of Lannan Foundation
and Wallace Action Fund.

Printed in Canada by union labor.

Library of Congress Cataloging-in-Publication data is available.

1 3 5 7 9 10 8 6 4 2

Table of Contents

To Michele, Sasha, and Jacob. You are all changemakers.
And to the people of Brazil fighting for their future.

"Victory is secondary. What matters is joy."
—Sócrates, Captain, 1982 Brazilian World Cup team

Acknowledgments

There is no way I would have been able to write this book without my research partner, Zach Zill. Zach traveled with me all the way to Rio and stuck with me back in the States even when I was ready to bury my laptop somewhere in my skull. He will write books, I hope soon, that will tear down walls.

This book could also never have gone to press without my editor Sarah Grey. She is the Pelé of book editing, or maybe Pelé is the Sarah Grey of soccer players.

Also this book could not have happened without the incredible support of the people at Haymarket Books. I wish every single aspiring writer had the privilege to write for a press that is as supportive, creative, and dynamic as Haymarket. Thank you, Rachel Cohen, Eric Kerl, Đào X. Trần, Jason Farbman, Julie Fain, Jim Plank, Rory Fanning, John McDonald, Jon Kurinsky, Bill Roberts, Ahmed Shawki, and Anthony Arnove at Haymarket Books, and the whole team at Consortium Book Sales and Distribution. And, in particular, thank you to Rory Fanning, who has believed in this book even in advance of actually reading it.

Thank you, especially, to everyone at the *Nation* magazine for their unflinching support as I shirked my duties as sports editor to travel, report, and write this text. Also big thanks to everyone at the *Progressive*, *SLAM* magazine, and Sirius XM Radio, especially Dan Baker, Mark Barry, and the Coach, Kevin McNutt, for their patience. Thank you to the people at the New Press as well. My book *Game Over*, published by the New Press, also includes some of my eyewitness reporting from past World Cups and Olympics and I am grateful to be able to use that same work in this text. Thank you especially to the late André Schiffrin, who founded the New Press and who passed away in December of 2013.

Thank you to Emily White and Keri Smith Esguia at Whitesmith Entertainment—and W. Kamau Bell for the introduction—for believing in this kind of work!

I also could not have written this without the assistance of the people in Brazil who showed me around and showed me the way. Thank you to Theresa Williamson, Catherine Osborn, and everybody at Catalytic Communities. Thank you, Christopher Gaffney. Thank you, Professor Marcos Alvito, for being the most quotable interview in the history of interviews. And thank you, Kay Alvito, for being such a wonderful host. My next-to-last thank-you goes, without question, to all the people in Brazil who showed me such incredible kindness. To every person who stopped to speak with me during an extremely tumultuous time in your country, thank you so much. This book is, of course, dedicated to you and your struggle for social and economic justice. I am so grateful that I was able to see and learn for myself that your country is so much more than a brand for export. You possess an invaluable tradition, culture, and history worth treasuring and worth fighting for.

Lastly, thank you to Michele, Sasha, and Jacob. Love you.

List of Abbreviations

AMPAVA	Association of Residents, Fishermen, and Friends of Vila Autódromo
ANC	African National Congress
AOC	American Olympic Committee
CBF	Brazilian Football Confederation
CUT	United Workers' Federation (Central Única dos Trabalhadores)
FIFA	Fédération Internationale de Football Association
FTAA	Free Trade Agreement of the Americas
GDP	Gross domestic product
ICC	Indigenous Cultural Center
IMF	International Monetary Fund
IOC	International Olympic Committee
LGBTQ	Lesbian, gay, bisexual, transgender, and queer
MST	Landless Workers' Movement (Movimento dos Trabalhadores Rurais Sem Terra)
PSOL	Socialism and Freedom Party (Partido Socialismo e Liberdade)
PT	Workers' Party (Partido dos Trabalhadores)
SUDERJ	Superintendent of Sports of the State of Rio de Janeiro (Superintendência de Desportos do Estado do Rio de Janeiro)
UN	United Nations

Finding Michael Jackson in Rio

Tell me what has become of my rights
Am I invisible because you ignore me?
All I wanna say is that
They don't really care about us

—Michael Jackson

On my first day in Rio de Janeiro, my research assistant Zachary Zill and I were jet-lagged out of our minds and had no clue what to do, so we decided to look for Michael Jackson. Not the man himself, who had passed away the previous year, but a statue of him that we had heard was located high up in Santa Marta, one of the famed *favelas*, or informal working-class communities, that are rooted throughout the city. Finding this particular Michael Jackson statue seemed worth the effort. In March 1995, the King of Pop released his ninth studio album, *HIStory: Past, Present, and Future, Book I.* It is remembered today mostly for the song "Scream," which brought Michael and his sister Janet together, or the queasy video for "You Are Not Alone," a song penned by R. Kelly, in which Michael disrobed with Lisa Marie Presley for a series of uncomfortable cuddles. Lost in the collective memory is *HIStory*'s searing protest song, "They Don't Care about Us." It has a stark immediacy as Jackson sings in a sharp staccato voice about protest, prisons, and state-sanctioned violence with a global vision and awareness. In Jackson's own words, it was "a public awareness song . . . a protest kind of song."[1]

What does this have to do with Rio? In 1996, Jackson, along with the video's director, Spike Lee, wanted to film in Santa Marta, a favela or "slum." This caused agitation in Brazil's corridors of power for multiple reasons. There was fear that by highlighting the favelas, Jackson would spread an image of Rio defined by crime and poverty. Then there was the even greater fear that, short of a military occupation, there would be no conceivable way to guarantee the safety of Jackson, Lee, and their crew in Santa Marta. In other words, government officials did not want the city to look unsafe, but they also didn't want people to "get the right idea" (so to speak) about its actual conditions.

It is true that at the time, by almost every metric, Rio was one of the least safe cities on earth. Brazil's government was also desperate to project Rio as a global megacity suitable for hosting high-profile international events. For decades, instead of fighting the poverty and inequality that give rise to crime, Rio cracked down on the urban poor using elite police squads. The primary contact residents of the city's favelas had with public authorities was by way of the police, particularly through violent police incursions where innocents were routinely killed and tortured and lives were constantly interrupted by stray bullets, shutting down schools and rendering homes unsellable. This led to the third anxiety related to Michael Jackson's visit: that his very presence would shed light on this "cleaning out" of the favelas, ironically—or perhaps intentionally—one of the themes of the song.

In 1996, Rio was making a serious bid to host the 2004 Olympics. Local authorities saw Michael Jackson's presence as the turd in the proverbial punchbowl. The Brazilian state leapt into action: a judge issued an injunction to stop the filming. Soccer star Pelé, then minister of sports, even weighed in, saying that the video shoot should not go ahead as planned. International news footage of Jackson wearing a surgical mask (because of his anxiety over a conjunctivitis outbreak in Rio) did not exactly help ease concerns about his effect on the city's image.[2] While the government tried to move every lever to keep Jackson from filming, residents of Santa Marta had the opposite reaction. They welcomed Jackson both for his stardom and for the possibility of improving their lives through the publicity his video would generate. As one woman quoted in the *New York Times* said, "They're ashamed of the conditions here, and they'll have to do something."[3] A Santa Marta samba instructor described the favela as "a poor world surrounded by a rich world, an island of misery surrounded by wealth."[4]

Jackson and Lee did film their video and, for all of the drama, Santa Marta is on screen for just a few fleeting moments, with Jackson scampering up the steep and narrow favela steps as if he is fleeing from an attacker. But it does not look like an exposé of the poverty in Santa Marta. In the context of the video, it appears more as if Jackson is fleeing to safety and searching for refuge amid the favela's poverty and community, and away from the injustice and "fame monsters" attempting to swallow him and his sanity whole. It is favela as oasis from the jarring indignities of his utterly unreal reality. In 1996, that would have been quite the unusual take; one would not have been wrong to accusé Jackson of romanticizing the poverty of a favela that no one would confuse with Neverland Ranch. Today it feels more like prophecy. Today developers are indeed chasing people up the favela steps in Rio's elite Zona Sul (South Zone) in an effort to get their hands on what has become incalculably valuable real estate. Today the favelas are for many an escape from a city and a country where public space is dwindling, people are getting removed from their homes, and the poor are being marginalized in an effort to turn Rio into the megacity of the International Monetary Fund's (IMF's) dreams.

We will get to all of this, but back to the King of Pop. Zach and I wanted to see the statue commemorating the moment when Michael Jackson and Spike Lee negotiated with both the Brazilian state and the local drug kingpins and ventured into the favela. We took the bus to Santa Marta in the neighborhood of Botafogo in the Zona Sul, just north of Copacabana and just east of the famous hundred-foot statue of Christ the Redeemer, and arrived at Santa Marta, home of thousands of residents—population estimates vary, anywhere from eight to thirty-five thousand—whose houses cling to one of the steepest hillsides in the city.

Back in 1996, Michael Jackson had to helicopter in to get to the top of the hillside. Now Santa Marta has a funicular tram. Then Santa Marta felt hidden behind a dark curtain. Now it is on official tourist maps of the city. In fact, there is a tourist checkpoint at the bottom of the hillside along Rua São Clemente, complete with multilingual guides who hand out maps of the favela and offer tips to visitors. The guides were, granted, lonely; there did not appear to be a rush of people clamoring to see the favela up close. Their brochures welcome people to the "Rio Top Tour" (in English) and promise to point out "historic community landmarks."

We ventured up ourselves, since neither of us knew where the Michael Jackson statue was. At first we decided to walk up the steep hill, testing my lung capacity. (Zach is a soccer player and his ability to walk quickly without losing his breath soon filled me with murderous thoughts.) I made the case that we should wait for the tram, to "have the experience." The wait was long; we were behind a group of young men carrying massive speakers that eventually filled half the tram by themselves. Most of the other half of the tram was filled by cases of beer. No one waiting seemed particularly put out by this. It was Saturday night and all of this was for a huge outdoor party that evening on the hilltop.

Two men in delivery uniforms were waiting alongside us with a mammoth mattress and matching box spring. There was also a group of moms with small children and grocery bags. Once we made it onto the tram, I argued that we should go to the top for the view and then find the Michael Jackson statue by traversing downhill. (Again: it was *steep*.) Maybe my motives were cardiovascular, but no one would have argued with the results. We walked out to an astounding view of one of the most beautiful cities on earth. The panorama unfolded in front of us: brown granite hills jutting up dramatically from gentle green slopes, a thick urban patchwork of roads and buildings, the shimmering water of the Lagoa Rodrigo de Freitas, and then the ocean just beyond.

Kids were throwing paper planes off the hillside and chasing after them as they floated gently down. Music echoed off the squat little houses, cobbled together at odd angles. Neighbors shouted to each other across a passageway. Of course there was a dusty soccer pitch at the top of the hill, just beyond the small plaza where the tram ended. Looming over the pitch was a new-looking building painted bright blue and emblazoned with the abbreviation UPP. We were to learn a great deal about the UPP, the "Pacifying Police Unit" making the favelas safe for tourists and real-estate speculators alike, in the days ahead. The UPP building was perhaps the largest in the community; its roof was festooned with high-tech surveillance and satellite equipment.

Just to the left of UPP headquarters, we had a clear view of the highest grouping of houses on the hillside, roughly fifty yards away from our perch. Massive painted protest slogans were grouped in front of them, almost certainly visible for miles. The signs read "SOS" and then, in Portuguese, "What kind of 'model favela' is this?" "Peace without a voice isn't peace, it's fear," and "Don't erase our history." We thought that the signs were protesting the UPP and the evictions and demolitions leading up to the World Cup and Olympics. We learned later that these very homes, which had stood for more than fifty years without falling, had been slated for removal on the pretext of "landslides." There was a rumor (accepted as common sense) that the real reason these homes would be destroyed was that a Brazilian billionaire wanted to build a private estate.

We ogled the view for a few more minutes and then decided to descend the hillside in an attempt to find what our map called "Michael Jackson Square." Our tourist map, however, was utterly incapable of guiding us through the narrow passageways and staircases jutting at seemingly impossible angles between, across, and through the squat houses. The compactness of the space in the favela was an incredible experience in itself, at least for Americans unaccustomed to this type of urban environment. It was a vast assemblage of humanity. We passed a cafe selling soda, beer, and grilled meats. We saw young boys playing an arcade game, a young family sitting around a grill, a door that opened directly onto a tiny, cramped bedroom. The smells of open sewage and of delicious cooking food intermingled. As we walked past a large boulder with two tiny kittens huddling on top of it, a rat that looked like the kittens' big brother waddled by. It was the first favela we visited. It would not be the last.

Finally, after asking directions from many bemused people sitting outside their homes, we arrived at Michael Jackson Square, a small plaza built into the hillside with another incredible view. To the left was a wall with a large mosaic depicting Jackson; just beyond the wall, on a small patch of concrete jutting out over the hillside, was the statue of the King of Pop. It was . . . small. Maybe five feet tall. Jackson was smiling, sunglasses resting on his surgically pointed nose, with none of the rage he showed in the video.

As metaphors go, this is good as any. Rio is being sanitized. To a New York City boy who does not recognize the place where he was raised, the signs felt all too familiar. Not even Michael Jackson's rage is permitted for public consumption. He smiles, his hand reaching out over a view of the entire city, almost as if he is saying, "The world is yours." But wipe that happy smile off his face and he could also be saying, just as clearly, "They don't care about us."

Brazil Is Not for Beginners

Of course I needed to write a book about Brazil. In fact, according to family, friends, and colleagues, it would be irrational if I *didn't* write a book about Brazil. I had done investigative journalism in Vancouver before the 2010 Winter Olympic Games, in South Africa before the 2010 World Cup, and in London before the 2012 Olympics. I had also written extensively on the Greek Olympics in 2004, China's 2008 Beijing Games, and Vladimir Putin's Sochi Winter Games in 2014. With the news that Brazil would host not only the 2014 World Cup but also the 2016 Olympics, the first country in the twenty-first century to attempt the daunting "twofer," this story seemed to demand a deeper level of analysis and examination. A country world-renowned for its ability to throw a party would be host to two of the most raucous global celebrations in existence. When you factor in the incredible role of soccer in Brazil's history and the drama that normally surrounds the funding and staging of these events, it just seemed like just too good a story to miss.

Brazil's economy, I knew, had grown dramatically over the last decade, barely slowing a whit with the Great Recession of 2008. I also knew that the demands of the World Cup and the Olympics—the massive increase in security funding, the displacement and eviction of the city's poorest residents, and the explosion of costs—would be a recipe for tensions and conflicts that would be difficult to keep under wraps. And I was fascinated by how the staging of the World Cup, in a dozen cities across the country, would differ from that of the Olympics, entirely situated in Rio. I wondered how the various construction projects and pressures would complement and complicate each other. I assumed that in Rio the World Cup would set the stage for the Olympics, with soccer-loving Brazil saying nary a word about the Cup; I reasoned that protests, if any, would be laser-focused around the Olympic Games. Factor in Brazil's unique political, economic, and social history and bada-bing: I would have myself a book.

It all seemed so very straightforward. But then I told my plan to Marcos Alvito, a professor and lecturer with expertise in both sports and the country's labyrinthine history. He looked at me for a long time and said, not without kindness, "Brazil is not for beginners." His words were meant to temper my ambitions. They were also an act of mercy. There are people who spend their entire lives studying and attempting to comprehend this remarkably complex country and still come up lacking a full understanding of what they see. It is a country whose very vastness is not only about geography but also a history that defies easy understanding. If Brazil were a movie, it would be the Coen brothers' *Miller's Crossing*: you have to see it and experience it repeatedly, and every time you look you notice something that affects what you thought you understood.

Understanding Brazil is particularly difficult for people from the United States. Brazil is like a funhouse mirror of the United States (or maybe the United States is a funhouse mirror of Brazil—it's all about on which side of the equator you stand). Like the United States, Brazil is a mammoth landmass of incalculable wealth and seemingly inexhaustible resources. Like the United States, its land was developed through the slaughter and displacement of the Indigenous population, followed by the African transatlantic slave trade. But imagine a United States where the fight to decolonize was led by the royal family of the colonizing country. Imagine a United States with huge areas of Indigenous land never brought under centralized control. Imagine a United States more than half of whose population was enslaved. Imagine a United States where, instead of criminalizing "miscegenation" or "race mixing," the state had actively encouraged interracial relationships (albeit using similar pathologies of social Darwinism and white supremacy). Imagine a United States without Jim Crow, where the cultures of the many celebrated in more than just a superficial manner. Imagine a United States without the pall of Puritanism, where, under the watchful eye of a hundred-foot Jesus Christ, a Carnival of masks and sexual fluidity flourishes. Imagine a United States where twelve families own the overwhelming majority of the land. Imagine a United States where a small group of oligarchs makes all of the decisions, ignoring any formal concepts of democracy (all right, maybe that's a little easier to imagine).

No, Brazil is not for beginners. It is a country of two hundred million people on an area larger than the continental United States. It possesses the largest economy in the Global South and the fifth-largest on the planet. It has more people of African descent than any country on earth outside of Nigeria, more people of Japanese descent than anywhere outside of Japan, and more Italians anywhere outside of Italy.[5] It is the friendliest nation you could ever hope to visit—and its police have killed ten thousand people in the last decade.[6] It has a history more complicated than a Russian novel and no less difficult to grasp.

There is no way I can fully explain every nuance of this country. It is simply not knowledge I possess. What I *can* do is demonstrate why the World Cup and Olympics come at an extremely perilous time for Brazil, a time when every nerve is exposed. I can talk about the way the needs of the World Cup and Olympics reveal like nothing else the profoundly different interests of different sectors of Brazilian society. I can show how the twenty-first-century, post–9/11 demands of the Fédération Internationale de Football Association (FIFA) and the International Olympic Committee (IOC), the governing bodies of the World Cup and the Olympic Games, have exacerbated all of these concerns. I can also attempt to show just how the World Cup and Olympics can bring a country together only to tear it apart.

To get this done, I start by writing about some of what is happening right now in Brazil, with an emphasis on Rio de Janeiro. Then in chapter 2 I sketch a very basic history of Brazil, which I believe is an absolutely essential prerequisite for understanding everything that is roiling the nation right now—in particular the existential fear that the current moment is yet another tenuous boom for Anglo-European consumption of Brazil's exports, soon to be followed by a bust that breaks the nation's back.

Chapter 3 explains just what is happening to Brazil's current "economic miracle" under the leadership of the Workers' Party (Partido dos Trabalhadores, or PT), with an emphasis on whom Brazil's recent economic growth has benefited and who is being left behind. Chapter 4 discusses the central role of soccer (or *futebol*) in Brazil's history and culture, as well as the roles of some of its key figures. Chapter 5 looks at the history of the Olympics, while chapter 6 focuses on recent sports mega-events, including both Olympic and World Cup events, and their effects on host countries to make clear why the World Cup, the Olympics, and twenty-first-century Brazil are such a combustible mix. In chapter 7 we'll look at the displacements and evictions I witnessed in Brazil, as well as some of the stories I had the privilege to hear about how the poorest residents of one of the most economically unequal countries on the planet have fought back. These struggles laid the groundwork for what in 2013 became the largest protests the country had seen in decades, coinciding with its hosting the Confederations Cup soccer tournament.

The sight of millions of Brazilians in the streets, marching on a soccer stadium, was enough to give President Dilma Rousseff and the powers that be at FIFA and the IOC night sweats. These protests also had the support of 75 percent of the Brazilian population.[7] This book looks at what exactly sparked that anger and made those protests so historic. If *Brazil's Dance with the Devil* can spark a discussion that challenges the conventional wisdom that hosting these kinds of sporting mega-events is something to which countries should aspire, then the flights, the interviews, and the patience and understanding of my family will not have been in vain.

One thing is certain. My respect for the people I met in Brazil—the fighters for social justice, the community organizers, the residents trying to save their homes—is infinite. No, Brazil is not for beginners. But we all have to start somewhere—and attempting to understand Brazil is critical for understanding what is happening in cities across the world.

CHAPTER 1

Brazil: "A Country for Everyone"

The City [of Rio] makes the poor even poorer, cruelly confronting them with mirages of wealth to which they will never have access—cars, mansions, machines as powerful as God or the Devil—while denying them secure jobs, decent roofs over their heads, full plates on the midday table.

—Eduardo Galeano[1]

In September 2012, I walked through one of the most destitute favelas in Rio. For all its poverty, there was also a sense of community one would be hard-pressed to find elsewhere in the wealthier communities of Brazil—or the United States, for that matter. This particular favela was situated on a hill in one of the city's most upscale areas. The close proximity of these contrasting communities had a dizzying effect when I exited the favela. It was as though I was stepping through a portal from one world into another. Around the corner was a Starbucks with an armed guard out front, so the wealthy of Rio could get their lattes in peace. He had a hundred-yard death stare for anyone who paused to look longingly through the lightly frosted glass. In just yards, I had gone from open doors and hillside soccer games to bullets and baristas.

Walking to the Metrô, I passed yet another of Rio's seemingly endless construction projects. I have been living in gentrifying cities for most of my life, so massive, dirty, congested landscapes are nothing new. What is different about Brazil is that the construction operations are usually branded with slogans that speak to a kind of "we're all in this together" national unity. This one had a banner that read, "Brasil: Um Pais de Todos" (a country for everyone). It's like Orwell for gentrifiers.

This particular mass of rubble was one of the many development projects in motion to get Rio ready for the 2014 World Cup and the 2016 Olympics. It cannot be overstated just how invested Brazil's elite are in seeing these games come off without a hitch. Hosting mega-events is about projecting a message that reaches far beyond the sports pages. Larry Rohter proclaimed, in his book *Brazil on the Rise*, that the country "conceives of the two coming events as a sort of giant coming-out celebration announcing Brazil's arrival as a player, not just in athletic competition but also on the global stage."[2]

When Brazil won its bid to host the 2016 Olympics, the country was heralded as a capitalist success story, with the *Financial Times*, the *Wall Street Journal*, and other organs of the 1 percent engorged over a nation whose stock market, Bovespa, had grown at a rate of 523 percent over the previous decade. My favorite example of this neoliberal ardor was the *Economist*'s cover article "Brazil Takes Off," illustrated with an image of Rio's iconic Christ the Redeemer statue zooming into space like a rocket.[3] Brazil, the article informed us, was once a country with "a growth rate as skimpy as its swimsuits, prey to any financial crisis that was around, a place of chronic political instability, whose infinite capacity to squander its obvious potential was as legendary as its talent for football and carnivals," but which was now "on a roll."[4] For so many in Brazil, this was long overdue. Hosting these sporting events was about international recognition that Brazil's day had come.

Georges Clémenceau, France's prime minister during the last years of the First World War, was once famously quoted as saying, "Brazil is a country of the future, and always will be."[5] For Brazil's wildly popular outgoing president, Luiz Inácio Lula da Silva, and the fifty thousand *cariocas* (the nickname for Rio's denizens) who jammed together and cheered as the decision was announced, the chance to host the

Olympics was about putting Clémenceau's infamous maxim to rest once and for all. Lula, as he is known, was in tears upon learning the news and spoke for many when he said, in a choked voice,

> Today I have felt prouder of being a Brazilian than on any other day. Today is the day that Brazil gained its international citizenship. Today is the day that we have overcome the last vestiges of prejudice against us. I think this is the day to celebrate because Brazil has left behind the level of second-class countries and entered the ranks of first-class countries. Today we earned respect. The world has finally recognized that this is Brazil's time.[6]

Lula himself had completed an utterly improbable journey: from working-class labor leader during a time of military dictatorship to the heights of political power. He ran for president four times before winning, and some joked his gravestone would someday read, "Here lies Lula, the future president of Brazil." But Lula made it to the presidency and impressed the IOC enough to win the right to host the Games. With national soccer icon Pelé at his side, Lula had presented Brazil's case and faced down the ghost of Clémenceau, not to mention some heavy hitters from Chicago: newly minted US president Barack Obama, first lady Michelle Obama, and, even more impressively, Oprah.

Yet those heady days in Copenhagen and among the throngs of Rio now seem like several lifetimes ago. Lula is no longer president; after serving out his terms he was diagnosed with throat cancer (now in remission) and stepped back from the spotlight. Brazil, whose 7.5-percent growth rate—even in the wake of the 2008 Great Recession—had made the *Economist* swoon, saw its economy sputter in 2012 toward a growth rate of just 0.9 percent.[7] Despite the near-absence of economic expansion, spending on stadiums and infrastructure projects intended for the 2016 Olympics in Rio and for the 2014 World Cup in twelve cities across the nation has not skipped a beat. The facts on the ground in Brazil have changed, yet, ravenous and remorseless, the World Cup and Olympic golems continue to feed. Projections for how much they will cost the country keep ticking upward at a taxi-meter pace. It is difficult even to keep up with the parade of stories of dissatisfaction, waste, protest, and tumult that appeared almost daily as this book was going to press. They express what I saw with my own eyes.

Danger: Stampeding White Elephants

When I was in Brazil, I spoke with workers who were deeply concerned about the rush to build twelve new "FIFA-quality" World Cup stadiums. Their concern did not stem only from the fact that this country already has no shortage of well-equipped fields. They were also concerned about the round-the-clock hours, the exhaustion of those operating heavy machinery, and the unsafe working conditions. Then, in November 2013, a crane collapsed into Arena Corinthians (Corinthians Stadium) in São Paulo,[8] sending an avalanche of newly cemented concrete to the earth below. This tragedy, which took the lives of two men, Fabio Luiz Pereira and Ronaldo Oliveira dos Santos, could have been far worse. One of their coworkers, José Mario da Silva, said, "I walked right underneath the crane on the way to lunch. If it hadn't collapsed at lunchtime, a lot more people would have died."

A reporter who happened to be present as the crane was collapsing snapped pictures with his cell phone. The instinctual response from an engineer for Odebrecht, the powerful Brazilian construction company in charge of rebuilding the stadium, as well as from several stadium security workers, was to assault the reporter and delete the photos from his phone.[9] Yet they could not keep the story quiet; in short order it was international news. Sepp Blatter, the reptilian chief of FIFA, said that he was "deeply saddened" by the deaths, and FIFA issued its own statement that the "safety of workers is a top priority." It is worth noting that Blatter voiced these comments just as FIFA faced international scrutiny about revelations of slave labor and multiple deaths during stadium constructions in Qatar, where the 2022 World Cup will take place.[10] Weeks after the accident, we also learned that the crane operator had been working for eighteen straight days, just another cog in Brazil's 24/7 sprint to complete stadium construction. Brazil's sports minister, Aldo Rebelo, said nothing after the tragedy about confronting fatigue or labor abuses on work sites. Instead, he assured the media that "the stadiums shall be built on time." As for the dead, Rebelo sent a tweet expressing "solidarity with the families of the victims."[11]

The only true solidarity that the government has shown, however, has been with FIFA—to get the stadiums done, no matter the cost. As Romário, star of the 1994 World Cup, put it:

> FIFA got what it came for: money. Things like transportation that affect the public after the tournament is over? They don't care. They don't care about what is going to be left behind. . . . You see hospitals with no beds. You see hospitals with people on the floor. You see schools that don't have lunch for the kids. You see schools with no air-conditioning. . . . You see buildings and schools with no accessibility for people who are handicapped. If you spend 30 percent less on the stadiums, they'd be able to improve the other things that actually matter. . . . They found a way to get rich on the World Cup and they robbed the people instead. This is the real shame.[12]

What took place at Arena Corinthians was not an isolated incident. In April 2013, a worker was killed doing upgrades at Arena Palmeiras in São Paulo. At Arena do Grêmio in Porto Alegre, eight fans were sent to the emergency room when a guardrail collapsed. In Rio, Arena Engenhão, which will be used for both the World Cup and the Olympics, "had to be closed for repairs six years after it opened due to reports showing winds of 63mph could rip off a roof that is already suffering from corrosion."[13] In Salvador, right by the location of last December's World Cup draw, where the groupings of the thirty-two participating national teams were announced, the roof of the brand-new Arena Fonte Nova collapsed. What provided the almighty structural pressure that caused it to fall? Rain.[14]

Judges have tried to halt the opening of stadiums deemed unsafe in several cities. Yet even the judiciary has been unable to slow down the FIFA-ordered sprint to the World Cup. After one judge attempted to stop a "friendly match" between Brazil and England because of unsafe conditions at a new "FIFA-quality" stadium, it went ahead as planned, despite areas "with scaffolding, cables and bolts jutting out from concrete."[15] In Curitiba, a conservative city in the south, a judge stopped the building process at Arena da Baixada because "countless infractions" put workers at risk of "being buried, run over and of collision, falling from heights and being hit by construction material." The judge was overruled and construction began again.[16]

The need for compliant, cheap labor has led to even more embarrassing tales making it onto the international wires. There are stories about the use of slave and prison labor to make sure that the stadiums get built on time. In 2012 and 2013, according to the Associated Press, several thousand prisoners across the country were working to help construct several of the twelve new World Cup stadiums.[17] The greatest embarrassment of all is that it is the ruling PT, a political party founded out of trade-union struggles and the popular resistance to Brazil's dictatorship, that has overseen these appalling labor conditions.

Yet even though it is "their party" making these demands, workers have taken no small amount of industrial action and the speedups have led to strikes and walkouts at almost every stadium. I arrived in Brazil not long after a four-month university strike against the government. Frayed banners with strike slogans could still be seen from university windows. As one university employee said to me, "At least half a dozen stadiums have had work stoppages. The Workers' Party government is now very against syndicalist movements and works actively to take apart unions. Which is an incredible irony. Just an incredible historical irony."

Priorities

The stories emerging out of Brazil also speak to the irony and the oddity of building stadiums in cities where there are other, far more pressing needs. Multiple media outlets have been reporting from Natal, a city of one million people in the north, where dissatisfaction with the cost and waste of a new stadium has locals up in arms. One customs official told a reporter that the new stadium is "like a spacecraft [that] has crash-landed in the middle of our town."[18] Natal is yet another place where a perfectly good playing field was bulldozed to build a new one that would be up to "FIFA standards." Jan-Marten Hoitsma, a project manager brought in to make sure Natal's stadium gets finished on time and under budget, explained, "There are no big football teams here—the biggest team gets gates of around 5,000 and we're building a 42,000-seater World Cup stadium."[19] In a city with immediate health care and education imperatives, where the absence of hospital beds, overcrowded classrooms, and high rates of illiteracy are a fact of life, the effort and attention devoted to the new stadium strike many residents as obscene. Graffiti around Natal, which urgently needs forty thousand housing units, reads, "We want 'FIFA standard' hospitals and schools." Outside the stadium's entrance someone has scrawled, "We want 'FIFA standard' work."[20]

These are the continuing echoes from the summer of 2013, when thirty thousand people took to Natal's streets—one link in a national chain of protest that brought millions into the streets. Regional economic secretary Rogerio Marinho said, "When the World Cup came to Natal, we felt as if we'd won a huge prize. The federal government had a specific plan for every city. We were going to get better streets, better public transport, all sorts of benefits. Most of those projects will not be ready in time."[21] Since the economic promises will not be met, Hoitsma has tried a different route: attempting to enlist the poor youth of Natal to train as "World Cup stewards" in order to "win over the community." One thing the government is *not* doing to "win over the community" is paying the 1,900 construction workers a living wage. Most are working for the minimum wage and have undertaken wildcat strike action in protest.[22]

Then there are the airports. Brazil's government sold two of the country's main airports to private consortiums in November 2013 to bring down its World Cup and Olympic budget deficits. At a cost of nine billion dollars, they will now be owned by a Singaporean company called Changi and, of course, Odebrecht—the same Odebrecht whose staff members assaulted a reporter for daring to record the collapse at Arena Corinthians.[23] As one environmentalist said to me, "If you think about the twelve World Cup cities and how they're going to be stitched together, there's no rail project whatsoever. Because there is no Brazilian rail system and no passenger trains, it is all going to be done with the airlines . . . so that the highest percentage of investment in transportation is air, and only the wealthy can really afford it."

Protests are also now a regular feature as FIFA officials visit the country in the lead-up to the World Cup. Not even being accompanied by Brazilian soccer stars Ronaldo and Bebeto could shield FIFA secretary general Jérôme Valcke and other officials from being picketed when they arrived at the Arena Pantanal construction site in Cuiabá. A large group of teachers arrived with handmade banners reading "FIFA go home" and "Less World Cup, more health and education." Their demonstration, although small, garnered international media play—partially because every crisis related to the World Cup will inspire attention, but also because the previous day police had attacked mass protests for higher wages in Rio. Teachers were among those tear-gassed and beaten.

Clearly the old ways are not going to cut it in Brazil. For every story of waste, corruption, and workplace accidents, there are even more stories of home evictions and new security protocols that would make Dick Cheney blush. I saw much of this with my own eyes. It paints a collective picture of a country that is attempting to use the World Cup and Olympics to both present itself externally to the world as a grand new power of the twenty-first century and continue internally a process of state-directed neoliberalism that puts profiteering ahead of human needs.

As Marcelo Freixo, Rio's radical mayoral candidate (more on him later), said to me,

> The truth is that the preparations are attending to the interests of big corporations and not of society. We had the experience of the Pan American Games in 2007 where no benefits were brought to the city. We have currently a city with enormous investments, but also enormous social aggravators. The federal ministry of health recently released a study showing that Rio has the worst public health system on offer in all of Brazil. Additionally, we have precarious and very expensive public transport. We also have a very low-quality education system—one of the worst. So it's a city with enormous investments taking place, but one that can't guarantee a minimum standard of living for its citizens.

All of this is happening, without so much stopping for a breath, in the aftermath of the largest series of protests Brazil has seen in thirty years. It is also happening with the partnership and encouragement of President Dilma Rousseff and her ruling Workers' Party. They still push ahead, with FIFA deadlines as the lodestar of their actions. They still see it as Lula did five years ago when he said, of the Olympics, "It's an opportunity like we've never had before to show the world what we are capable of, strengthen our self-esteem, and achieve new advances."[24] No one in power is adapting to the new economic reality, in which growth has slowed dramatically. No one is echoing the words of Romário, who said, "There's no good schools, there's no good hospitals—how can there be a World Cup?"[25] There is no recognition that prioritizing the games above all else has rendered every new "white elephant" World Cup stadium a potent symbol of just how much people feel they are being left behind.

Dilma and the Workers' Party were supposed to be different. Instead they continue the tradition expressed in a longstanding joke:

> When God was creating Brazil, St. Peter was behind him, watching. God said, "I'm going to put beautiful mountains here."
>> Peter said, "Great."
>> "Beautiful beaches," he said.
>> "Great."
>> "A lot of land, producing everything. No desert."
>> Peter said, "Great."
>> God said, "Nice climate, lots of sun. . . What, Peter?"
>> "Lord, with all due respect, I must disagree."
>> "Why, Peter?"
>> "You're giving these guys too much."
>> "Just wait, Peter. Wait to see what kind of government I'm going to put there."

Brazilians are outraged that services like transportation, education, and health care are inefficiently run or woefully underfunded, yet spending for the World Cup alone could reach the fifteen-billion-dollar mark—which would make it more expensive than the previous three World Cups combined.[26] In Rio, the legendary Maracanã Stadium has received a five-hundred-million-dollar facelift, with construction crews working around the clock to make the site of the 1950 World Cup final a twenty-first-century, "FIFA-quality" stadium. The construction companies, which are the largest political donors in the country, want to see this happen by any means necessary. Security firms have been hired to keep unsightly poverty out of view of the coming international audience. This means that new high-rises are going up, new high-tech security systems are being installed, new roads are being paved, and dozens of favelas have been demolished because they were built in areas deemed "high-risk" or "designated for public use." Both of these phrases are extremely misleading. A "high-risk" area can mean anything from gang activity to landslides. Evicting people from spaces "designated for public use" is particularly ironic when you consider that razing a favela will eventually lead to the private development and ownership of highly valued hillside real estate. Author Bryan McCann quotes Paulo Muniz, a resident of Favela Vidigal, about the ways such threats have historically been used as excuses for ethnic cleansing. "They came with that story of risk of landslide," said Muniz. "But if Vidigal was at risk, so were half the favelas in Rio, along with many of the luxurious homes in Gávea [a middle-class residential neighborhood nearby]. When we found out they had plans for development, we knew it was really about profit."[27]

The human cost of designating areas as either "high risk" or "for public use" is starting to leak out into in the international press. Across Brazil, as many as two hundred thousand people are scheduled to be evicted from their homes as a direct result of the World Cup. The displacement toll on Rio, where the intersection of the World Cup and the Olympics will be most disruptive, is already touching off some of the most dynamic organization and acts of resistance the coastal megacity has seen in decades.

Renato Cosentino, a member of the World Cup and Olympics Popular Committee of Rio de Janeiro wrote,

> Today Rio de Janeiro's poorest live in a lawless city. It's as if a card emblazoned with the Olympic logo has given city authorities superpowers to ignore the Federal Constitution, international agree-

ments signed and ratified by Brazil, and the recommendations of the United Nations. The federal government pretends not to see it and the International Olympic Committee hasn't spoken out about the charges of human rights violations caused by the preparations for the Games.... At a time when Rio de Janeiro has a chance to show the world that it can overcome the social inequality that has marked its history, it is instead reinforcing that inequality.[28]

As one street sweeper, using his own job as a handy metaphor, said to me, "What is wealth for them? For them, it's a red carpet, covering up the trash beneath it with a pretty cover. So the rich and the powerful walk on their red carpet, and they're not really looking at what's going on. Critical people need to lift up the carpet to look at what's underneath."

This process is more than immoral: it is actually unconstitutional. Brazil has some of the toughest squatters' rights laws in the world. Anyone who built a house more than five years ago is supposed to be protected, according to both the Brazilian Constitution and local legislation, known as the Organic Municipal Law. If a resident accepts compensation, then, at least in theory, it is supposed to allow them to get comparable housing of at least equal value elsewhere. But that is not what is happening. As one Rio housing activist, João, said to me,

> Money is handed to you and you take it or leave it. People have to live in the favelas because of the proximity to wealth. They need to be close to where their jobs are and they cannot afford transportation. For the wealthy, it's like your Mexican immigrants in the United States: they hate the favelas but they need the individuals in the favelas to do all the work they do not want to do. The time they are serving the rich people, they are good; the time they are living nearby, they are bad and it's the same people.

One of the main focuses of World Cup and Olympics development appears to be creating physical space between the favelas and the wealthy areas. This process is slightly more complicated in Rio, where the favela plans operate on numerous fronts. In tourist zones, there is a full-court press to pacify, sanitize, and Disneyfy the favelas. The goal is to incorporate them into the city, open them up to the formal market, and slowly gentrify them. This process involves evicting the pesky people who have to live in the favelas, the *favelados*, who are being pushed out to the distant edges of the city and beyond. To connect these people to their jobs, a new bus line is being built—and its construction is also displacing people.

"Now we have BRT, Bus Rapid Transit," João said to me. (Yes, its name is in English.) "We don't need to spoil [the wealthy areas] with another favela. It means that rich people can live their lives without acknowledging the slums on the hill. . . . It will be like magic: the favela where one in five of us live disappears, and the people disappear as well."

This accelerated change from third-world city to first-world economy is also fundamentally changing the time-honored ways Brazil does business, known as the "Brazilian cost"—a system involving patronage, bribes, personal connections, and, if you are so inclined, charity and a helping hand. As Larry Rohter wrote, "There is a growing tension between the old highly personal way of doing things and the new, which calls for impartiality."[29] In neoliberal Brazil, the worst part of the Brazilian cost—the cronyism and corruption—remains, while the part that emphasizes the humanity of everyone involved, even at the expense of efficiency and the bottom line, is gone.

As Graça da Guarda, a guide at a local museum, said to me, "Our whole city is going to became just a venue for mega-events and the price we are being asked to pay is the price of evicting people. . . . Even when Brazil was at its most impoverished, when we had the highest poverty rates in the world, there was this thing called a legitimate middle-class existence. Now the mere thought of that is a joke." Not long after we spoke, during the stadium protests of 2013, the so-called "middle classes" hit the streets out of fear for their own survival. Their fears are grounded in the changing world around them. As the *New York Times* noted, Rio's mayor, Eduardo Paes,

> is saying all the right things about combating sprawl, beefing up mass transit, constructing new schools, and pacifying and inte-

grating the favelas, where one in five city residents lives, with the rest of the city. But as months of street protests illustrate, progressive ideals run up against age-old, intractable problems in this city where class difference and corruption are nearly as immovable as the mountains. This is a city divided on itself."[30]

The *Times* is correct that the city "is divided on itself," but it is incorrect to ascribe progressive ideals to Paes and the integration of the favelas. Instead, Paes's model of urban planning has far more in common with the *Times*'s own backyard, New York's Times Square, and former mayor Michael Bloomberg's gentrification mission to build a city that can only be enjoyed as a "luxury good."

This effort to turn Rio into a Bloomberg-esque "luxury good" is seen not only in the spiraling real-estate prices, constant construction, and agita-producing upheaval, but also in the presence of police officers calmly patrolling these areas with body armor and machine guns. The most heavily armed of these watchmen are overseeing a four-billion-dollar redevelopment project surrounding Rio's port. This project aims to take a historic, ethnically mixed neighborhood defined by cobblestone and masonry and turn it into what is being called "Little Manhattan," a commercial real-estate hub anchored by something ominously called the Museum of Tomorrow. It speaks volumes that the Museum of Tomorrow will be lavishly funded, while a museum that aims to examine Brazil's past at that same port operates as a bare-bones operation and a labor of duty and love.

The Museum of the Slaves

The Rio port area has in recent years been a working-class district, home to artists and squatters as well as regular workers. It has twenty-first-century Brooklyn's feel of creative ferment without its odor of ethnic cleansing. Street murals everywhere express discontent about the construction efforts and evictions in the area.

I am there to investigate a small, unassuming building known as the Museum of the Slaves. Once a family home, this museum houses Rio's first and only known slave burial ground. Not too long ago, the owners planned renovations and started digging under the foundation. Just below the surface they found a monstrous number of skeletons. When they contacted the city government, nobody showed any interest in finding out the story behind the bodies buried under their house, so they contacted archeologists at one of Rio's universities. The archeologists determined that these bones were old—and that they belonged to enslaved Africans who had been brought across the Atlantic by force to work in the American colonies. The sheer number of those who died on the Middle Passage or shortly after arriving still holds the power to shock. They were buried here, within walking distance of the port's bustling slave market. At this particular site it is estimated that, over sixty years, one hundred thousand dead Africans were buried. There were so many corpses that the slave runners had to use fire and compression to break them down and make room for more.

Since this site reveals a history that the city government would rather go unremembered, it has declined to take part in its preservation or to invest funds in deeper excavations. It has chosen to ignore this incredible feat of historic and cultural preservation. The family who originally found the bones bought the house next door and opened a modest museum with the help of the university. The museum showcases the history of slavery in Brazil, along with stories of individual Africans who arrived in Rio under bondage.

While the walls are packed with exhibits, the museum centers on the floor: sections of it are made of glass, and you can look down and see piles of broken bones beneath your feet. The mass grave has been maintained as a reminder of a history many want forgotten. Even with the glass, the work of cataloging the bones and attempting to figure out who is underground continues. It is remarkable that this research is being done almost entirely with personal resources. The state, finally—after the museum had been open for a decade—made a single donation, paying for the glass over the dig sites.

A hidden history of violence lies just under the surface of modern Rio. Life is cheap. We've spent the past few hours walking through sites of intense violence and death—the passageway where drug traffickers walked their execution victims to die; the cliffs from which the dead were thrown, the staircase where cops had shootouts with gangs; the slave cemetery where the lifeless bodies of those stolen from their homelands were unceremoniously dumped, crushed, and burned. It is a past that today's urban developers and mega-event funders desperately want to leave in the ground, to build over and push out of sight.

It is a laudable goal to try to create a city in which such violence is a thing of the past. It is hard to imagine that happening, however, through a renewed set of violent dispossessions or by organizing amnesia about the nation's past. But that is the price of the real-estate speculation taking place across the country. "It is sharper in Rio but it is happening everywhere," said Marcos Alvito.

> It's in every city, certainly every World Cup city, it's unbelievable what's going on. Belo Horizonte, same thing. São Paulo, same thing. Cuiabá, in the middle of freaking nowhere . . . hotter than balls, in the winter it's forty degrees [Celsius] there. It is hotter than balls. Real estate is going through the roof! And it's all the same kind of development, closed condominiums. So there's this homogenization of lifestyles that's happening across Brazil.

But nowhere is the symbolism of what Brazil was, compared to what it is becoming, more acute than at soccer's Taj Mahal, the most holy site of Brazil's national obsession: the Maracanã.

The Maracanã and the Death of Crowds

All stadiums have ghosts. Every game, every brawl, every collective howl is a new phantom that adds an imperceptible layer of energy to the structure. That is why an old stadium makes you feel that buzz of anticipation when you enter its gates. That's also why a new stadium, no matter the architect's intention, can feel as sterile and antiseptic as a hospital bathroom. Rio's Maracanã Stadium, otherwise known as the "Sistine Chapel of international football," has hosted some of the most famous matches and concerts in the history of the world. It is also undergoing a "five-hundred-million-dollar face-lift"—but this is less a nip and tuck than full-scale vivisection.

The reinvention of the Maracanã has been happening for fifteen years, but Rio activist and former professional soccer player Chris Gaffney described it to me better as the "killing of a popular space in order to sell Brazil's culture to an international audience." In 1999, the Maracanã had a capacity of roughly 175,000, although total crowds could reach near 200,000 when people jammed themselves into the standing-room-only open seating on the top level. Most famously, a 1963 contest between historic rivals Flamengo and Fluminense drew a record 194,000 people. The energy of that day is discussed in the hushed tones of folklore.

In 2000 the number of seats was reduced to 125,000. In 2005, it was reconfigured to seat only 85,000, at a cost of two hundred million dollars,[31] to get Brazil ready for the Pan American Games. Now, as epicenter of the World Cup Finals and the Olympic Games, it will seat only 75,000 and will also include a shopping center. In an eerily symbolic construction move that mirrors the erasure of the favelas, the upper deck, once the famed low-cost open seating area for ordinary fans, will now be ringed by luxury boxes. An area that once sat thousands will, according to FIFA dictates, be a VIP-only section where modern Caesars can sit above the crowd. Those boxes will, in true US fashion, be sold off to private business interests after the 2016 Games.

Gaffney has researched and written extensively about the history of the stadium. He pointed out to me that "the Maracanã was known for its large crowds, and many people refer to games by the number of people that were there to see them, not necessarily by what happened on the pitch." Yet when soccer fans discuss "what happened on the pitch," they do so with emotion. The Maracanã entered Brazilian lore as a place "born in traumatic circumstances." It was built to host the 1950 World Cup—a massive engineering project intended to showcase Brazil's potential as an emergent South American nation in the wake of World War II. At the 1950 finals, Brazil lost to Uruguay 2 to 1 in front of an estimated 220,000 spectators, one-tenth of Rio's entire population at the time. As Alcides Ghiggia, who scored Uruguay's winning goal in that decisive final game, put it: "Down through its history, only three people have managed to silence the Maracanã: the Pope, Frank Sinatra, and me." The Maracanã is where the four major soccer clubs of Rio—Botafogo, Flamengo, Fluminense, and Vasco da Gama—have played out their historic rivalries. It is where Pelé scored his one-thousandth goal.

The stadium has come to symbolize the national character of both soccer and celebration. It is also seen as a reflection of Brazil's worst problems during the time of dictatorship. In the 1970s, 1980s, and 1990s, when Brazil's cities suffered from mismanagement and capital flight, so did the Maracanã. Despite the fact that it was falling apart, and even after a section of the stands collapsed in 1992, it was still home to the largest crowds in the world. As Professor Alvito explained to me,

> When Brazil started to enter more into the global economy and FIFA started to host events here, starting with the Club World Championships in 2000, there was a tremendous external pressure to eliminate the standing sections: you had to put in luxury boxes. And so it started undergoing these reforms, these middle-aged reforms, the sort of "nip and tuck" (which is also a very Brazilian thing to do). Dye the hair, stick in some fancy bits, sell yourself again to an international audience.

What is being "nipped and tucked" is the *populares* section. This is where the masses have always stood together. The change—from the masses standing as one in the upper deck to a ring of luxury boxes—could not be more jarring for followers of the sport and devotees of the Maracanã. Just as the Maracanã's dramatic alterations symbolize, to many, a new, two-tiered Brazilian culture that excludes the masses, it can also be seen as an example of something being transformed to sell its "Brazilianness" at the expense of actual living, breathing Brazilians: another economic example of a Brazil in thrall treating its very culture as an export commodity to market abroad.

Limiting the Maracanã's capacity has obvious, blaring, subtle-as-a-blowtorch symbolic implications. Brazil has always—from its beginnings, as we will see—chosen to present itself as a mass mosaic, as opposed to the "melting pot" ideal promoted in the United States. Teddy Roosevelt famously railed against a multicultural ideal, saying that "there is no room in [the United States] for a hyphenated American," but Brazil has always taken a different approach that pushes back against assimilation as an ideal. Brazil would be a multitude of different groups, but all together: something even greater than the sum of their parts. The Maracanã was the place where that mosaic of the cultural multitudes could form, where people could see themselves in the context of their adopted country. For that to change in such a dramatic fashion is difficult enough. To have it happen because an external, European body—FIFA—says that "no international sanctioned match can take place if people are standing" is really more than many cariocas can possibly bear. This, as we will see in the next chapter, speaks to an area of profound sensitivity in Brazil, rooted in its very founding as a country: the idea that Europe would exercise power over any hopes of sovereignty Brazilians might possess. As Graça said to me, "It's like canceling your culture because of FIFA." Or, as Gaffney put it, it's "an insult to the rich culture of the stadium."

Brazil is now left in a situation very familiar to those of us in the United States whose cities have built mega-stadiums with public funding: the people who pay the taxes that made a new Maracanã now cannot afford tickets to the Maracanã. "A modern stadium that we cannot enter," as Gaffey called it. Alvito, his voice riddled with pathos, pointed out that the Maracanã "was made for crowds; crowds roar. Crowds litter. They cry. It is not just two hundred thousand to seventy-five thousand that is the issue. It is who is going to be allowed in. It is the death of crowds."

On a sunny weekday in September 2012, Chris Gaffney took me down to the Maracanã for a sanctioned tour of the construction taking place inside the stadium. He provided running commentary about what he clearly believed to be a sacred space. "For fifty years, this was the largest stadium in the world," he said. "But now we have developers and the government that are blinded by money, blinded by the project, and blinded by this neoliberal way of thinking about the world." As we approached the stadium, we saw, heard, and felt the thrumming rhythm of neoliberal Brazil: jackhammers and construction trucks, shuttling back and forth on suspension that magnifies the rumble of their engines. Among the cranes was a sea of workers in matching blue hard-hats. Chris informed us that the stadium construction employs five thousand workers. Gutting and rebuilding the Maracanã is a twenty-four-hour job: three eight-hour shifts, with a constant flow of workers punching in and punching out. They have had to go on strike on several occasions, to protest not only for higher wages but to get the toilets un-clogged and make the cafeteria food edible.

But before we could see the inside, we got a taste of the "Brazilian cost": we were denied entry, as well as our formal media tour, because someone did not tell someone else we were arriving. We had to reschedule for later that week, but this misfortune proved to be an unbelievable blessing. Gaffney suggested we go next door to the Indigenous Cultural Center (ICC), where we met Carlos Tukano.

Carlos is about fifty. He is an Indigenous Brazilian, born in the state of Amazonas, who has worked for thirty years to build a collective organization of Brazil's dozens of Indigenous groups. When Carlos lived in Rio at the ICC with eleven other families, he had a hard time sleeping—the stadium renovation to end all stadium renovations was taking place right next door, at all hours of the night. But the noise wasn't the only reason Carlos couldn't sleep. He and the other residents feared they would be swept away with the construction's debris. (Their fears eventually came to pass when, a year later, the ICC was torn to the ground.)

When I met them at the still-standing ICC, the families were living in trailers next to the museum in protest of its dilapidation, disrespect, and neglect. Founded in 1910, the ICC is an achingly beautiful three-story structure with twenty-foot ceilings; like the old Maracanã, it vibrates with history. The original museum was dedicated as a space for Indigenous studies just two decades after the country formally abolished Indigenous enslavement. Teddy Roosevelt—apparently not terrified by "hyphenated Brazilians"—visited the locale with Cândido Rondon, the great Brazilian explorer, supporter of Indigenous rights, and first director of Brazil's Indian Protection Agency.

Even though the formal museum was shuttered by 2012, Carlos and the other occupiers were holding lectures and displaying several makeshift cultural exhibits. Most of this happened in the yard outside the building because its interior was in terrible disrepair, the floors covered in rubble. The wrought-iron stairs still had their skeletal shape, but the handrails and marble stair treads had been ripped out. Climbing them was like going up sixty feet on a diagonal ladder, and it was a long way down. I made it up, but kept my eyes straight ahead.

In 1977, the property was abandoned in the wave of economic crisis and decay plaguing Brazil at the time. The following year a new Indigenous museum was opened in a different part of the city, the Botafogo neighborhood. For many years this building fell into disuse and disrepair.

In 2006 Indigenous families arrived from across the country to retake the space. For one year they lived in total peace. That changed in 2007, when FIFA announced that Brazil would host the 2014 World Cup. Despite rumblings that the Maracanã would need a serious upgrade, Carlos and everyone at the ICC believed that they would be left alone. Sure enough, they were entirely unbothered between 2007 and 2010. They simply held the space and opened their own makeshift museum. Student groups, tourists, and researchers came to learn about the history of Indigenous Brazil and participate in cultural events. Its new curators resuscitated this place of profound historical importance.

In 2010 the pressure to move out began, with eviction notices and political harassment becoming a regular part of life for the occupiers. The activists attempted to meet with government officials but were not granted a meeting until 2012. The Sport and Leisure Ministry, the only people with any real say over the building and the space, chose not to attend, which sent a loud-and-clear message that the museum would be reduced to rubble to make way for World Cup and Olympic parking lots. The squat then became an occupation as the activists made clear their intentions to occupy the space as a peaceful protest. "We speak to the government and they just put us off," Carlos told me. "But we will not leave because we want a place to show the power, history, and pride of the Indigenous people."

In a country of two hundred million people that purports to celebrate its diversity like few other places on earth, it's as if a velvet rope keeps Indigenous people out of the Carnival. The most recent census counted between 650,000 and 850,000 Indigenous people in all of Brazil, which is ludicrously low; Indigenous people in cities tend to not disclose their ethnic heritage because of the institutional racism and disrespect they still face.

The entire structure of the ICC building, with its gorgeous architecture and historical importance, could have been rebuilt as a locus of pride. Developers estimated the cost at a mere ten million dollars—a pittance compared to the Maracanã rebuild. It could have become a symbol of Brazil's rich and diverse history. It could even have attracted tourists coming to Rio for the World Cup and Olympics, a feel-good advertisement for the beneficence of the Brazilian state. Instead, it's slated to become parking lots.

The same logic that would bulldoze the ICC has also shaped the Maracanã renovation. We managed to tour the inside several days later, after much persistence, this time without Chris Gaffney. Although he is a walking encyclopedia of its history, I was grateful Chris was not there. He treasures this stadium for what it was—and what we saw in the bowl of the Maracanã was its negation. From the field to the upper decks, the history of the Maracanã was being unceremoniously ripped apart. The level of demolition was particularly shocking because of the two hundred million dollars spent on repairs just a few years earlier—yet another example of needed resources getting flushed in favor of cosmetic stadium rebuilds.

As I watched the destruction I thought about one of the Indigenous occupiers, a young, fiercely intelligent man named Arrasari, who said, "I am not moving. I will stay until I am no more than a pillar of salt. They think we'll go because they've cut us down like trees. But the root remains."

It is true that if you need to uproot a tree, you don't try to cut it down: you bring a bulldozer. That is exactly what the Brazilian state did to the ICC. In March 2013, the bulldozers, backed by men with guns, stormed the cultural center. Two hundred police officers dressed in military garb, firing tear gas canisters and using pepper spray, took the center. Chris Gaffney was quoted in the *New York Times*: "By resorting to force, this reflects the general attitude of state authorities toward the people getting in the way of their sports projects."[32] I was relieved that Chris's voice was a part of the article. The *Times*, however, quoted neither Carlos Tukano nor Arrasari. They were invisible to the end.

Environment

The environment is an extremely sensitive subject in Brazil, home to the "lungs of the earth." The Amazon rainforest creates 20 percent of the earth's oxygen and 25 percent of its drinkable fresh water.[33] It has also been razed and burned with shocking speed as Brazil's economy has hummed.

It is, of course, not difficult to understand why the last thing people in Brasília, Brazil's capital, want to hear on the subject are lectures from the Global North. Lula once said, "What we cannot accept is that those who failed to take care of their own forests, who did not preserve what they had and deforested everything and are responsible for most of the gases poured into the air and for the greenhouse effect, they shouldn't be sticking their noses into Brazil's business and giving their two cents' worth."[34] He certainly has a point, although it says something damning about our world that the logic of our system dictates Brazil's sovereign right to destroy the "lungs of the world." By making statements that make destroying rainforests sound like a bold act of Global South defiance, Lula also disregards the powerful history of Brazil's own environmental community, which was critical in the founding of his own Workers' Party and has been fighting for decades to preserve the Amazon. As legendary Brazilian environmentalist

Chico Mendes put it, "At first I thought I was fighting to save rubber trees; then I thought I was fighting to save the Amazon rainforest. Now I realize I am fighting for humanity."[35]

The World Cup—which is a national operation, as opposed to the Rio-centric Olympics—means greater stress on this critical ecosystem. This can be seen most sharply in the efforts to build a "FIFA-quality stadium" in the middle of the Amazon rainforest. Brazil will be spending $325 million, almost forty million more than the original estimates, while uprooting acres of the most ecologically delicate region on the planet. Are the "lungs of the world" really the best place for a new stadium? Even those in Brazil who advocate for the national autonomy of the rainforest region, without interference from international environmental bodies, are crying foul. This particular stadium does not only defy environmental needs, it defies even its own logic. The Amazon is already home to a stadium that draws far less than its capacity. Why do all this for just four World Cup matches? Romário, our soccer star–turned–politician, called the project "absurd": "There will be a couple games there, and then what? Who will go? It is an absolute waste of time and money."[36] Since this particular "white elephant" seems to be uniting opposition of both the "wasteful spending" crowd and the "pro-breathing" crowd, the government is looking for options for the stadium after the World Cup that seem fiscally sound. One idea being floated is to turn the entire stadium into a massive open-air prison—a use with a notoriously bloody echo in Latin American history, one not lost on those protesting the priorities of both FIFA and the Brazilian government.[37]

Security

Then there is the question of security, a word that means different things to different people. When the planners of the World Cup and the Olympics discuss security, they are speaking about the security of the wealthy to travel to Brazil and feel as safe as they would in a gated community. *USA Today* wrote, without attribution, that Brazil "has the seventh-highest homicide rate in the world and only eight percent of reported crimes are solved."[38] Every lurid new story from Brazil, including two grisly (yet entirely unrelated) beheadings, now receives more publicity in the United States than any crime in Brazil's history, precisely because these stories are framed in terms of whether World Cup tourists will feel safely sheltered.

Yet the question of security, as we will see in chapter 6, is less about keeping tourists feeling unthreatened and unscathed than about introducing a profoundly intrusive "new normal" of surveillance. At a cost of nine hundred million dollars, the twelve World Cup host cities will be equipped with surveillance and integrated command centers staffed with police and military personnel, in addition to two large security centers in Rio and Brasília that will monitor security nationwide. More than a thousand surveillance cameras will be installed in Rio de Janeiro alone. "Because of the size of the event and the need of integration between the forces, strategic planning for it began nearly a year ago," Rio state security secretary José Mariano Beltrame told *USA Today Sports.* "We bet on the modernization of police, from the academy to the fleet." Beltrame does not mention that the police will be under the command of the military, an idea that last had currency during the dictatorship. He also doesn't mention that drone surveillance planes will be flying over Rio, as they did for the Olympics in London. He especially does not mention that all of this will cost almost ten times the price of security at the 2010 World Cup in South Africa. (I was in South Africa right before play started, and I cannot imagine what that security scenario would look like multiplied by ten.)

The security plan also includes creating "exclusion zones" around the stadiums, guarded by 1,400 armed troops, as well as "World Cup courts" aimed at fast-tracking judicial proceedings to charge, prosecute, and convict crimes ranging from robberies and assault to "ambush marketing in contravention of FIFA's regulations."[39] That means open season on Brazil's "informal economy" of street markets and stalls. Ramping up security also means ramping up police brutality, not a small concern since numerous recent incidents have drawn widespread public outrage. As Travis Waldron wrote,

Along with excessive spending and inequality, police brutality and corruption were among the complaints in last summer's protests. According to government numbers, Brazilian police killed one in 229 suspects they arrested last year, one of the highest figures in the world (U.S. police kill one in every 31,575). Protests erupted in June against police over the death of a 17-year-old São Paulo boy killed in an earlier demonstration, then again in August over the case of Amarildo de Souza, a Brazilian man whose disappearance and subsequent death was blamed on police officers (25 were charged with his murder in October). Typical police responses to protests—tear gassing, pepper spraying, and excessive force—were also rampant throughout the demonstrations, drawing even more opposition from the protesters.[40]

These fears of police brutality cannot be found in the mainstream media, but graffiti and murals across the city speak about it, going up in the night faster than they can be painted over. "The walls," as Eduardo Galeano wrote, "are the publishers of the poor."

Older Brazilians see in this new security regime a jarring echo of the days of military dictatorship, yet with one critical difference. This time, instead of crushing revolutionary movements, the authorities are focusing their repression on squelching spontaneous rage at the priorities of commerce and on making sure the trains—and planes—run on time. If this all sounds very "Big Brother," it is worth noting that the security operation at Maracanã goes by the official name of, yes, "Big Brother."

Yet no matter the stated goals of World Cup security, the major concern is that the security protocols will remain even after the party ends and everyone has gone home. There are no external military threats against Brazil, and a standing, aggressive military and national police command structure can really only be aimed in one direction: inward. The internal threat, as the 2013 protests made clear, is that people are dissatisfied with the government taking public money and giving it to private corporations. If you want to keep that kind of anger bottled up, you have to militarize the cities.

To know the human cost of such an arrangement in Brazil, one only has to go back to the 2007 Pan Am Games and the Complexo do

Alemão massacre. During the Pan American Games, the police staged a large-scale invasion and occupation of the Complexo do Alemão, a series of interlocking favelas in northern Rio. The pretext was a crackdown on drug traffickers, but police killed forty-four people, some of them execution-style. Many of the dead were later found to have nothing to do with drug trafficking or illicit activity.[41]

These instances of police brutality, harassment, and murder have also fallen disproportionately on Brazilians of African descent, who make up half of the country's population. Henry Louis Gates, in his 2011 PBS series *Black in Latin America*, said that Brazilians "wanted their national culture to be 'blackish'—really brown, a beautiful brown blend . . . in each of these societies the people at the bottom are the darkest skinned with the most African features."[42] This dynamic, as we will see, is deeply rooted in Brazil's history.

Seizing land and homes, running roughshod over the rights of those of African and Indigenous descent, opening the doors for foreign plunder, the buzzsaw development of the Amazon, exporting Brazil's culture, declaring an end to public space, militarizing the cities: all of these can be facilitated through laws described as "states of exception," like those historically passed for the Olympic Games in which the usual rules (and constitutions) no longer apply. This is why mayors like Michael Bloomberg in New York City and Richard Daley in Chicago—both cities pinnacles of gentrification—wanted the Olympics so desperately and why Lula fought so hard for them at the end of his presidency. In a rush of excitement, the land grab and the privatization of public space could proceed with abandon. These objectives touch on the deepest and rawest nerves in Brazilian history. The next chapter endeavors to give non-Brazilian readers some sense of that history, which is critical for understanding the present.

CHAPTER 2

"There Is No Sin Below the Equator"

If the past has nothing to say to the present, history may go on sleeping undisturbed in the closet where the system keeps its old disguises.
—Eduardo Galeano[1]

The Brazilian flag, with its uniquely radiant colors, is featured in murals and street art throughout the country. Its green symbolizes the lush rainforests of Brazil's interior; yellow stands for the gold once believed to reside under its earth in inexhaustible abundance. In the flag's center is a blue globe with *Ordem e Progresso*, or "order and progress," in small lettering across its circumference, making it one of the few flags on earth emblazoned with a slogan: a cartoonist's dream. I saw it replaced with with "Corruption and Anger," "Disorder and Retreat," "Smash This State," or—one that elicited laughter when I asked for a translation—"Revolution in the Streets and Bedrooms."

The quest for "order and progress" goes on amid a national history more defined by a series of extremes: booms and busts, the beautiful and the brutal, the anarchic and the totalitarian, the joyous and the tragic. In Brazil, the search is not for a "more perfect union" but for how to harness (and, yes, exploit) its remarkable wealth, culture, and resources—while becoming more than just the beaten-down junior partner of the United States and Europe.

In this brief chapter, I am not going to attempt to summarize Brazil's incredibly complicated whirling dervish of a five-hundred-year history. I do want to take a highly selective tour through this past, though, to help those outside Brazil understand why the spending, security practices, and evictions that have come with hosting the World Cup and the Olympics provoke such a strong reaction. Some Brazilians are excited about their country being recognized, through hosting, as the world power it is. Some are fearful that this is yet another instance of euphoria before the bottom falls out of the economy. Others are repulsed at the United States and particularly Europe—seen as the power behind FIFA and the IOC—descending once again on their country like spring-breakers at Carnival. Many in Brazil see FIFA and the IOC as no different than Justin Bieber, whom the paparazzi caught stumbling out of a famous Rio brothel in October 2013—nothing on their minds but how to take a piece of the country and leave some cash on the dresser on their way out the door.

Understanding the psychology of Brazil has to start with the awe Europeans felt on the first day they stepped off their boats and saw a verdant beauty beyond their extent of their imaginations. One Jesuit priest reputedly said in the early 1500s, "If there is a paradise here on earth, I would say it is in Brazil."[2] Yet the people who first came to its shores were not here to spread a religious gospel. They believed they had found a country bursting at the seams with riches—not to mention several million Indigenous people incidental to that quest. The story of the next few centuries is one of single-minded plunder of each of the nation's resources until the soil, workers, or slaves were exhausted and could give no more, then moving onto the next. Its plunderers truly believed there would be no end to this bounty. There is even an old Brazilian proverb that speaks to this: "God repairs at night the damage that man does by day."[3]

Slavery in Brazil

There is a (very) old joke about a lumberjack who brags to a prospective employer that his previous job was in the Sahara Forest. When the boss say, "Don't you mean the Sahara Desert?" he replies, "Exactly!" Brazil, along these lines, is named for a tree that for almost all intents and purposes no longer exists: the Brazilwood tree. The Brazilwood was once so plentiful that it dominated the Atlantic rainforest. The Atlantic rainforest is also a tiny fraction of its former size. The reddish Brazilwood was a critical source of red dye for the textile manufacturers of Europe, who chopped them down until the forests were incapable of regenerating. If you want to see a Brazilwood tree in 2014, your best bet would be a botanical garden. Whether Brazilwood, rubber, coffee, diamonds, gold, or—today—cattle, soy, oil, and the Amazon rainforest, Brazil's bounty has long been plundered by adventurers, colonists, and oligarchs. FIFA and the IOC are only the latest groups to come from foreign shores and look upon the remarkable vistas of Brazil with dollar signs in their eyes.

To get an idea of how early European arrivals saw Brazil's Indigenous population, we can look to the most influential chronicle of their lives: German explorer Hans Staden's 1557 book titled, in the understated style of the times, *The True History and Description of a Land of Savage, Naked, Fierce, Man-Eating People Found in the New World*. Staden's text, as subdued as its title, is filled with pulpy, overheated, fabricated stories of orgiastic cannibalism. The book had a ready audience, however, among the Catholic hierarchy and the Portuguese throne. Plunder became an act of humanizing, civilizing mercy; the Europeans saw the Indigenous people of Brazil as deserving to be both enslaved and conquered. If you want to understand how a soccer stadium could be built in the middle of the Amazon or how an Indigenous museum could be evacuated with military force and then torn to the ground, here is where that starts.[4]

In Portugal, people heard tales of "endless fertility" and riches for anyone willing to take them. The problem with Portugal, as anyone who has ever seen a map can tell you, is that it is somewhat smaller than Brazil. How much smaller? Portugal is roughly thirty-five thousand square kilometers. Brazil is almost three and a half *million* square kilometers, more than half of what would become known as South

America. This difference in size determined how conquest was organized; its repercussions have lasted until today. Rather than try to overwhelm the Indigenous population militarily, the Portuguese created a network of trading centers, each backed by the military, and attempted to graft a European-style feudal system onto the areas developed around these trading posts. In 1534, Portugal's King Dom João III tried to organize this sprawling, ecologically diverse landmass by dividing it into twelve hereditary captaincies, with grantees controlling each section. It was not successful, but this sixteenth-century practice of decentralized domination was reflected in the oligarchic fiefdoms that defined the country for centuries.[5]

In 1500, when Europeanss first arrived, Indigenous cultures comprised more than a hundred language groups. Anthropologists disagree about the size of Brazil's Indigenous population, but estimates range from five hundred thousand to two million people, with some estimates as high as eight million. These numbers dropped dramatically after the Portuguese conquerors reached their shores. The smallpox and measles that traveled with them thinned the ranks of Indigenous people dramatically. Then there were the more direct means of subjugation. Indigenous tribes who resisted conquest were slaughtered without mercy. While this brutality took place, Portugal's King Manuel I wrote, "My captain reached a land where he found humans as if in their first innocence mild and peace living."[6]

A land does not plunder itself, however. The Portuguese explorers needed workers and attempted to transition Brazil's Indigenous population into slave labor. This did not exactly work. Brazil's tribes were horizontally organized hunter-and-gatherer tribes. They responded to efforts to enslave them and pound work discipline into them by escaping, which they did not find to be especially difficult. They ventured into the interior, deep into the Amazon rain forest, an area that the Portuguese regarded with atavistic fear. Instead, as the saying goes, they "clung like crabs to the coast."[7] This fear of the interior meant lucrative work for specialized trackers who could brave the interior and bring back the body parts of native rebels. For the Indigenous people, thus began a life defined by the inconvenience of their existence. As Eduardo Galeano wrote, "Exiled in their own land, condemned to an eternal exodus, Latin America's native peoples were pushed into the poorest areas . . . as the dominant civilization extended its frontiers. The Indians have suffered, and continue to suffer, the curse of their own wealth; that is the drama of all Latin America."[8]

For the Portuguese court and its emissaries, the need for labor became an obsession. It was a question not only of the conquerors' mission but of their very survival as an impatient, sybaritic Portuguese court awaited its promised riches. The conquerors turned, just as their counterparts in North America would, to Africa and the transatlantic slave trade. While there were strong similarities between the North American slave trade and Brazil's—not least of which were the identical cruelties of the Middle Passage—we should not be blind to their differences, chiefly those of size and scope.[9] It is a fool's errand to try to quantify the relative inhumanities of different slave trades, yet we can say with confidence that there has never been a slave trade on earth that rivaled the scale as well as the brutality of the slave trade to Brazil and the conditions in which slaves there lived. The trade itself lasted almost three centuries, from 1580 to 1850, and the need for labor was so profound that, by the nineteenth century, African slaves and their descendants made up the majority of the country.

No country in the Western Hemisphere brought in more slaves than Brazil: estimates start at three and a half million. Half died during the voyage, creating a genocidal situation even beyond that of the United States. Once in the country, the life expectancy of the average slave was eighteen—three to four times less than in the United States. This was linked to both labor conditions and the appalling rates of infant mortality.[10] The brutality on display was justified through a series of newly formed ideologies about "inferior" and "infected" races that required subjugation in the name of human progress.[11]

The main barrier to genocide was resistance. Slave traders purposefully sought Africans from a variety of tribes and regions and then mixed them so that language barriers would hinder their ability to organize resistance and revolts. Yet the history of resistance is as long as slavery itself. The number-one method of revolt in Brazil was running away in groups and forming autonomous communities, known as *quilombos,* in the interior. One settlement lasted more than a century, until 1694, when it was conquered by Portuguese security forces.

This was far more possible in Brazil than in North America; in Brazil, incursions into the interior by settlers were infrequent. Unlike the United States, Brazil also never offered incentives for "settling" Indigenous land to upwardly mobile European indentured servants, making ventures into the Amazon for small-scale farming nearly nonexistent. By 1800, less than 5 percent of Brazil's land had been conquered by the Portuguese and the rest was home to escaped slaves and the Indigenous population.

Meanwhile, the developing oligarchy started to systemize what became its recurring pattern of monocultural agriculture, farmed by slaves and located primarily in the northeast of the country. This pattern of jumping from single crop to single crop, draining resources, and then moving on had the awful cost of extreme booms and busts. From 1600 to 1650 the key crop was sugar, which made up 90 to 95 percent of exports. Then in 1690, after gold was discovered in the Minas Gerais and Mato Grosso regions, Brazil went all-in on the mining industry.[12]

In the eighteenth century diamonds and gold became the national obsession, once again at an awful human cost. In the diamond and gold mines, under threat of whipping, torture, or death, slaves worked the mines until they died where they stood. This created a greater demand for slave labor, increasing a slave trade that resembled a meat grinder. In the United States, where the primary slave crop was King Cotton, there was a financial incentive to keep slaves alive: they were the most valuable "equipment" in the production process. After the United States banned the transatlantic slave trade in 1808, creating a sustainable family structure and a religious hierarchy that preached obedience in the slave community was especially important; the slave community had to be stable enough to reproduce its own labor. In Brazil, however, the primary "crops" were diamonds and gold. Sustaining the lives of slaves was secondary to getting as many of the precious stones and minerals out of the ground as humanly possible. If slaves died in the mines, they were dumped and new slaves brought in. That is why the life expectancy of slaves in Brazil was so cruelly brief by comparison to the United States.

This system generated wealth unlike anything ever seen. Yet, to the gnawing frustration of the settlers, that wealth did not go toward industrializing or modernizing their settlements. It also did not go toward buying new equipment, which would have dramatically cut the death tolls of the slaves in the mines—slaves being a very expensive part of the operation. Instead, the Portuguese royal court poured this unprecedented capital, mined at an unprecedented human cost, into conspicuous consumption. In order to pay off its mounting debts, the Portuguese court also used Brazil like a piggy bank, borrowing money from its treasury or cutting deals on its back. They saw Brazil's riches in the same way the oligarchs saw African slaves: as disposable, irrelevant, and replaceable. This practice had terrible long-term effects on the country's development. In 1703, Portugal signed the Methuen Treaty, assuring England a guaranteed place for its goods in Brazil. This calcified the monoculture economies that ensured the boom-bust cycles. Until 1715, the Portuguese royal court banned sugar refineries. In 1729, it was against the law to construct new roads that would facilitate mining. In 1785, if you owned your own spinning mill or loom, you were ordered to burn it or the state would do it for you. Let us be clear about why this was happening: forced industrial underdevelopment. Deliberately stopping Brazil from industrializing ensured that European industry would reign supreme and Brazil would be used almost exclusively as a source of raw material. This also meant that issues like education went unaddressed. Fear of a nonwhite majority and the absence of the need for an educated workforce meant that schooling was not on anyone's agenda. The Church banned printing presses until 1808. By 1818 only 2.5 percent of adult men had spent time in school.[13] Because of this dynamic Brazil was, as Galeano put it, "inexorably condemned to poverty so that foreigners might progress."[14]

The Beginning of the "Mosaic"

People in the United States are taught to think about race, racism, and what constitutes a "person of color" in a very rigid fashion. It is worth outlining how Brazil's conceptions of race have historically differed from those of the United States. The differences are dramatic, with profound implications for Brazilian social and cultural development. Brazil was predominantly settled by Portuguese men who made the journey across the ocean without wives or children (unlike North America, where settlers often voyaged with their families). As these men built settlements, the question of sex needed answering. The solution was seen as interracial coupling and procreation. In the United States, interracial sexual relations usually involved white settlers raping slaves and Indigenous women or keeping them as mistresses; in extremely rare cases, they built families with women of a different race. Brazil, on the other hand, celebrated the idea of European men procreating with Indigenous women as well as African slaves. This took every possible form, from voluntary marriage to using rape as a tool of social control. "There is no sin below the equator" was a popular saying among settlers.

These differences shaped how ideas of "race"—and practices of racism—formed in Brazil. Unlike in the United States, where even "one drop" of nonwhite blood consigned you to a lower status, Brazil had a host of color designations. Your color and your parentage, on a sliding scale, determined both status and access to economic opportunity. People designated as *mamelucos, caboclos,* or mulattoes (meaning mixed European and Indigenous or African heritage) developed a specific status as "intermediaries between whites and Indigenous or slave communities." As Henry Louis Gates described it, "In America one drop of black ancestry makes you black. In Brazil, it's almost as if one drop of white ancestry makes you white."[15] This visible and respected mixing in society, not to mention the minority status of whites, meant that the mixing of African and Indigenous influences, including through music, dance, and sports, was a part of Brazilian culture well before independence.

Twenty-first-century Brazil chooses to market itself in ways that imply that it has always celebrated African, European, and Indigenous culture in a progressive, beautiful, and even antiracist fashion. As one saying goes, "There are racists in Brazil. But Brazil itself is not racist." This mirrors the deeply influential work of Gilberto Freyre, whose 1933 book *Masters and Slaves* described Brazil as a "racial democracy" that would thrive precisely because it would grow to embrace its Indigenous and, particularly, its African heritage. As Freyre said,

> Every Brazilian, even the light-skinned fair-haired one, carries about him on his soul, when not on soul and body alike, the shadow or at least the birthmark of the aborigine or the negro, in our affections, our excessive mimicry, our Catholicism which so delights the senses, our music, our gait, our speech, our cradle songs, in everything that is a sincere expression of our lives, we almost all of us bear the mark of that influence.[16]

There was quite a lot of history to overcome to achieve this reality as a "racial democracy." The formal goal of the Catholic Church, which the Portuguese settlers took to heart, was to wipe out Indigenous culture. Their treatment of African slaves brought the barbarism of the practice to new heights. But because slaves from Africa were rapidly becoming the majority of Brazil's population, the settlers needed these different racial rules.

Rumblings of Independence

Portugal had become dramatically dependent upon Brazil, exhausting its resources to pay the debts of the crown. Among Brazil's colonists, the belief became widespread that their country only existed to be exploited by European powers. In 1788, the first plot to overthrow the "royal plantation" was led by wealthy landowners who were strongly influenced by the writings of Thomas Jefferson—explicitly because they saw him as a great leader who could preach freedom while practicing slavery. That was a message they could get behind.

Yet the liberatory language of the struggle, even in a country where less than 3 percent of the population could read, did inspire many more people than just the oligarchs. The Haitian revolution of "Black Jacobins," in particular, inspired slaves and "mulattoes" to revolt. There were slave revolts in several cities, but the experience of Haiti was not repeated in South America, where escaped or assassinated slaves were just replenished with more imports.[17]

Then came a happenstance so bizarre and so seismic that it altered Brazil's road to independence ineffably: its decolonization efforts against the Portuguese royal court were led by its king.

In 1808, the royal court of Portugal's King Dom João VI relocated to Brazil after Napoleon invaded Portugal to rule from exile. In 1822, after the constitutionalist Liberal Revolution in Portugal, João was called to return. Upon leaving Brazil, he told his son Pedro that if he were ever called upon to choose between returning to Portugal and remaining in Brazil, he should choose Brazil and rule this wealthy land as king. In 1822, this came to pass, and on January 9, Pedro made the iconic statement that now symbolizes Brazil's founding and opens its own Declaration of Independence: "*Diga ao povo que fico!*" ("Tell the people I'm staying!") With this, according to national lore, Brazil announced its autonomy. This was an unparalleled moment historically: a monarch would be leading a colony's movement for independence from what was technically his family's own monarchy.[18]

Brazil was able to establish its independence without a titanic conflict. There was no Bunker Hill, no Valley Forge, no grand battles against Portugal etched into the nation's psyche. All it required was a series of skirmishes across the coast before a financially overleveraged Portugal finally folded. Independence from Portugal was a victory, but it also cemented the power of the oligarchs. It also did not come without cost. Adding insult to injury, part of the peace treaty required Brazil to assume the debt that Portugal owed England. Portugal had accrued this debt because it needed funds to squelch Brazil's independence movement. In other words, the Brazilians were paying the British for the arms Portugal had just used against them. In addition, as part of its deal with Portugal, Brazil had to privilege imported British goods with miniscule tariffs, even at the expense of its own domestic goods.

Nineteenth-century US ambassador James Watson Webb summed up the two countries' relationship:

> Britain supplies all the capital needed for internal improvements in Brazil and manufactures all the utensils in common use, from the spade on up, and nearly all the luxury and practical items from the pin to the costliest clothing. British pottery, British articles of glass, iron, or wood are as common as woolens and cotton cloth. Great Britain supplies Brazil with its steam and sailing ships, and paces and repairs its streets, lights its cities with gas, builds its railways, exploits its mines, is its banker, puts up its telegraph wires, carries its mail, builds its furniture, motors, wagons.[19]

In addition, Brazil was required to import goods from Great Britain for no other reason than that they were made in Great Britain. The Brazilians were compelled to import wallets even though they possessed no paper money. They were also compelled to import ice skates, which didn't exactly suit anyone's needs. And, when visiting, Englishmen could live as imperial supermen, with truly "no sin below the equator": by law, Brazilian courts had no jurisdiction over anything British citizens did on Brazilian soil. Foreign debt was also beginning to smother Brazil economically. By 1850, debt payments comprised 40 percent of its budget. Most of the nation's borrowing was going toward building railroads to connect the ports with the centers of production, with scant resources aimed at internal development. This was a situation that can only be described as forced underdevelopment. Brazil had become not only a source of natural resources for industrializing Europe, but also a captive market for their manufactured goods.

Brazil as a Free State

Independence did not spark a flowering of education, emancipation, and urbanization, as in some other countries. The country was still ruled by the same monarchy, with the king now magically Brazilian instead of Portuguese. It remained an agricultural, slave-based economy, dominated by large-scale mines and plantations. There were very few artisans and small-scale independent landowners in the new Brazil;

the oligarchs made it difficult to do anything other than either work for them or join the new standing Brazilian army. Beneath the oligarchy, you had a symbolic royal court, an army (with mixed-race officers), Indigenous tribes in the interior, and slaves.

From the very beginning, there were tensions. The idea that a former colony of Portugal would be led by its royal family was too heavy a contradiction for the country to bear. Dom Pedro I attempted to mediate that by dividing independent Brazil into eighteen provinces, each led by a president—an oligarch—appointed by the king. Pedro was forward-thinking for a royal and had progressive ideas, but, in a twist of fate, the wealth and expanse of the country worked against his family's rule as the exploding coffee and then rubber trades enriched the oligarchs. Dom Pedro II managed to remain in power until the eventual end of the slave trade also signaled the end of royal rule.

Slaves were, it was said, "the hands and feet of Brazil."[20] There were sporadic slave uprisings during the nineteenth century, as the memory of the Haitian Revolution lived on in stories of Toussaint L'Ouverture's victory. These uprisings were squelched with a shocking level of brutality. Torture and mutilation, followed by your head being displayed on a pike as a warning to other slaves, was the punishment for "treason." [21] In this climate, "runaway slave hunter" became a burgeoning profession. Escaped slaves were hunted by the *bandeirantes*—their name derived from the fact that they organized themselves as part of a "band" of trackers and killers. Their expeditions were for slaves and gold, depending on which export was the more valuable at any given time. The bandeirantes could be recognized on sight because they were known to wear the ears of those they captured as necklaces.[22]

The brutality of Brazil's slave trade fostered pressure for abolition both at home and abroad, but it was a lot to ask of the oligarchs and plantation owners to give up their "hands and feet." The transatlantic slave trade to Brazil was technically illegal by 1826 but continued until 1850. By 1830, there were still more slaves than free people in Brazil, and it was still the largest slave economy on earth. The slave economy was so dominant in preindustrial Brazil, and Dom Pedro so indebted to the oligarchs, that every law was bent toward further concentrating land ownership and perpetuating the slave economy. This was very different than in the United States, where disputes about the benefits of free versus slave labor led to a civil war. It also led to the Homestead Act of 1862, which encouraged small farmers to take land and settle it. This challenged the westward expansion of the plantation class, at the expense of Native Americans. There was never a Homestead Act in Brazil, only more laws blocking the growth of any kind of small-scale land ownership.[23]

Yet despite the oligarchs' determination to maintain slavery, a number of factors finally accelerated its belated end. First, as mentioned above, a series of slave rebellions, not to mention hysteria after the victorious Haitian Revolution, left the royal court and the oligarchy completely unnerved about the possibility of rebellion. In addition, *quilombolas*, escaped slaves, were settling in camps on the very beaches of Rio.[24] *O Rebate*, an 1889 periodical, wrote, "Had the slaves not fled en masse from the plantations, they would today be still slaves. Slavery ended because slaves rebelled against it and against the law that enslaved them." The abolition "was nothing more than the legal recognition—so that public authority wasn't discredited—of an act that had already been accomplished by the mass revolt."[25]

Slavery was also creating an immigration crisis. European indentured servants who came to Brazil complained about the horrible conditions and being treated like slaves. This, in addition to a growing movement in Europe against slavery, led to Brazilian job recruiters being banned from countries throughout the continent. These servants' labor was so crucial that ending slavery became a life-and-death economic question of ending a labor shortage.[26]

Lastly, there was a growing moral revulsion toward slavery among Brazilians. Brazil's version of *Uncle Tom's Cabin*, a work of literature that inflamed people's opposition to slavery and achieved mass popularity, was a poem called "O Navio Negreiro," or "Slave Ship," by Antônio de Castro Alves, detailing the horrors of the

Middle Passage.[27] The king himself even wrote an antislavery article (under the pen name "The Philanthropist") in which he called slavery "the cancer that is gnawing away at Brazil" and insisted that it "must be eradicated."[28]

Abolitionist and antislavery societies were also beginning to form. Their method of moral suasion was to play on Brazil's ongoing obsession with its perception in the eyes of the rest of the world. As one tract argued, "Brazil does not want to be a nation morally isolated, a leper, expelled from the world community. The esteem and respect of foreign nations are as valuable to us as they are to other people."[29]

Then came the final straw: army officers in independent Brazil's standing army, many of them mixed-race, began to refuse orders to go after escaped slaves. Fear of Haiti-style revolts, labor shortages, and pressure from abolition societies inside and outside the country had all catapulted Brazil toward abolition. But the last factor that finally facilitated the end of slavery in Brazil was a fear of disease. The officers were terrified of the very thing that supposedly proved the weakness of the Indigenous people they were conquering: germs. Yellow fever and cholera were making their way over from Africa. This finally halted Brazil's lucrative illegal slave trade.

On May 13, 1888, Brazil became the last country to formally abolish slavery with what is known as the Golden Law. There was no civil war when abolition was finally decreed, just relief. The overriding agenda of the Brazilian state was abolition. Without abolition, there could be no industrialization, no acceptance by Europe into the emerging global economy, and no influx of European immigration and labor to push back against labor shortages as well as change the racial balance of forces. Given these needs, all concerned were feeling quite pragmatic about the need for change.[30]

Yet even this change did not take place without controversy. In 1891, in a hotly contested action, "the Brazilian Minister of Finance decreed the abolition of history; he ordered the destruction of every document which dealt in any way with slavery or the slave trade; a nationwide burning of the books."[31] Some historians have argued that this was done explicitly to prevent the oligarchs from seeking compensation for abolition. This has had the more long-term historical consequence, however, of preventing any kind of movement for reparations or historical accountability from Brazil's wealthiest families. Accountability for genocide has thus largely been erased.

Once abolition became the new reality, there was no formally codified segregation, no equivalent to the US Jim Crow laws. Generations of intermarriage and carefully constructed racial hierarchies made rigid segregation impossible to enforce. Far more important and influential were ideas of white supremacy and social Darwinism, which became refracted through the lens of a culturally mixed nation. However, there also was no struggle over the political and economic status of the newly liberated people—it was just "slavery's over, now fend for yourselves." This created a mass influx of propertyless, impoverished ex-slaves into Rio and other cities. It also meant the creation of Brazil's still-flourishing sex trade: the massive expansion of the prostitution and exploitation of women of African descent. This emancipation, in which people were given "nothing but freedom," laid the basis for the extreme inequality of Brazilian society today.

As this precarious new underclass formed over the nineteenth century, ideological tracts called for more European immigration to "whiten" and therefore improve the Brazilian population, Abolishing slavery did lead to a mammoth 500-percent explosion of immigration, largely made up of Italians, Germans, and, starting in 1908, Japanese. Between 1890 and 1930, Brazil's population grew by 160 percent to more than thirty-four million people.[32]

The end of slavery also opened the door for two dramatic developments. The first was end of royal rule: the armed forces removed and replaced the monarchy without bloodshed. This meant that Brazil's very founding as a republic was under a military government. The army voted to increase its own size by 50 percent and double its own salaries. It then disestablished the Roman Catholic Church as the "official" church of Brazil, weakening its position significantly compared to other Latin American countries (no sin below the equator!).

The beginning of the Brazilian republic coincided as well with the beginning of Carnival, a six-day party that today draws as many as five million people into the streets throughout the country. Carnival mixes elements of Catholicism (it is held the week before Lent, ending the Tuesday before Ash Wednesday) with the pagan festival of Saturnalia as well as elements of Indigenous and Afro-Brazilian culture. Like the samba dancers who lead its processions, Carnival is a celebration of how Brazil chooses to see itself in its best light: as a beautiful mosaic of different cultures that have come together to produce something uniquely beautiful and life-affirming. It is also a day of masks, where sexuality and identity are fluid and under the protection of anonymity, so people can experiment without fear.

Today, it is understandable why so many Brazilians are rankled by the modern commercialization of Carnival as a brand, just another export for global consumption, kind of like a super-sized Mardi Gras. But this would come later. In the late nineteenth century, the military government had no problem with the masses having their Carnival in the streets. They were concerned with setting up this new republic in ways that would establish continuity with the past. They could not have known that the echoes of their blueprint would reverberate into the twenty-first century. The army adopted a constitution that was a model of "radical decentralization." This had the effect of preserving the old oligarchic power in the new Brazilian military republic, while continuing to stymie any attempts to industrialize. In addition, the oligarchs proclaimed themselves part of the army: they were now officially colonels.[33]

Though the military republic was content to remain an agricultural economy in an age of industrialization, Brazil's rulers did have their eye on developing one part of the country: Rio. In 1902, 590 buildings were destroyed and thousands of families displaced on this prime piece of coastal real estate.[34] Because the interior was largely left to the landed estates and the Indigenous people, what little industrialization there was took place on the coast. The presence of labor unions and other workers' organizations was extremely modest, mostly on the docks or among the railway workers attempting to connect the coast to the interior one track at a time. The union movement that did exist was imported into the country with the European immigration wave, which included many people with experience in the revolutionary anarcho-syndicalist or socialist movements in their home countries. The anarcho-syndicalists congregated in São Paulo, while the socialists tried to find purchase in Rio de Janeiro. The reaction of the military was to repress them both in brutal fashion.[35]

Unions' and radicals' initial inability to find a home in Brazil was mirrored in industry's inability to expand: the country was still too decentralized, the oligarchs still too powerful, and the country as a whole still too addicted to its single-crop export economy. This absence of industrialization also meant that while its neighbors poured funds into public education, Brazil did not. The oligarchical mentality was to keep workers as poor and disempowered as possible. By 1920 only one-quarter of Brazilian workers were literate, a figure that had not moved in a generation.[36]

Yet Brazil still believed that, due to its size and the wealth it produced, it should be afforded respect. After World War I, Brazil expected to be granted a leading place in the League of Nations. It withdrew in 1926, angry and insulted, when this was denied. Respect on the international stage would only come under the leadership of doomed dictator/president Getúlio Vargas.

The Time of Vargas and the Military Dictatorship

Each drop of my blood will be an immortal flame in your conscience and will uphold the sacred will to resist. To hatred I reply with pardon, and to those who think they have defeated me, I reply with my victory. I was a slave to the Brazilian people, and today I am freeing myself for eternal life. But this people, whose slave I was, will no longer be slave to anyone. My sacrifice will remain forever in their souls and my blood will be the price for their ransom. I fought against the exploitation of Brazil. I fought against the exploitation of her people. I have fought with my whole heart. Hatred, infamy and slander

have not conquered my spirit. I have given you my life. Now I offer you my
death. I fear nothing. Serenely I take my first step towards eternity and leave
life to enter history.

—From the suicide note of Getúlio Vargas[37]

In 1930, in the wake of the Great Depression, Brazil experienced another military coup. Initially bloodless, it installed the leader who would leave a greater mark on Brazil than anyone until Lula: the charismatic, savvy, and ruthless Getúlio Vargas. Vargas was a fascist sympathizer who admired Hitler and Mussolini. He did not believe that democracy was a feasible option for Brazil. Seeing what he believed to be models of success in Germany and Italy, he held that only a strong national hand could finally conquer Brazil's interior and industrialize the country. He also said—and this resonated with Brazil's masses—that liberal democracy was inherently intertwined with corruption and fraud. Vargas was canny enough to introduce women's suffrage in 1932, although it was a "suffrage" without democracy. Far more illustrative was that he did so while repressing the very new women's movement: Vargas "smashed the first small wave of feminine activism" fighting for suffrage.[38] As we will see in chapter 4, he also banned women from playing soccer, symbolically shutting them out of a cultural space that was generating both national pride and a sense of national identity.

Despite his sympathies, Vargas sided with US president Franklin Delano Roosevelt and the Allied powers in World War II. Roosevelt was deeply concerned, given Vargas's fascist proclivities as well as Brazil's growing German émigré population, that Brazil could well side with the Axis powers and serve as a beachhead for Hitler in the Western Hemisphere. Vargas leveraged this fear to cut a lucrative deal with FDR for Brazil to become the number-one rubber producer for the US war effort. Vargas was thrilled that FDR and the United States had been forced to come to him, hats in hand. Yet the people who paid the price for this deal were the Brazilian citizens conscripted to make the journey into the rubber plantations of the Amazon. Known as the "rubber soldiers," they worked in slave conditions for the war effort and are still fighting for reparations to this day. As one of them explained in 2010, "An army official came to my town and told us we could join the fight on the front line in Italy or go to the Amazon. He said we would become heroes in the rubber battle and get rich tapping rubber." Once numbering fifty-five thousand, today the rubber soldiers are down to their last several thousand survivors.[39] ·

Vargas, it must be noted, was also the first leader of Brazil who understood the value both of nationalism and of actively fostering a sense of national identity. Perhaps this resulted from his careful study of Europe's fascists, but either way, he plowed funds into creating a "unique" Brazilian culture. He funded national organizations to promote and teach soccer as well as supporting Brazil's internationally renowned samba schools. Samba is a Brazilian dance and music that combines cultural elements from Africa and Rio; Vargas emphasized the African contribution and celebrated the idea of a country as a mosaic that brought together disparate cultural elements to create a greater whole.[40] But even as he celebrated samba and soccer, Vargas also cracked down militarily on any efforts to create cultural space he did not define as "Brazilian"—such as Japanese and Jewish schools and newspapers. These he had eliminated, seeing them as a threat to "Brazilian identity." Communist and other dissident political parties were also outlawed and strikes remained illegal from 1937 to 1946. When some still took place, particularly in São Paulo, he met them with intense repression, arresting, torturing, and even killing union organizers.

Vargas was eventually forced out of office in 1945 thanks to spiraling inflation that saw the cost of living in Rio double and São Paulo triple. Dissatisfaction and resistance to Vargas were also rooted in anger over the conditions of the health care and education systems (sound familiar?). Literacy levels still hovered around 25 percent and life expectancy was just forty-six years. In one of the most stunning political reinventions imaginable, Vargas was reelected in 1950 as a born-again populist and a major supporter of labor unions. He started the national oil company, Petrobras, under the left-populist slogan "The oil is ours." He instituted a minimum wage and formed the Brazilian Labor Party, which was seen as the political party for workers and the peasantry. The man who had outlawed strikes became known as the "Father of the Poor."[41] But his administration faced a variety of corruption scandals and the economy was in disarray due to the plummeting price of coffee, then the single cash crop. Vargas took his own life with a gunshot in 1954. In his suicide note, he wrote, "The crisis of coffee production came and the price of our chief product went up. We tried to defend the price, and the answer was such violent pressure on our economy that we had to give in."[42]

Vargas's problem was not limited to local corruption scandals and an economy that was eroding his popularity. It was his inability to manage and control the fundamental trend warping his dreams of national mission and prominence on the global stage: massively expanding social inequality. Any effort to address this inequality, like the raising the minimum wage, met with implacable resistance from the oligarchs, the new industrialists, and the military. This exploding inequality grew up side by side with urbanization and the creation of the favelas. The interior remained more or less the Wild West, with Brazilians still seen as "clinging to the coast like crabs."[43]

After Vargas's suicide, Brazil elected a radical left-nationalist president named Juscelino Kubitschek. Known by his initials, JK, he ruled from 1956 to 1961 and is still remembered with great affection as one of the fathers of modern Brazil. Born in poverty, JK was a medical doctor before becoming immersed in politics. When elected, he saw the critical importance of breaking up the oligarchs' power and diversifying the economy. His slogan was that the nation needed to make "fifty years of progress in five." JK succeeded in building a new national capital in Brasília, which symbolically lies in the interior of the country—a national dream since the initial 1891 constitution. Placing the capital in the interior sent a message that the nation was no longer comprised of "crabs clinging to the coast" but that the entire land had in fact, after 450 years, finally been brought into an actualized nation-state.

The Kubitschek presidency created a period of economic optimism in which Brazil's economy experienced explosive growth and seemed to break out of its historic patterns of underdevelopment. Galeano described it in *Open Veins of Latin America*:

> Those were the days of growth euphoria. Brasilia emerged as if from a magician's cauldron . . . highways and great dams were built; automobile factories produced a new car every two minutes. The industrial curve climbed steeply. Doors were flung open to foreign investment, the dollar invasion was hailed, the dynamism of progress was felt in the air. . . . The leap forward was financed by inflation and a heavy external debt that would be unloaded on the backs of successor governments.[44]

This was true. Eighty percent of all investment between 1955 and 1962 came from state-guaranteed loans, which meant borrowing the money from successive generations, who would have to pay the bill when it came due. The optimism of the JK years was also tightly connected to Brazil's success on the international soccer stage and its victory in the 1958 World Cup, led by two wildly charismatic teenagers called Garrincha and Pelé—more on them in chapter 4. Soccer historian David Goldblatt notes that "money was pouring into football" during this period: "The legacy of the Vargas years, in which black and mulatto players had been integrated economically and stylistically into a professional game, was strengthened by the influx of resources and new urban migrants and the booming popular cultures they helped create."[45]

Like so many of Brazil's rulers before and since, JK was plagued by rumors of corruption. (He would be the last president to finish a term in office until 1998.) None of the charges were ever proven, but his successor came to office in 1961 with a promise to "sweep the corruption out of the country."[46] He resigned in short order and was replaced by João Goulart, a left-wing economic nationalist who attempted to enact a "Basic Reforms" plan with an emphasis on redistributing land, improving adult literacy, extending voting rights to people who could not read, and taxing multinational corporations. Goulart also pledged to be a global leader on nuclear disarmament and vowed to stand up to the IMF and the crippling debts it was imposing on the country.[47]

In this Cold War climate, with the United States and the USSR competing for influence in Latin America, such radical "antibusiness" policies attracted the attention of the White House. Sure enough, in 1964, Goulart was deposed by a military coup, with the approval if not the direct support of the United States. There is audiotape of President Lyndon Johnson saying that the United States needed to take "every step that we can" to ensure Goulart's overthrow.[48] LBJ recognized the new military government as legitimate within hours of the coup. In fact, Goulart had still neither resigned nor left Brazil when Johnson, unable to restrain himself, sent a congratulatory telegram to military puppet Pascoal Ranieri Mazzilli, who had provisionally assumed the presidency.[49] Barely a month after the coup, US ambassador Lincoln Gordon, touring Brazil's army barracks, said that deposing Goulart "might be included with the Marshall Plan proposal, the Berlin blockade, the defeat of Communist aggression in Korea, and the solution of the Cuban missile crisis as one of the most important moments of change in mid–twentieth century world history."[50] As the coup took place, in an operation code-named Operation Brother Sam, the United States kept an aircraft carrier, the USS *Forrestal*, waiting just off Rio's coast in case its military muscle was needed.

The military dictatorship held political power in Brazil for the next twenty-one years. The nation's economic director, Roberto Campos, said in 1965 that "the era of charismatic leaders surrounded by a romantic aura is giving place to a technocracy."[51] A friend of Galeano wrote him a heartbreaking letter in 1966, describing the conditions for ordinary Brazilians: "We are a beaten, dominated, conquered, destroyed nation. The regime had to ban strikes and destroy unions and parties, to jail, torture, and kill, to cut workers' wages by any means necessary."[52] This era was also, not coincidentally, when Brazil began selling off millions of acres of the Amazon rainforest to US business interests. Galeano notes that "before 1967 . . . foreign capitalists bought, at $0.07 an acre, a tract larger than Connecticut, Rhode Island, Delaware, Massachusetts, and New Hampshire put together. . . . Par for the course in Latin

America: its resources are always surrendered to imperialism in the name of its lack of resources."[53]

The establishment of the military dictatorship did not spur the mass killings and slaughters that took place in subsequent years in places like Chile, Bolivia, and Argentina. The "disappeared" in Brazil numbered in the hundreds instead of the thousands, and there was no "great leader" like Chile's Augusto Pinochet. Instead, a series of five generals controlled the nation in this period. However, because it was the first country in the Southern Cone to fall to dictatorship, Brazil was used as a base to launch subsequent coups. As Noam Chomsky and Edward S. Herman note, "From Brazil, and with continuing U.S. assistance, torture spread throughout much of Latin America in the 1960s and early 1970s, with Brazil serving as a torture-aid subcontractor."[54] In 1970, Brazil won the World Cup, which, along with a spike in economic growth, contributed to a general mood that there would be no alternative to military rule. The dictatorship adopted slogans such as "Forward Brazil" and "Brazil: Love It or Leave It" to hammer the point home.

Goodbye to All That: The End of the Dictatorship

The military government effectively used torture and repression to smash the revolutionary left by 1974, but even without consistent political challenges, change was roiling the country. Brazil was finally on the path of industrialization. In addition, the population exploded from forty million people in 1960 to eighty-two million in 1985. The country was becoming younger, poorer, and far more restive. Much of this population growth was in the area most difficult for the military to control: the favelas. "The favela association movement became a vanguard in the national mobilization against the dictatorship.... The wave of mobilization for urban reform ... helped pressure the military government to legalize the formation of new political parties in 1980, and to hold democratic elections for state governors in 1982."[55]

The era of military rule was also marked by corruption and an inability to address problems of education and healthcare or to tame the

inflationary nature of the boom-and-bust, production-for-export economy. The year 1984 saw millions in the streets rallying for the right to
vote: the biggest political protests the country would see until the Confederations Cup protests of 2013.[56] The protestors had a simple, unassailable slogan: "I want to vote for president." A leading figure at the
rallies was soccer star and 1982 World Cup captain Socrates, whose
team, Corinthians, proudly operated on democratic principles and took
a formal position against the dictatorship. Soccer announcers also addressed the crowd, cementing the connection between soccer and politics of which Vargas had dreamed, though perhaps not for the ends
Vargas had in mind.

　　Like the end of royal rule and the end of slavery, the dictatorship
did not end in the fires of war but with a pragmatic acceptance. João
Figueiredo, Brazil's last military leader, who governed from 1979 to
1985, took small steps every year to reestablish civilian rule. Political
prisoners and those in exile were granted amnesty and six new political
parties were founded. In 1985, civilian rule was enacted with the indirect election of Tancredo Neves, who died of a heart attack before he
could take power. Yet civilians' ability to vote for their leaders could
not tame the economic cycle of booms and busts that still scarred the
economy. In 1988 inflation was more than 1,000 percent, and there
was a "brain drain" as educated young people emigrated to find work
and a stable economy in other countries. In 1989 and 1990, currency
values jumped 2,700 percent in one twelve-month period. One worker
famously said, "What good does it do to have a shopping bag full of
money if all I can do is buy a kilo of beans?"[57]

　　With hyperinflation and hypercorruption came a crime wave as
well as a series of epic gun battles between drug dealers and the police.
Brazil became internationally infamous for an explosion of homicides
and the kidnappings of wealthy residents and tourists, though the level
of police violence was little known outside the country. This rising violence was, as Bryan McCann wrote, rooted in the "partially demobi-
lized security forces of the Latin American dictatorships [which]
became interest groups in the new Latin American democracies, ex-

acerbating violence in attempts to secure their own position," as well as an "an expanding illegal economic sector" in which "the two principal commodities were cocaine and guns."[58] The well-heeled refused to venture out of their gated communities without armed escorts, creating images of a nation hopelessly divided against itself. Yet the real war—with a real body count—was not the criminals kidnapping and murdering the rich, but the police acting with extreme prejudice against the poor.[59] As McCann writes,

> Favelas became stigmatized as the source of pervasive urban violence . . . deeper class divisions did not disappear. Instead, those divisions hardened into new forms of discrimination and exclusion . . . the border between the favela and the rest of the city was increasingly enforced through heavy armament. Rio's elite retreated into closed condominiums, private schools, and shopping malls guarded by private security; they fortified their apartment buildings and coveted armored vehicles and personal weapons.[60]

The dirty secret of state violence and police brutality seeped out into the open during the night of July 23, 1993, when Rio police attacked sixty sleeping street children. Eight were killed. All of the children, part of the city's exploding homeless population, were sleeping in an area that they believed to be safe: the steps of Rio's Candelária Cathedral.[61] At the time this massacre garnered international headlines, São Paulo's police department had the highest homicide rate of any force on earth.[62]

Amid this decay, Brazil's education and healthcare system was by almost every marker actually worse than it had been in the 1970s. Racism, although little discussed, still defined opportunity and access; Afro-Brazilians held very few positions of power or influence out of the music studio or off of the athletic fields. The year of the attack by police on sleeping homeless children, inflation hit 2,500 percent.[63] This nation of unimaginable wealth was in free fall. If someone had said in 1993 that this country would not only be able to stabilize its economy, but also raise millions out of destitution and even pave the way for an economic boom, people would have looked at them as if they were daft.

How did Brazil do it? Before we go through the mechanics of how this was done, I should be clear that it is highly debatable, given the current state of its economy, just how secure Brazil ever actually was and how much of this recovery was illusory. Either way, to understand the current state of affairs in advance of the World Cup and Olympics, it is worthwhile to figure out just how a country with a 2,500-percent inflation rate rescued itself from an economic free fall in just a few short years.

President Fernando Henrique Cardoso, popularly known as "FHC," tamed hyperinflation by taking the radical step of scrapping Brazil's currency and starting with an altogether new system of exchange. Switching currencies wasn't radical in itself: Brazil had been changing to a new currency every few years due to inflation. This was known as O Plano Real—the Real Plan ("real" being the name of the new currency it introduced).

Cardoso first introduced the Real Plan in 1994, when he was finance minister under President Itamar Franco. It was meant to address the economic instability caused by historically high inflation rates. Foreign and national investment in Brazil had slowed to a standstill because when inflation is high, production costs spiral, eliminating any prospect for profit and reinvestment. In addition, high inflation deeply damages the banks because the amount they lend is drastically reduced in purchasing power by the time it's paid back. These kinds of inflationary spasms had plagued Brazil for decades, though never so severely, thanks to a program of indexation the military dictatorship implemented and used in the 1970s that ensured that the prices of goods and wages were pegged to rise and fall together. They thought this could tame inflation, but this practice just locked it in and made it worse—as did the military's penchant for printing more money any time one of its state-run enterprises ran aground.[64]

Cardoso decided that the only solution was a dramatic departure. The Real Plan not only created a new currency, the real, but also implemented a mass austerity program, which included auctioning off state enterprises and dramatically reducing government spending. Cardoso also jacked up the nation's interest rates. Foreign currency began to flow: investors could make money simply by parking their cash in Brazilian banks. These currency streams made it easier for Brazilian banks to lend money to businesses. The real gained value as greater numbers of people converted their savings into Brazil's smoking new currency. A stable and valuable real also made imported goods cheaper for local consumption. Japanese-made electronics, because of Japan's own crisis, flowed into Brazil throughout the 1990s. These cheaper imported goods also acted as a control on inflation, forcing Brazilian producers to keep prices low in order to compete with imports.

All of this taken together allowed Brazil's inflation to fall from those highs of over 2,000 percent into the single digits. Once inflation had dropped, Brazil began to create a new kind of internal consumer market, where working people were able for the first time to open bank accounts and buy goods on credit. There would be no point in opening an account during a period of high inflation because the longer you would save, the more worthless your money, yet without a bank account it was impossible to get a credit card. It was around this time that the country also expanded the practice of giving individual residents of favela dwellings titles and assigning them value, so the properties would not be seen or perceived as "community owned." These consumption patterns would have a dramatic effect on Brazilian life and culture, even as they simultaneously made Brazil the neoliberal darling of international capital and its media organs, which lustily described Brazil as "thrust[ing]" into "the forefront of the global trend toward open markets and free trade."[65]

Cardoso's Brazil was also trying to send a message to international capital that was heard loudly and clearly by FIFA and the IOC in the following decade: that Brazil is a safe place to hold your mega-events and that the government will allow the neoliberal games to operate as they wish without government interference or restraint. The contradiction of this entire plan, however, is that it was also predicated on an attack on working-class living standards and unions the likes of which the military could have only dreamed. Wages and social services were casualties of the market. Not long after Cardoso left office, Brazil held the ignominious ranking of "most unequal country on earth," with 31 percent of the country living below the UN poverty line.[66]

These attacks on working-class living standards were doubly impacted by the fact that initially the Real Plan sputtered on its own terms. The entire plan was predicated on making a country attractive for foreign investment and Brazil's economy was slammed by the global downturn of the late 1990s, which hit the "Asian Tiger" countries Brazil was courting particularly hard. In the end Cardoso's Brazil had to be saved from catastrophe by a $41.5 billion loan from the IMF. The bailout was hugely unpopular in Brazil for reasons that echo deeply into Brazil's history: the idea of being trapped in the chains of foreign debt held by the powers of the Global North. Its unpopularity was fueled even further by the fact that the bailout did not work; the economy continued to slump.

Cardoso's response was the equivalent of putting out a fire with gasoline. He rushed to relaunch his campaign to make Brazil friendly to foreign investors. This meant even sharper reductions in government spending, even more privatizing of state industries, and even more driving down workers' wages. In short, more austerity. This caused terrible pain among the Brazilian masses. When Cardoso's government privatized and sold off the steel, telecom, and mining industries, the consequences fell on the shoulders of the most vulnerable. Historian Kenneth Maxwell noted the "perverse effects" of these decisions: "Many industrial workers were displaced as imports flooded the consumer market. Not only did the service sector expand, but many industrial workers were forced into the informal sector. Subsequently, unemployment increased dramatically."[67] Cardoso's losing streak was so acute that even Brazil's soccer team, defending their title as World Cup champions after winning it all in the United States on July 4, 1994, lost in the 1998 finals to underdog France.

The true beneficiary of this period of austerity was Lula, who, after years of running for office, now finally completed his unique journey to the presidency. In Lula, the people of Brazil saw change. They also experienced far more continuity than anyone expected.

CHAPTER 3
Oh, Lula!

The ghosts of all the revolutions that have been strangled or betrayed through Latin America's tortured history emerge in the new experiments, as if the present had been foreseen and begotten by the contradictions of the past.
—Eduardo Galeano[1]

You can't understand why the presence of the World Cup and Olympics jangles every frayed nerve in Brazil without understanding the presidency of Luiz Inácio Lula da Silva. Lula served as president from January 1, 2003, to January 1, 2011, and left office as the most popular living politician on earth with an eye-popping 80 percent approval rating.[2] Yet, even at his peak, discontent rumbled beneath the surface of Lula's presidency. As long as growth rates continued to hum, everyone cheered the "Lula model" of leadership, despite concerns about corruption, health care, and education. Today, as growth begins to sputter and the nation pours billions into hosting the World Cup and Olympics, the current president, Lula's anointed successor from the Workers' Party, the less charismatic, more technocratic Dilma Rousseff, has paid the price. Despite continuing Lula's policies, a unique amalgam of social democracy and free-trade neoliberalism, her popularity sits at less than half that of her mentor.

Let's talk Lula.

Lula's Rise

Luiz Inácio Lula da Silva is known by a single nickname, Lula, in the style of the nation's great soccer players. And like soccer in Brazil, his reign as president feels larger than life, with the tall tales becoming even more burnished depending on who is doing the telling. It seems that almost everyone, friend and enemy alike, has a personal favorite story involving the labor leader turned head of state. To me, the most evocative, if unflattering, Lula story starts in 1998. That year Brazil, still reeling from record inflation, was granted the largest rescue package in history of the IMF, as described in the last chapter. The loans totaled more than forty-one billion dollars, and the conditions tied to them included deep cuts in Brazil's already tenuous social safety net. Lula, like all labor leaders, was on the front lines protesting the aid package.

A decade later, under Lula's rule, Brazil officially became an IMF creditor—not a debtor—after securing the purchase of ten billion dollars in bonds. In other words, Brazil was buying a profitable piece of the debt of the poorer nations of the world. Lula, deploying the swagger that made him formidable when he was on the other side of the barricades, strutted like a peacock and said, "Don't you think it's chic for Brazil to lend to the IMF?" He laughed and said that he looked forward to "go[ing] down in history as the president who lent a few reals to the fund."[3] It is difficult to find historical precedent anywhere on earth for Lula's leadership in Brazil, primarily for what he accomplished and the way he accomplished it. There may be similar leaders, and parts of his social agenda may have found echoes in other places, but the Lula experience has been unique. Lula was a true neoliberal social democrat. He stitched together left-wing and right-wing economic prescriptions to bring millions out of abject poverty, but did little to solve some of the country's most pressing social problems. And he did so in a context that few—perhaps no—other social-democratic leaders faced in the 2000s: extremely high growth rates and a commodity boom that left the country flush with cash. To know how he and the country arrived at this point, you need to know the man.

Lula was born on October 27, 1945, the seventh of eight children all raised in poverty in Brazil's impoverished Northeast. When he was seven, his mother moved the whole lot of them to São Paulo, traveling for thirteen days in the back of a flatbed truck. Lula had to leave school in the second grade to work and support his family, but taught himself to read at the age of ten—the beginning of his impressive intellectual life as an autodidact. At nineteen he lost a finger in a factory accident and, according to lore, ran from hospital to hospital, doors slamming in his face. This experience was transformative, spurring him to become involved in union activities, a nine-fingered firebrand determined to improve conditions for workers and fight the antilabor priorities of the military dictatorship.[4]

No matter where the mythmaking ends and the reality begins, there is no question that Lula's rise was meteoric. He was elected president of the São Paulo steelworkers' union at twenty and brashly expanded its numbers, despite organizing under the conditions of a military dictatorship. During this time, young Lula was imprisoned for a month for organizing what the dictatorship's Labor Courts deemed an illegal strike. In February 1980, he helped found the party that would catapult him to the presidency, the PT (Partido dos Trabalhadores, or Workers' Party), at age thirty-four. The PT brought together reformists, revolutionaries, trade unionists, socialists, environmentalists, and liberation theologists into an electoral as well as activist political organization. It became home to some of the leading theorists and academics in the country, who attempted to articulate just how Brazil, with all of its natural wealth and radical multiculturalism, had arrived at this point of military dictatorship and economic crisis.[5]

Lula further built his base in 1983 by launching the CUT (Central Única dos Trabalhadores, or United Workers' Federation), now the largest union federation not only in Brazil but in all of Latin America, with seven and a half million members. He ran for president unsuccessfully three times before being elected in 2002 in a landslide, with 62 percent of the vote. In that election, Lula received more votes than anyone who had ever run for public office *in the history of democratic politics.*

When Lula took office, he inherited a country in crisis. Inflation had stabilized, yet more than one-third of the population lived under the UN poverty line—the highest rate of inequality in the world. Argentina had just declared the largest sovereign default in history and Brazil, many predicted, would follow suit. Lula's immediate agenda was to assure international financial institutions and investors that he was no flaming radical and that Brazil would honor its debts—the very IMF debts he had protested as usurious and immoral. To make sure the international loan sharks were paid, Lula selected a motley crew of economic conservatives and globalists to head his Central Bank and Ministry of Finance. On his orders they went even further than what the IMF demanded, raising interest rates and slashing public spending. He became known as "the IMF's favorite president." The *Financial Times* was so besotted with him it suggested he be named to head up the World Bank.[6] It was a bitter pill to swallow for many in the PT and the social movements that had propelled him to power.

By the time Lula left office, the number of Brazilians living in poverty had dropped dramatically. As millions were lifted out of poverty, inequality lessened even as business boomed (according to—disputed—government statistics). During Lula's tenure, from 2002 to 2010, while many of the world's economies drooped and the United States poured more than a trillion dollars into its war in Iraq, international capitalists chose Brazil's stock market as their favorite place to park their currency. Between 2009 and 2011, Brazil vaulted from fifteenth to fourth on the list of countries receiving the most foreign direct investment. In 2011, that figure totaled sixty billion dollars. In 2011, Brazil also surpassed Italy and Great Britain to become the fifth-largest economy on earth.[7] Today, three-fifths of Latin American industrial production takes place in Brazil. This is remarkable when you consider that industrialization was not even a tangible reality in the country until 1950.[8] São Paulo, all by itself, is now larger and has a higher gross domestic product (GDP) than the next two biggest South American countries, Argentina and Colombia. Brazil now exports more beef than any nation on earth, with Russia its largest single customer.[9]

In the context of this stunning growth, Lula sought to identify himself as a personification of the Brazilian masses. When he left office, he said, "If I failed, it would be the workers' class which would be failing; it would be this country's poor who would be proving they did not have what it takes to rule."[10] As self-serving as that statement is, there is at least an element of truth in it. You cannot understand Lula's rise from union militant to the highest office in the land without understanding that this was not the triumph of an individual, but the culmination of what historian Perry Anderson calls "the most remarkable trade-union insurgency of the last third of a century"[11]—the same insurgency that toppled the Brazilian dictatorship in 1985.

And yet, as much as this seemed like a storybook rise of man, economy, and nation, there was a rot beneath the surface, seen most publicly in a series of corruption scandals. With the election of Lula and the PT, many expected that a page had been turned and that organized graft in Brazilian politics would become a thing of the past. Instead, corruption emerged so quickly and virulently that the Lula era almost ended just as it was getting started.

First, in the spring of 2005, José Dirceu, the head of Lula's cabinet, and Delúbio Soares, the PT treasurer, were caught conducting a "cash for votes" operation, using an illegal slush fund to wire money to the deputies of the smaller parties in Congress.[12] Then there was the resignation of Antonio Palocci, a key PT leader, in the spring of 2006. Palocci was running a "party house" near Brasília that operated as a den of prostitution and bribery. Instead of coming down on this with the full weight of the presidency, Lula made a massive effort to keep Palocci. In typical Lula style, he compared Palocci to the soccer star Ronaldinho, making the case that, whatever his faults, he was too valuable a player to give up.[13] (Lula has never hesitated to use soccer to make his points, whether through metaphor, criticizing certain players, or just wearing the color of his favorite team, Corinthians. Like Vargas before him, he knows that the cultural value of soccer should never be underestimated.) But as further details emerged, Palocci had to step down. He was eventually acquitted by the nation's

Supreme Federal Tribunal—yet this only added to the cynicism about the "new day" Lula had promised. As Anderson detailed:

> Of the eleven current members of the tribunal, six of them appointed by Lula, two have been convicted of crimes in lower courts. One . . . made legal history by guaranteeing immunity to a defendant in advance of his trial, but was saved from removal by his peers to "preserve the honor of the court." Another supported the military coup of 1964, and could not even boast a law degree. A third, on casting a crucial vote to acquit Palocci, was thanked by the president in person for assuring "governability." . . . Scenes like these, not vestiges of an older oligarchic regime, but part and parcel of the new popular-democratic order, preclude complacency about the prospects ahead, without abrogating them.[14]

The scandal could have brought Lula down before he even started; many believed that, at the very least, it would cause the PT to get blown out of office in the 2006 elections. They were wrong. Lula won his second election with 61 percent of the vote, roughly the same number as before, although the composition of his voters was poorer and more elderly. Many in the middle classes were pushed away, according to polls, by the corruption scandals and the absence of progress on—this will sound familiar—education and health care.[15]

In the period prior to the 2006 elections, the Brazilian economy improved dramatically. Credit for this goes less to the austerity programs IMF officials and *Economist* editors advocated than to the discovery of massive oil deposits and to China's unprecedented economic growth. No matter who was in office, Brazil would have benefited dramatically from a China desperate for two of Brazil's most plentiful exports, soy and iron ore. It also became a major buyer of Brazil's cattle reserves. All of this production for export meant that the country's average growth in Lula's first three years as president was 4.3 percent and climbing (compared to just 1.6 percent in the 1990s). With these numbers, Lula was going to win again—and win he did.[16]

Unlike Venezuela's Hugo Chávez, who positioned himself as an opponent of unfettered globalization, the PT and Lula were avid participants in free-marketeering and international finance. This paid dividends in the mid-2000s, rocketing the Brazilian economy to unprecedented heights with growth of 8 percent per year. The country was flooded with consumer goods from its new partners in China and East Asia; employment, as well as consumer spending, was on the rise. This also provided the economic basis for Lula's highly popular social policies aimed at combating economic inequality—the very inequality aggravated by some of his own earlier policies.

Lula may have been the IMF's "favorite president." He did not, however, fit easily into the neoliberal mold. Lula emphasized modest social programs. He also insisted on a level of state economic control that would be distasteful to neoliberals in the United States—though, again, his record here is inconsistent at best. But his quest to make Brazil a friendly center for capital investment and a key trading partner for China showed its benefits most sharply when Wall Street crashed in 2008: in Brazil, it was no more than *uma marolinha*, a ripple.[17] Lula said, "Crisis? What crisis? Ask Bush. It's his crisis."[18] While the United States hemorrhaged half a million jobs per month in early 2009, Lula's Brazil continued its rapid growth—even US treasury secretary Tim Geithner was praising its economy for leading the world out of a recession.

Lula the fire-breathing radical had become a darling of the *Economist* and *Financial Times* crowd, who regularly contrasted his leadership with that of the "irresponsible" Chávez. Many on the left believed that, like so many left-wing Latin American reformers before him, he would at some point have to "face a decisive choice": either to lead a workers' struggle for economic justice or to serve the interests of the markets.[19] But Lula never had to face that choice while in office.

Negotiating Neoliberalism: Lula's Foreign Policy

How did Lula do both? How could he feed the ravenous appetites of neoliberalism while raising the living standards of the poor?

To understand this, first we need to talk about what neoliberalism is. In the United States, when we hear the term "liberal," it's usually coming from Republicans who are talking about Democrats—a political term that means you lean left but aren't a radical. The liberalism in "neoliberalism," on the other hand, is *economic* liberalism, which describes people who want "free-market" capitalism to rule economic life—meaning (to greatly simplify it) that they want to expand the private sector and shrink the public sector as much as possible. (Translation: sell off the public schools to the highest bidder and start drilling for oil in national parks.) "Corporatist" is probably a better term. The neoliberal philosophy as we know it today was crafted and honed beginning in the 1960s by the economist Milton Friedman and his disciples at the University of Chicago, known collectively as the Chicago School. In the fevered imaginations of its proponents, the workings of the market are a "celestial clockwork"[20] that regulates itself perfectly when left alone. As Naomi Klein put it:

> Like all fundamentalist faiths, Chicago School economics is, for its true believers, a closed loop. The starting premise is that the free market is a perfect scientific system, one in which individuals, acting on their own self-interested desires, create the maximum benefit for all. It follows ineluctably that if something is wrong within a free-market economy—high inflation or soaring unemployment—it has to be because the market is not truly free. . . . The Chicago solution is always the same: a stricter and more complete application of the fundamentals.[21]

In practice, the "fundamentals" amount to taking money and power out of the hands of ordinary people and putting them in the hands of the rich, whose "self-interest" creates wealth that Ronald Reagan famously claimed, following Friedman's advice, would "trickle down" to the rest of us.

The problem, of course, is that the "trickle" promised to workers never does seem to materialize. The wealth stays at the top—and in return, the masses of people are expected to make enormous sacrifices. Neoliberalism's top priorities include crushing unions, privatizing health care and education, abolishing worker protections like safety rules and the minimum wage, and removing environmental protections—all of which stand in the way of truly "free" trade. In the developing world (and, increasingly, poor areas of rich countries, like the southern United States), neoliberals' freedom to pursue wealth has them pushing governments to create "free-trade zones," "promise zones," and so on—areas with nice names in which bosses get a break from tax and labor laws, so they can run nonunion sweatshops where workers have literally no rights. If anything, the wealth trickles up as services that the wealthy do not depend upon (like public transportation and public education) are eliminated. As Klein points out, "Because of the obvious drawbacks for the vast majority of the population left outside the bubble, other features of the corporatist state tend to include aggressive surveillance . . . , mass incarceration, shrinking civil liberties and often, though not always, torture."[22]

As you might imagine, neoliberal economics tend to be pretty unpopular with the electorate. This is especially true in the Global South, where people are well aware that neoliberalism is designed to give international financial institutions, the "great powers," and particularly the United States the upper hand. Left to their own devices, people tend to vote for things that make their lives better, like sharing wealth and resources and ensuring quality health care and education for all. Nobody wins elections by promising to turn the country into a sweatshop zone. So in order to put neoliberal policies in place, the world's elite need a strategy—some clever sleight of hand to get what they want before anyone can object. Enter the shock doctrine.

The idea is simple: people who are traumatized are more likely to agree to authoritarian measures, to suspending democracy, to doing whatever it takes. The trauma can be unexpected, like a natural disaster or a terrorist attack, or planned, like massive budget cuts or a military coup—anything that

> puts the entire population into a state of collective shock. The falling bombs, the bursts of terror, the pounding winds serve to soften up whole societies much as the blaring music and blows in the torture

cells soften up prisoners. Like the terrorized prisoner who gives up
the names of comrades and renounces his faith, shocked societies
often give up the things they would otherwise fiercely protect. . . .
After the tsunami, the fishing people in Sri Lanka were supposed
to give up their valuable beachfront land to hoteliers. Iraqis, if all
had gone according to plan, were supposed to be so shocked and
awed that they would give up control of their oil reserves, their state
companies and their sovereignty.[23]

While people are reeling, trying to figure out how to survive, corporations and the corporatist state walk through the open door and take
what they please. In New Orleans, in the wake of Hurricane Katrina,
the shock doctrine meant that huge swaths of prime real estate went
from the hands of poor black residents to rich developers and the public
school system was completely gutted.[24] After the 9/11 attacks, the shock
doctrine allowed the Bush administration to pass a wide-ranging set of
laws that restricted civil liberties on an unprecedented scale and created
the multibillion-dollar "homeland security" industry. And across the
developing world, international financial institutions are key players in
implementing the shock doctrine: when an economy falls into crisis,
the IMF and World Bank show up prepared to lend enormous sums—
if the country agrees to a harsh new regimen of "austerity," privatization,
and neoliberal reforms.

The Chicago School trained economists from all over the world
in shock doctrine tactics—and treated Latin America like its own dedicated laboratory. It engineered a coup in Chile (another 9/11 tragedy,
this one on September 11, 1973), then fanned out across the continent
establishing and training military dictatorships, including in Brazil.
But in recent years, the military dictatorship model has become less
necessary: political liberals, from Obama to Lula, have been more than
willing to embrace the logic of neoliberalism.

Lula's tenure in office coincided with the George W. Bush presidency's careening from one crisis to the next, borrowing unprecedented sums from China, getting itself mired in the Middle East,
and racking up more than a trillion dollars in debt. This gave Brazil

a historically unprecedented opportunity to shake the yoke of perpetual peonage to a United States that had neither the economic nor the military capital necessary to keep South America in line. Chávez in Venezuela, Evo Morales in Bolivia, and other leaders were signaling a new leftward shift throughout the region. Lula's former radicalism and continued ability to speak the language of the left allowed Brazil to maintain a good relationships with Morales, Chávez, and even Cuba's Fidel Castro.

Lula cannily positioned himself as a buffer between the extremes of US imperialism, on the one hand, and a radical regional anti-imperialist bloc, on the other. The negotiations over the Free Trade Agreement of the Americas (FTAA) stand as the quintessential example of Brazil's new power to mediate and even demobilize the radical wave on the continent while also presenting itself as a thorn in the side of the United States. The FTAA marked the hemispheric expansion of the controversial North American Free Trade Agreement (NAFTA), which in 1994, over the opposition of labor and environmental groups, created a "free-trade" bloc and eliminated tariffs between the United States, Canada, and Mexico. As the FTAA was hammered out over the course of the last decade, it sparked antiglobalization protests wherever negotiators met. Cuba, Venezuela, Bolivia, Ecuador, the Dominican Republic, Nicaragua, and Honduras all bitterly opposed it. But Brazil managed to lead a "moderate bloc" in conjunction with Argentina and Chile that for all intents and purposes scrapped the FTAA and, in its place, instituted a series of bilateral trade deals. This was not just an embarrassment for the United States; it established Lula's Brazil as the key power broker in future trade negotiations within Latin America. While Lula pursued his brand of neoliberalism economically, he used his foreign policy as a way to assert his nation's independence from the United States. Under Lula, Brazil recognized Palestine as an independent state. He also refused to take part in economic blockades of Iran. He promoted trade pacts that excluded the United States and strengthened relations with the its greatest headaches on this side of the Atlantic: Venezuela, Bolivia, and Cuba. Most symbolically, Brazil promoted and even held meetings of a new formation known as BRIC (Brazil, Russia, India, and China, a title invented by Goldman Sachs), which set about constituting a more-than-credible counterbalance to a global economy dominated by the United States and European Union.

Just as Lula was able to position himself at the crest of a surging wave of Latin American power, he also asserted Brazil as a twenty-first-century subimperial power in its own right by sending troops to occupy Haiti after President Jean-Bertrand Aristide was deposed in 2004. Lula even sent the Brazilian national soccer team over for a friendly match. Hundreds of thousands waited for hours to see Rivaldo, Ronaldinho, and other Brazilian stars defeat Haiti 6 to 0. Brazil's team was escorted to the stadium by a convoy of white tanks. They called it the Match for Peace. Here is how the *Washington Post* described the scene:

> On Wednesday, U.N. forces—most of them Brazilian—surrounded the stadium in full combat gear. Armored personnel carriers were stationed about 100 yards apart around the stadium, which was protected by fences and barbed wire. Haitian police patrolled with German shepherds and Rottweilers, and helicopters flew overhead. Blue-helmeted peacekeepers carrying shotguns ringed the field inside the stadium.[25]

If you're hearing echoes of the old nineteenth-century tactic of US troops bringing baseball bats and balls to the Caribbean, you're not far off. Many have also pointed out that Brazilian troops in Haiti are using and honing methods developed for controlling large, densely concentrated poor populations—which could be very useful back home, for example in the favelas.

For the next seven years, until 2011, several thousand Brazilian troops aimed to, as one UN official admiringly put it, "turn Port-au-Prince into Disneyland."[26] For all of the UN's admiration, it must be noted that it bears responsibility for a cholera outbreak in Haiti and that its troops were also used to repress labor demonstrations and protests, among numerous other scandals.[27] The cost of this occupation was roughly 450 million dollars per year, in the poorest country in the

Western hemisphere—Haiti has 70 percent unemployment and an average income of three dollars per day.

Lula's Domestic Policy: Image and Reality

At home, Brazil's rapid economic growth allowed Lula to spend freely on social programs that challenged inequality and made his administration incredibly popular among his base of supporters, despite the stubborn facts that inequality and poverty still plagued the country. Once the economic upturn began to gain steam, Lula launched the social program called Bolsa Família. This is the policy most frequently used to explain Lula's popularity among the poor. Much of what it encompasses also existed under his predecessor Cardoso, but it was not "branded" in the same fashion. Bolsa Família, which translates roughly to "family purse," provides direct payments to 13.8 million impoverished families—fifty million people in total— but only if they are able to prove that their children attend school until age seventeen and go to health clinics for basic vaccinations and regular checkups. As the *Christian Science Monitor* reported, "the stipend is then deposited into the recipient's bank account (preferably that of a woman)," which has "helped raise 36 million Brazilians out of extreme poverty."[28] Between 2001 and 2011, the infant mortality rate did fall by 40 percent. In the impoverished Northeast it fell by 50 percent, a historic accomplishment. Malnutrition has also dropped, although numerous factors led to this improvement in the quality of life for Brazil's poor. The program only cost 2.5 percent of the nation's GDP, but its image mattered even more to Lula's presidency than its substance because, as Perry Anderson wrote, of "the symbolic message it delivers: that the state cares for the lot of every Brazilian, no matter how wretched or downtrodden, as citizens with social rights in their country. Popular identification of Lula with this change became his most unshakeable political asset."[29] The question that tortures analysts is whether Bolsa Família is a fig leaf on an otherwise neoliberal agenda or whether its existence marks a fundamental departure from neoliberalism itself.

Far more economically substantive, even if less symbolically powerful than Bolsa Família, was raising the minimum wage, which Lula increased by 50 percent between 2005 and 2010.[30] Other programs also acted as an economic stimulus to the poor and the working class, such as the *crédito consignado*, which guaranteed bank loans for household purchases to those who had never before held bank accounts, with repayment automatically deducted from monthly wages or pensions. Lula also required colleges to offer scholarships to poor students, which opened higher education to more than seven hundred thousand poor and working-class students. This collectively brought millions of Brazilians into an income bracket above seven thousand dollars per year, which the government was quick to classify as "middle class." It was estimated to cost 0.5 percent of GDP. As Lula liked to say, "It's cheap and easy to look after the poor."[31]

The sum total of these programs—the Bolsa Família, an increased minimum wage, and new access to credit—"set off a sustained rise in popular consumption, and an expansion of the domestic market that finally, after a long drought, created more jobs."[32] It also, even more importantly, created a popular impression that Lula genuinely cared about the poor—even as he was turning Brazil into a neoliberal paradise and the engine of an ailing global capitalism. Lula's supporters are quick to point out that progress for the poor under his administration, while rife with contradictions, was truly substantive. They point to numbers that, on paper, appear staggering: government data show the number of people classified as "poor" dropping from fifty to thirty million in Lula's first six years in office; the number of those described as "destitute" was cut in half.[33]

Yet when examining just how successful Lula was at "tackling inequality" while achieving growth, it is worth looking closer and remembering something Marcos Alvito told me: "Statistics are like a bikini. They show so much, but they hide the most important parts." First, the inequality numbers pointedly do not include the new stratum of Brazil's superrich, a rapidly growing class of billionaires, who have purchased the H. J. Heinz ketchup company, Anheuser-Busch, and other multinational companies. After buying Heinz and laying off hundreds of workers at its Pittsburgh headquarters, the wife of one employee rushed to early retirement referred to the situation as "the Brazilian plague." Meanwhile, between 2006 and 2008, the number of Brazil's millionaires increased by 70 percent—more than that of India. Taxes are also highly regressive for working people—another reason the excessive taxation to pay for new soccer stadiums spurred protests in 2013. If you live on less than twice the minimum wage, half of your income is taxed. In contrast, if you make thirty times the minimum wage, only a quarter of your income is taxed.[34]

One result of all this growth on capitalist, neoliberal terms has been that the oligarchy—the social class that has dominated Brazil since its founding five centuries ago—has actually become more powerful. This is particularly the case in Rio. The 2016 Olympic site is the only region of the country where inequality actually worsened under Lula's rule. The oligarchs' land ownership has not only increased but has become more concentrated than it was fifty years ago, a result of Brazil's transforming into one of the leading agribusiness and beef-producing countries on earth. As a part of this land grab, Lula and his successor Dilma Rousseff have been far tougher on the landless peasant movement than his right-wing predecessors.

In addition to the oligarchy's traditional power base, the countryside, over the last decade they have also ventured into the cities, where real-estate speculation reigns. Urban real-estate speculation, as anyone in Brazil's megacities will be quick to tell you, has followed an even more aggressive pattern, with a rush to seize urban land. When I was in Brazil, I visited comfortable middle-class apartments with rents that would make a New Yorker blanch. At one, on the twenty-first story of a high-rise, the elevator had been "out" for months, forcing people to walk up and down the stairs. It is like a slow-motion version of the age-old practice of landlords burning tenants out of their apartments. "They think they can turn this place into a luxury hotel," the residents told me. "So they are doing what they can to make us move. It is happening everywhere."

Not to shock anyone, but real-estate developers and construction workers are the biggest contributors to Lula's Workers' Party. Chris Gaffney described the situation to me:

> It's important to remember that Brazil, twenty-five years ago, was still a dictatorship . . . so the consolidation of democratic institutions is recent and they're still very weak. It's very easy to criticize, especially from a North American perspective, what we perceive as the neoliberalization of the Brazilian economy. But before, there was really no stability, so inflation's been under control for fifteen years, the economy has grown, it is more stable, but at the same time that there are people that have left poverty, the rich are more rich than they've ever been. Lula and the PT gave out scraps to the left that allowed them to really open up the country for massive profits on the right.

A Political Root Canal

During his second term in office, Lula expanded both his social welfare projects and Brazil's importance on the global stage after the discovery of massive offshore oil deposits in 2007 and 2010. With eighty billion barrels of oil and gas deposits for export, Brazil joined rarefied company among energy-producing countries.[35] The PT has pursued an aggressive program of offshore drilling (even though environmentalists were critical players in founding the Workers' Party), with a terrible toll on Brazil's environment.

Lula also dramatically slowed the gains of the Landless Workers' Movement (Movimento dos Trabalhadores Rurais Sem Terra, or MST). The MST has, for twenty-five years, been one of the most important organizations for social change in Brazil. It has 1.5 million members and a presence in twenty-three of Brazil's twenty-six states. Under Cardoso, a series of violent confrontations with the government turned the MST into an international cause. The attention did not stop Cardoso from criminalizing the movement, meeting its occupations with armed assaults. Believing Lula and the PT to be a friendly government, the MST shifted its strategy away from occupying public lands and began focusing on the areas gobbled up by agribusiness. Yet Lula resisted meeting with the MST until 2005. The meeting was hostile, with MST leaders pledging afterward to return to their confrontational ways. But they had been weakened by their earlier alliance with the PT.

Given that Lula was tough on labor unions, the environment, and the MST, one might think that grand social movements challenging these imperatives would mark his presidency. One would be wrong. Lula succeeded in dismantling any kind of popular response to his agenda. This point is critical, because it explains the spontaneous, disunified, and youthful nature of the 2013 protests.

Lula was able to demobilize the opposition to his neoliberal policies first and foremost by thoroughly transforming both the PT and the main trade-union federation that he helped found, the CUT. He "converted the party from a 'movement-party' to an electoral party."[36] These bureaucracies became a part of the ruling apparatus of the government and in return they were Lula's great defenders. The PT was now a political machine, in charge of accruing votes and doling out twenty thousand highly paid federal jobs. The CUT was now officially in charge of the country's largest pension fund. They were "inexorably sucked into the vortex of financialisation engulfing markets and bureaucracies alike. Trade unionists became managers of some of the biggest concentrations of capital in the country. . . . Militants became functionaries enjoying, or abusing, every perquisite of office."[37] The union paid a price for this. During the 1980s, under a period of dictatorship, the CUT represented more than 30 percent of Brazil's workers. Today, after a decade of Lula and the PT in power, that number is now 17 percent.[38] That is in many respects the most stunning statistic of Lula's presidency. The bitter fruit of neoliberalism—and its siblings, austerity and inequality—is that when these economic policies flourish, even under a "workers' party," the workers suffer.

The majority of the Brazilian left supported the PT from its formation in the 1970s through the election of Lula. The general impact of Lula's presidency was to throw this left into disarray and to confuse and demobilize social movements. Lula retained the loyalty of important sections of the left with large social bases, like the MST and the CUT, even as he carried out policies aimed at satisfying the international financial powers at the expense of Brazilian workers and failed to follow through on the agrarian reforms the MST had turned into an international issue. The PT was able to keep its core, but this new organization led to a massive disconnect with the working classes and shop floors from which the PT grew. I spoke with Marcelo Freixo, Rio's mayoral candidate from the left-wing Socialism and Freedom Party (Partido Socialismo e Liberdade, or PSOL), which formed after splitting from the PT. Freixo is an elected lawmaker in Rio who has repeatedly risked his life to expose the city's powerful militias; he even had to flee the country in 2011 because of his work.[39] He told me,

> The arrival of Lula in power actually weakened social movements initially because it co-opted them. These were people who had historically fought side by side with the PT and with Lula. So they naturally wanted to go with Lula, but many of them were co-opted as Lula moved to the right during his time in office. One of the damaging aspects of this is that for young people, it looks like all parties are the same. That they all form coalitions and come to power and behave in a similarly corrupt way. Lula is now allied with Fernando Collor, who was impeached in the early 1990s, and with [José] Sarney, who was a corrupt politician, Brazil's first democratically elected president [after the end of the military dictatorship]. They're all now aligned in the government. This generated amongst the population a sense that "they're all the same." That's very difficult to reverse. We are working on this, trying to reverse this perception: that's why our campaign has involved social movements as well as many young people.

The PT also lost many of its theorists and academics, who abandoned the party in despair. Radical Brazilian sociologist Chico de Oliveira, one of the historic founders of the PT, left the party in protest. When Perry Anderson asked Oliveira whether Lula's effect on the left could be compared to Franklin Roosevelt's New Deal in the United States, Oliveira replied that

> a more appropriate analogy . . . [is] the South Africa of Mandela and Mbeki, where the iniquities of apartheid had been overthrown

and the masters of society were black, but the rule of capital and its miseries was as implacable as ever. The fate of the poor in Brazil had been a kind of apartheid, and Lula had ended that. But equitable or inclusive progress remained out of reach.[40]

In 2004, expelled PT members formed the aforementioned Socialism and Freedom Party, an electoral left party that has had some electoral successes and important, albeit not extensive, connections to the broader social movements in the country. Its divisions from the MST can be seen in the comments of João Pedro Stedile, an MST leader, who said, "The PSOL tried to reconstruct a PT of the left but did not manage to do so, because the tactic, the [electoral] path is defeated. We will not accumulate the forces to vie for power through institutional paths."[41]

The social movements also suffered because Lula provided something the nation had not experienced in decades of economic upheaval and military dictatorship: stability. Brazilians' widespread desire for stability in the 2000s cannot be ignored. As one veteran movement activist said to me:

> Social movements throughout Brazil have been eviscerated under the PT, absolutely eviscerated. One of the reasons is . . . that people assumed they had a friend in power, and why would that person betray them in the way that Lula, or the PT, has? Once you assume power, you don't need to fight anymore. And so all these long-term social structures stopped, or they were co-opted, or they were given power so now the struggle needs to go against them. But the struggle against them comes from the right. So you either go all the way back to some mixture of fascism or Marxist/Leninism, or you just conform to the increase of the power that you've got and your struggle's over.

When Lula left office, the 2014 World Cup and particularly the 2016 Olympics were seen as his swan song: a signal that the world was finally granting Brazil the respect it felt it had deserved for almost a century. Tragically, the World Cup and Olympics are not symbolic successes. They walk hand in hand with graft, austerity, security crackdowns, and a set of spending priorities that would have made the young Lula blush.

Yet he also had the good fortune to win the bids for these mega-events just before the end of his term of office—meaning he avoided the much more difficult task of their implementation.

The Election of Dilma

Lula's political career brings to mind a line from the movie *The Dark Knight*: "Die a hero or live long enough to become a villain."[42] Lula did not die, but term limits pushed him out of office before economic stagnation, scandal, or the fallout from hosting the World Cup and Olympics could be pinned directly on his legacy. That has fallen on the shoulders of his chosen successor, Dilma Rousseff, popularly known as Dilma. Unlike Lula, Dilma was born into the upper middle class, her father a Bulgarian entrepreneur. After the military coup of 1964, seventeen-year-old Dilma became a socialist and an urban guerrilla. She joined the militant left-wing group Colina (Comando de Libertação Nacional, the National Liberation Command). Unlike Lula, who spent one month in prison during the dictatorship, Dilma was behind bars from 1970 to 1972, where she was tortured by the very government she would someday lead.[43] When Lula chose Dilma to succeed him, she was largely a political unknown, the last person standing to hold the banner of the Workers' Party after a series of scandals struck down more obvious contenders. It was a testament to Lula's legacy, the economic boom, and the social movements' inability to find purchase that Lula could sell the public on electing a veritable political unknown to lead the nation. Not only did Dilma win the first election after Lula left office, but the PT also emerged as the largest political party in Congress.

While Lula was basically able to have his cake and eat it too—both neoliberalism and social programs—Dilma has been president of the post-party hangover.

The *Economist*, the magazine of the neoliberal consensus, now blasts its former darling Brazil for being "a stagnant economy, a bloated state" with "the world's most burdensome tax code." Its editors sniff that "the markets do not trust Ms. Rousseff." Most hilariously, they tie the mass protests of 2013 to her lack of "fiscal rectitude," comparing her unfavorably to "the pragmatic Lula."[44] They do not see that, while they may have the right diagnosis for why her approval rating has fallen from 65 percent to a low of 30 percent—that is, taxation, corruption, health care, and education—the austerity they claim as a cure would, without question, bring people back into the streets. They didn't consider that her pledge to hold down the minimum wage and place strict boundaries on public spending might also have something to do with it.[45] Or that possibly, with the economy dragging, people who have clamored for years for massive public investment in the cities aren't pleased to see all that money getting plowed into hosting the 2014 World Cup and 2016 Olympics. They certainly didn't consider that maybe, *just maybe*, Brazilians don't want to spend billions on new stadiums while the poor are being displaced—especially when it's all for the benefit and service of the twenty-first-century version of the same European powers that have been stripping the country of its skin for four hundred years.[46]

"I used to be a fan of Dilma," a Rio teacher said to me, adding:

> But I lost respect for her when she sided with the mayor's plan for Olympic development. There are some huge contradictions between her federal policy and the local impact of the Olympic development, which she supports. . . . Dilma is just a capitalist. And this is just capitalism, it's all about making money. The poor are the ones who built this city. You couldn't be here without the poor of Rio. But now, the people who built the city are being pushed out. You can't have a positive legacy of the Games when the poor who created this city aren't part of that legacy.

Brazil has long sought respect on the international stage. At a state dinner held in his honor in Brasília in 1982, Ronald Reagan raised his glass to toast to Brazil and instead, whether by accident or as an act of condescension, toasted "to Bolivia."[47] Those days may be done, but international respect has its price. The neoliberal price, paid by Lula and continued by Dilma, is what laid the groundwork for the explosive 2013 Confederations Cup protests.

CHAPTER 4

Futebol: The Journey from Daring to Fear

> *Brazil has the most beautiful soccer in the world, made of hip feints, undulations of the torso and legs in flight, all of which came from capoeira, the warrior dance of black slaves, and from the joyful dances of big city slums. . . . There are no right angles in Brazilian soccer, just as there are none in the Rio Mountains.*
>
> —Eduardo Galeano[1]

The relationship between soccer and Brazil is not so much about sports as it is about national identity: it is the connective tissue in a country defined by different cultures crashing together in violence and beauty. This nation is Indigenous, African, German, Italian, Japanese, Lebanese, and Eastern European. When people consider what makes them "Brazilian," soccer operates much as baseball did in the United States decades ago: as a portal to a sense of belonging and a different national identity than their ancestors.

Soccer crosses into all aspects of Brazilian life. It is inextricable from the country's political, economic, and cultural history throughout the twentieth century. No other country is more identified with the sport that is a global obsession. Only Brazil has qualified for every World Cup since the tournament launched in 1930. Only Brazil has won the *Copa* five times. No other country has put its stylistic mark on the sport quite like Brazil. If you play the game in South Korea, Germany, or Zambia and you play it with flair, feints, and fakes, people will say you play in the "Brazilian style" and everyone will know exactly what that means. It was this "Brazilian style" that gave the sport its defining nickname, "the beautiful game."

Not surprisingly, soccer has also been a mirror reflecting Brazilian society. It has been put to use by military dictators and by those who resisted military dictatorship. Today, as Brazil gets ready to host the World Cup, its new soccer stadiums have become symbols of corruption, waste, and stagnation. Likewise, the homogenization of Brazil's beautiful game is a reflection of globalization, gentrification, and the way even a place defined by the Rio Mountains can become "flattened." It also reflects a colonial structure in which the best soccer players are developed in-country and then sold to the massive commercial conglomerates that operate the top clubs in Europe. The best players, who used to delight crowds at the Maracanã in between World Cups, are now another export.

To know soccer in Brazil is to know how Brazil sees itself, which is critical for the goals of this book and for anyone hoping to understand the current conflicts. As with all stories, we need to start at the beginning.

Soccer Comes to Brazil's Shores

> In Brazil, futebol's history falls into four broad periods: 1894–1904, when it remained largely restricted to the private urban clubs of the foreign born; 1905–1933, its amateur phase, marked by great strides in popularity and rising pressures to raise the playing level by subsidizing athletes; 1933–1950, the initial period of professionalism; and the post-1950 phase of world-class recognition accompanied by elaborate commercialism and maturity as an unchallenged national asset.
>
> —Robert Levine[2]

There is evidence that the elements of soccer stretch back to the Han Dynasty in China more than two thousand years ago. Different forms of the game have been seen in a variety of cultures and societies across the globe: there is something very elemental about trying to kick a ball into a goal. The modern sport as we know it today, however, was first codified in England in 1863. This was when representatives from schools and clubs across London met at the Freemasons' Tavern to expunge any elements of rugby from the sport. Before this time, some teams had played the game with rugby rules integrated, which included legal tackling, tripping, eye-gouging, and shin-kicking as much as kicking the ball. The rugby lovers were expelled and a set of widely agreed-upon rules about everything from the degree of contact allowed on the pitch to an absolute prohibition on the use of hands were finally established. From there, the sport then set about conquering the globe.

There are differing stories about how soccer found its way to Brazil. The most often repeated, and for many the most credible, story says that it all began with a young man named Charles Miller in 1894. Miller was the upwardly mobile son of a Scottish rail engineer working in Brazil to make sure that the trains could get goods to the ships for export. Miller arrived on Brazil's shores to work with his father. He also just happened to be an accomplished midfielder in Southampton, England. In tales that make him sound like Moses, he is said to have stepped off the boat at the port of Santos in São Paulo with two soccer balls, one in each hand: one a symbol of the game as it was in Europe, the other of what the game could become.[3] If Charles Miller really, honestly, and truly walked around thinking about his future iconography, then that is more impressive than any of his other accomplishments. What we do know is that Miller, out of boredom, started organizing "kickabouts" among his fellow expatriates living in São Paulo. (The city even has a street named after him.) These kickabouts attracted attention from locals fascinated by the sport, which they saw as similar in style and energy to the dance and martial arts popular in the country. Even though both men and women were, according to accounts, drawn to the game, play was a male-only exercise then and for decades afterward.[4]

Another origin story names Brazilian soccer's Prometheus as a Scottish dye worker named Thomas Donohue, who came to Brazil in

1893 to work at a textile factory in Bangu, on the outskirts of Rio. Richard McBrearty, curator of the Scottish Football Museum, contends that Donohue marked off a field near the factory and started to organize five-on-five matches in April 1894, six months before Miller's first game in São Paulo.[5] No matter whether one chooses to see soccer as having arrived on bourgeois or proletarian wings, the beautiful game arrived in Brazil as a part of that first post-emancipation wave of European migration—as industry was first expanding throughout the South American continent.

Some anthropologists argue that a form of the sport may have also existed in Indigenous culture, which gave it an air of familiarity to Brazilians. But one thing is clear beyond all shadow of a doubt: as soon as soccer reached Brazil the people made it their own, and it spread as if they had been poised and crouched, just waiting to play. Brazil's first football club was founded in 1900. São Paulo launched its first formal league in 1902.[6] Charles Miller said with wonder in 1904, "A week ago I was asked to referee in a match of small boys, twenty a side. . . . I thought, of course, the whole thing would be a muddle, but I found I was very much mistaken . . . even for this match about 1,500 people turned up. No less than 2,000 footballs have been sold here within the last twelve months; nearly every village has a club now."[7]

People of African descent were excluded at first, but the thrill of the game, along with the fact that poverty was not an obstacle to play, made it irresistible. After slavery's abolition in 1888, newly liberated Afro-Brazilians migrated in droves into the cities, creating a mass of urban poor for the first time in Brazil's history. These cities were very much under the cultural influence of the British Empire because of the treaty made for Brazil's independence fifty years earlier (see chapter 3). Soccer was present on fields throughout the citie, yet it did not become the "beautiful game" until Afro-Brazilians made it what we know today as "Brazilian." Their feints, fakes, and flair were reminiscent of the slave martial art of capoeira. In addition, many have theorized that because soccer was an integrated space in a racist society, Afro-Brazilian players took great pains to make no physical contact whatsoever with their opponents, lest they risk reprisals. That meant playing with a style that people found both aesthetically pleasing and effective. The widespread embrace of the Afro-Brazilian style—and, remember, newly emancipated slaves made up roughly half of the population—gave Brazil something it had never had during its period of royal independence: a national identity. A country in which one in two people had until recently been held in slavery, ruled by an oligarchy with unthinkable wealth, a country with historic connections to Portugal but really under the economic umbrella of the British empire: soccer brought these disparate strands together to create a connective tissue and a common Brazilian experience.

The sport continued to spread through Afro-Brazilian life. People made their own soccer balls and played without shoes, toughening the soles and sides of their bare feet with calluses and scar tissue. In many neighborhoods today, little has changed. I saw young people playing soccer in the favelas with beat-up, half-deflated balls. So much of play is in the body, the hips, that the ball becomes secondary to the act. By 1910, precisely because it was embraced by Afro-Brazilians, Rio had more makeshift soccer fields than any city in South America. The debut of Brazil's national team came in 1914, in a game against the British club Exeter City. Ten thousand spectators came out to watch Brazil beat the British club 2 to 1. Newspapers called the electric buzz in the stands "simply indescribable."[8]

Rio, not coincidentally, was also the site of the first club to field Afro-Brazilian players. It was called the Bangu Athletic Club, started in 1904 by the British managers of the same textile factory where Thomas Donohue had labored a decade earlier.[9] Many factories started soccer clubs in this era, another factor that brought the game to the Brazilian masses. This practice was seen in the United States as well: managers creating sports clubs in factories as a way to keep labor grievances at bay.

But if the game was flowering as a multicultural space on the public fields, racism and restriction dominated official league play. Like in the early decades of the Olympics, rules for admittance ensured that the sport remained aristocratic and white. As soccer historian Alex Bellos has written, "Football provided a justification to reconsolidate theories of white supremacy, which had been thrown into doubt by the abolition of slavery. The first nonwhite players on the big clubs tried to flatten their hair and whiten their skin. To this day, the Rio club Fluminense bears the nickname 'Rice Powder' because that is what opponents would chant at Carlos Alberto, the first 'mulatto' to play for the club."[10] These color lines and white supremacy started to wither only when integrated teams began achieving greater success. Vasco da Gama, a Rio club started by Portuguese-Brazilians, was the first league team to integrate formally. It won the championship with much fanfare in 1923, with a team made up of "three blacks, a mulatto, and seven working-class whites."[11] After Vasco won the championship, the other big Rio clubs set up a separate league excluding it. Vasco eventually journeyed back into the league and continued using black players despite rules designed to exclude them—such as requiring players to be otherwise employed and to be able to sign their names, as well as requiring each team to have its own stadium. The Portuguese community that supported Vasco found employment for its black players and even provided remedial education for them. The players' most lasting legacy to the sport, however, was the practice of referring to players by their first names or using nicknames; the Portuguese expats were said to have difficulty with the black players' multisyllabic last names. This is perhaps the origin of the uniquely Brazilian tradition of calling players by a single name, like Pelé, Ronaldo, or Ronaldinho.[12] This practice now extends to other sports as well: the Brazilian NBA basketball player Nenê Hilario is now known only as Nenê. It also operates in politics, as the last three presidents— FHC, Lula, and Dilma—can attest.

Once integration began in soccer, it was a tidal wave. This was quite different from the integration of sports in the United States, where twenty-five years after Jackie Robinson broke baseball's color line in 1947, Jim Crow laws were still in effect and teams had quotas on the number of African American players they would sign. Many of Brazil's teams set about the task of full integration as soon as it was allowed.

After 1938, when any pretense of stopping integration ended, the Rio club Bonsucesso fielded a team of eleven Afro-Brazilians without any fear about quotas or appearances.

Now, as Alex Bellos argues, "*futebol* was not the game that Charles Miller imported in 1894. *Futebol* was the sport that was played as a dance; it was the sport that united the country and that showed its greatness."[13] Bellos's description of the "Brazilian style" is stunning; he illustrates

> a game in which prodigious individual skills outshine team tactics, where dribbles and flicks are preferred over physical challenges or long-distance passes. Perhaps because of the emphasis on the drib-ble, which moves one's whole body, Brazilian football is often de-scribed in musical terms—in particular as a samba, which is a type of song and a dance. At their best, Brazilians are, we like to think, both sportsmen and artists. Since most Brazilians learnt from in-formal kickabouts, it was likely that they would play in a way less constrained by rules, tactics, or conventions. Since many started playing using bundles of socks, it was also likely that their ball skills would be more highly developed and inventive. Alternatively, one could explain the flashy individualism by pointing to the na-tional trait of showing off in public.[14]

The obvious point of comparison, as noted above, is the Brazilian martial art/dance of capoeira, devised by slaves as a dance that masks the use of lethal force. Today in Brazil, *capoeiristas* gather on beaches and in studios to practice this unique martial art. The movements in both Brazilian soccer and capoeira demonstrate the art of "hiding in plain sight." In both cases, the imprint of African culture, history, and influence cannot be overstated.

Soccer achieved even higher prominence with the ascension of mil-itary dictator Getúlio Vargas. Vargas understood that soccer was be-coming a national obsession and was the first major politician to see the political benefits of being identified with the sport. He started the National Sports Council in 1941 to fund a network of soccer clubs, with the goal of developing talent and making sure the national team had the best possible training and facilities. If we want to understand why Brazil is, as of this writing, the only country to have won the World Cup five times, part of the answer is certainly Vargas. He made sure that all of these leagues and federations were under his central control. He also pointedly and publicly subsidized all expenses for the national team's trip to France for the 1938 World Cup. This was a savvy move, as the country was enthralled by the thought of its team returning historic favors and conquering Europe. Brazil flourished in the 1938 tournament, coming in third after getting knocked out in the first round of the previous two World Cups. The tournament also made a star out of Leônidas da Silva, winner of the World Cup's Golden Ball award for most outstanding player as well as the Golden Boot for the tournament's top scorer. This was a particularly satisfying honor given that European teams held the majority of the votes. Leônidas was a national celebrity, symbolizing the very essence of what being Brazilian could mean in the twentieth century. He was also Afro-Brazilian and his nickname, Black Diamond, was a celebration of this dual heritage. Leonidas is also credited—though the point is disputed—with inventing the "bicycle kick," a reverse kick that to this day only the truly daring attempt and only the greats pull off.[15]

It would be two decades before Brazil actually won a World Cup, but the nation was now hooked not only on playing but also on the idea of setting an international standard, proving its worth to the parasitic powers that had bled it dry over the centuries. Soccer became synonymous with a certain kind of manhood. "Real men" played soccer and, by that transitive property, Brazilian men were equal or superior to any men on earth. (We will deal later in this chapter with the question of Brazilian women in soccer.)

Gilka Machado, an iconic Brazilian poet of the 1930s, wrote a poem about the 1938 World Cup. She celebrated the team's "entrancing, winged feet" and gave a glimpse into the rise of soccer and its place in the constellation of Brazilian cultural identity:

> Brazilian souls
> follow in your footsteps
> to the rushing ball,

to the decisive kick
of the glory of the Fatherland.

The players of the national team are playing for the manhood of a nation as they

Fix in the eye of the foreigner
The miraculous reality
That is the Brazilian man

The poem ends with a salute to the soccer players, the heroes of Brazil:

The soul of Brazil
Lays down a kiss
On your heroic feet.[16]

Then there was the 1950 World Cup final, where Brazil lost to Uruguay in front of a packed Maracanã filled to the rafters two hundred thousand strong, by a score of 2 to 1. Not unlike the Boston Red Sox fans who used to talk endlessly about the Curse of the Bambino and relive what they refer to as "Game Six" (of the 1986 World Series, that is), Brazil's soccer culture obsesses over this loss. It is considered the Maracanã's most famous moment. It even has its own name: the Maracanaço. Roberto DaMatta, a renowned Brazilian anthropologist, writes of the 1950 World Cup final as "perhaps the greatest tragedy in contemporary Brazilian history. Because it happened collectively and brought a united vision of the loss of a historic opportunity. Because it happened at the beginning of a decade in which Brazil was looking to assert itself as a nation with a great future."[17] Brazil's goalkeeper, Moacyr Barbosa Nascimento, suffered racist recriminations and was treated as a pariah for decades afterwards. "Under Brazilian law the maximum sentence is thirty years," Barbosa said in 2000. "But my imprisonment has been for fifty."[18]

To understand how deep this loss goes, consider the year 2000, which marked the thirtieth anniversary of Brazil's third World Cup victory in a final game that expressed all that is beautiful about the Brazilian way of soccer. That year, 2000, also marked the fiftieth anniversary of the Maracanaço. According to Bellos, the anniversary of the 1970 victory "passed barely without trace," while Rio newspapers published headlines commemorating the 1950 loss: "A HALF CENTURY OF NIGHTMARE."[19] The Brazilian novelist Carlos Heitor Cony wrote, "Survivors of that cruel afternoon believed they would never again be able to be happy. . . . What happened on July 16, 1950, deserves a collective monument, like the Tomb of the Unknown Soldier. These are the things that build nations, a people drenched in their own pain."[20] The 1950 loss carries such cultural weight that it is permanently imprinted on Brazil's national psyche; its international soccer team, as Alex Bellos writes, is "always playing against itself, against its own demons, against the ghosts of the Maracanã."[21]

One result of the 1950 loss was that Brazil tried to shake off the doldrums by redesigning its uniforms to the now iconic vivid yellow, blue, green, and white. Since 1970, with the widespread commercial availability of color television, their dazzling green and canary yellow shirts have signified a unique kind of soccer. For the world, no one wore that shirt with quite the panache of Edson Arantes do Nascimento, otherwise known as Pelé. Yet within Brazil, which revels in its own uniqueness, the real icon is someone far less familiar to casual and international soccer fans, someone as brilliant and as tragic as the Maracanaço. His name is Manuel Francisco dos Santos, but they call him Garrincha.

Garrincha and Pelé

To even have a cursory knowledge of Brazilian soccer or its place in Brazilian culture, you need to know the legend of Garrincha. Born in the impoverished rural town of Pau Grande, a region of Rio de Janeiro, Garrincha was the key player in Brazil's 1958 and 1962 World Cup victories. Many Brazilians regard the athletically gifted, personally flawed Garrincha as the greatest player to ever come out of Brazil, better even than Pelé. *Garrincha* is Portuguese for "wren," a bird defined by both its delicacy and its surprising speed. He has also been called "the Angel with Bent Legs" because he was born with spinal

defects that bent his right leg inward and made his left leg six cen-
timeters shorter than his right and curved outward. From this unlikely
start, he became a master of ball control and goal scorer without peer.[22]

Somehow, on his bent legs, Garrincha was also a speed merchant,
blending incredible balance and ability with an inability to be caught.
As teenagers, Garrincha and Pelé were on the same triumphant 1958
World Cup team. Stunningly, neither was played during the first two
games. They finally were put in for the third, against the USSR. At
the very beginning of the game, Garrincha hit the post after dribbling
around the field for forty seconds. Pelé also hit the frame of the goal
after a pass from Garrincha. This barrage ended mercilessly with a goal
by their teammate, striker Edvaldo Izídio Neto, known as Vavá. This
is considered the "finest three minutes" in Brazilian soccer history.

This entire 1958 World Cup squad represented a new, multicultural
generation filled with a promise of hope and social mobility unknown
to previous generations. David Goldblatt notes that the 1958 World
Cup squad was largely made up of

> the youthful elite of the new generation of football players who
> came of age in the boom. . . . The squad underwent intensive med-
> ical checks in Rio's leading hospitals which revealed an extraordi-
> nary catalogue of disease, neglect, and long-term malnutrition.
> Almost the entire squad had intestinal parasites, some had syphilis,
> others were anemic. Over 300 teeth were extracted from the
> mouths of players who had never been to a dentist, and but for this
> episode might never have gone. Epidemiologically, Brazil's '58 were
> a team of the people.[23]

Yet alongside their hope, tragedy also lurked in the poverty that mal-
nourished many of these players. Many of them discovered, much like
future generations of athletes, that once the cheering stopped, no one
was going to look out for their interests—and a fall from greater heights
could produce an even more jarring impact.

No one personified this familiar story of sports, economic adver-
sity, and misfortune more than the everyman Garrincha. He was, in
the brightest possible spotlight, a tragic figure, an alcoholic like his fa-

ther who spent himself to bankruptcy. Anthropologist José Sergio said, "When someone dies, you take stock of all the person's life. Garrincha was identified with the public. He never lost his popular roots. He was also exploited by football so he was the symbol of the majority of Brazilians, who are also exploited."[24] Garrincha's was a grand narrative: the wren picked apart by vultures who was not only an able player on crippled legs but beautiful. He lived life with reckless, wicked abandon. His legend is how some Brazilians choose to see themselves. Pelé is a different kind of role model, one Brazilians have been more apt to respect and resist simultaneously. Both are works of art, but Pelé is cold as marble.

The Cold Cool of Pelé

When Rio was chosen to host the 2016 Olympics, the man standing by Lula's side was Pelé. Who else could it possibly have been? Born in 1940 outside of São Paulo, Edson Arantes do Nascimento was raised in poverty. Unlike Garrincha, Pelé was a legacy athlete, the son of a respected Fluminense player known as Dondinho. In 1956, before his sixteenth birthday, he was already a prodigy, stuck with the nickname Pelé against his will for reasons that are still unknown (possibly because he had difficulty pronouncing the name of his favorite player, Bilé). The top scorer in his league in São Paulo at fifteen, he would score the one-thousandth goal of his career thirteen years later at the Maracanã.

Pelé's accolades, described in full, would fill an encyclopedia. He was named FIFA's player of the twentieth century, along with Argentina's Diego Maradona. He was voted World Player of the Century by the International Federation of Football History and Statistics. He finished ahead of people like Muhammad Ali and Michael Jordan and was voted Athlete of the Century by the IOC, in conjunction with the Reuters News Agency. By any statistical measure, Pelé was the most prolific player and scorer ever to live. A pro at fifteen, he joined the Brazilian national team at sixteen and won his first World Cup at seventeen. At that 1958 World Cup, Pelé became the youngest player to play in a World Cup final match at seventeen years and 249 days, scoring two goals in the final as Brazil beat Sweden 5 to 2. His first goal, a lob over a defender followed by a precise volley shot, was selected as one of the finest goals in World Cup history. When Pelé scored his second goal, Swedish player Sigvard Parling later commented: "I have to be honest and say I felt like applauding."[25] Pelé is still the only player to be a part of three World Cup–winning teams. He still holds the single-game record for goals in a game, with eleven scores (no, that's not a typo). In 1961, when Pelé was twenty, Brazilian president Jânio Quadros declared him "a national treasure," both to burnish his own presidency and to prevent Pelé from signing with a club in Europe.[26] This would be the first of countless times Brazil's political leaders would attempt to bask in his glow.

What Pelé was able to do like no one before him, or perhaps even since, was to transcend Brazil and become an international icon. His face became one with the most popular sport on earth. In the pre-Internet age, his global fame was rivaled only by, perhaps, Muhammad Ali. In 1967, the two armies of the Nigerian Civil War declared a forty-eight-hour ceasefire in honor of—and so they could attend—an exhibition game that Pelé was playing in Lagos. His stardom contributed to black athletes' new heightened status in Brazil: "Promoted by intellectuals, the media, and the dominant classes as a symbol of Brazilianness, *futebol* achieved the fullest extent of its influence when blacks, like Pelé, were given full recognition within the system. The outpouring of national pride and self-esteem which accompanied the three World Cup victories could not have been imagined under other circumstances."[27]

During the 1970s, a survey showed that Pelé was the second-most recognized brand name in Europe, after Coca-Cola. By nineteen, the Brazilian Coffee Institute had already asked him to be its international emissary. He was the first athlete to trademark his own name. He also made himself a blank political slate as well as a "brand." In this Pelé was ahead of his time, paving the way for superstar athletes of African descent like Michael Jordan and Tiger Woods: the neoliberal superstar in an age before neoliberalism. Becoming an international icon was very profitable for Pelé, but it also had the effect of distancing him from Brazil's masses. If he belonged to international commercialism, then he could never really belong to them.

This was not all that would distance him from the masses.

There is no doubt Pelé was an incredibly powerful symbol of pride and excellence at a time when few Afro-Brazilian faces were accorded such status. But he never used his hyper-exalted platform to challenge any of the racism in Brazilian society. Instead, Pelé had an army of publicists programming his every move off the pitch. Even as "the revolt of the black athlete" was on everyone's lips in the 1960s, Pelé was criticizing Muhammad Ali for resisting the draft and refusing to fight in Vietnam.[28] In an era where the rulers and rules of the world were being challenged, Pelé met and entertained European royalty. He allowed Brazil's dictatorship to use his image on postage stamps and went on "goodwill tours" to newly independent African republics on behalf of whichever of the rotating dictators happened to be in charge. He dressed in African garb, celebrating a Brazil in which the position of the Afro-Brazilian masses was dire.

It is not that Pelé was a hardline, heartless right-winger as much as he was someone who chose to risk very little. The Brazilian government was, ultimately, his most important patron, and he sided with the ruling power in his country, right or wrong, time and again. He was an industry unto himself—partially owned and subsidized by the state. When asked by a foreign journalist, as he invariably was, about poverty in Brazil and the mushrooming growth of the favelas, Pelé's stock answer was that God had made people poor and his function was to use his God-given athletic greatness to bring joy into their difficult lives. Textbooks for schoolchildren invariably included his picture "not only as a sports hero but to emphasize teamwork and the virtues of hierarchy."[29]

When Pelé scored his one-thousandth goal in 1969, this hero worship reached levels best described as galactic. "In a schmaltzfest of tears and declarations," Goldblatt writes, "Pelé dedicated the goal to the children of Brazil. A Brazilian senator composed a poem in his honor and read it from the floor of Congress. The following day's newspapers, which in every other country on the planet covered nothing but the second Apollo moon landing, were split down the middle in Brazil. Apollo 12 on one side, Pelé on the other."[30] This was life under dictatorship: for all the beauty and democracy he represented on the pitch, Pelé allowed himself to personify a dictatorship. His thousandth goal was Brazil's moon landing.

After Brazil's victory in the 1970 World Cup, the military dictatorship pulled out all the stops to use the national team to solve what Goldblatt calls "the problem of securing popular legitimacy."[31] Addressing the nation, military dictator of the moment Emílio Garrastazu Médici said:

> I feel profound happiness at seeing the joy of our people in this highest form of patriotism. I identify this victory won in the brotherhood of good sportsmanship with the rise of faith in our fight for national development. I identify the success of our [national team] with . . . intelligence and bravery, perseverance and our technical ability, in physical preparation and moral being. Above all, our players won because they know how to . . . play for the collective good.

Médici was so ham-fisted in his efforts to ride the popularity of Brazil's team that many on Brazil's left rooted for the country's opponents. Medici repeatedly attempted to use the team as a way to symbolize Brazil's economic miracle.[32] Even as his government rounded up political dissidents, it also produced a giant poster of Pelé straining to head the ball through the goal, accompanied by the slogan *Ninguém mais segura este país*—"nobody can stop this country now."

Pelé was no unconscious actor in this. When asked in 1972 about the dictatorship, he responded, "There is no dictatorship in Brazil. Brazil is a liberal country, a land of happiness. We are a free people. Our leaders know what is best for [us], and govern [us] in a spirit of toleration and patriotism."[33] Keep in mind that when Pelé was saying this, twenty-five-year-old Dilma Rousseff was being tortured in prison. One wonders if this has ever come up in conversation.

In 1974 President Médici and FIFA president João Havelange begged Pelé to play in the World Cup, but he refused, choosing instead to play for the New York Cosmos. In 1978, from his safe New York City perch, he still addressed the dictatorship in favorable terms, this time saying that in a country as uneducated as Brazil, the masses were better off not voting.[34] At his final game, an exhibition match at Giants Stadium between the Brazilian team Santos and the Cosmos in which he played one half for each team, Pelé spoke to the crowd, asking them to say the word "love" with him three times—the unbearable banality of the politics of Pelé.[35] (This is why soccer great–turned–rebel politician Romário once said, "Pelé is a poet as long as he stays silent."[36])

There is one exception to Pelé's history of tying himself to power—yet even this extraordinarily uncharacteristic act derived from dovetailing social justice with financial self-interest. It happened when he took on the Brazilian Football Confederation (CBF) and its entrenched, deeply corrupt president of twenty-three years, Ricardo Teixeira. Teixeira's father-in-law happened to be the aforementioned president of FIFA, João Havelange. In 1993 Pelé and his sports company sought the TV rights for the Brazilian domestic soccer leagues. Pelé claimed that Havelange and Teixeira made it very clear during the negotiations that bribes and other assorted sleazy goings-on were a prerequisite to securing the rights. This was tradition, the sports version of the "Brazilian cost." It also underlines the words of renowned soccer journalist Juca Kfouri: "I have always said that God put the best players here and the worst bosses to compensate."[37]

As he explained to the public, Pelé resisted and lost the bid. Enraged, he went public with charges that the CBF was corrupt in a 1993 interview with *Playboy*.[38] In retaliation, FIFA shut him out of the 1994 World Cup launch ceremony and celebrations. He was a pariah—not only as a public figure, but also economically. In 1995 he attempted to exact a measure of revenge, accepting an appointment from President Cardoso as Extraordinary Minister for Sport. Pele devoted his four years in the post to campaigning for what became known as the Pelé Law. This involved forcing clubs to open their books and converting clubs listed as nonprofit or charitable trusts into private limited companies. It also involved systematizing and regulating contracts in favor of the players as well as reorganizing domestic Brazilian soccer leagues and competitions. In proposing these reforms, "Pelé was attacking the interests that kept Teixeira in power. Pelé became the figurehead of football's 'modernizers.'"[39] The Brazilian Congress passed an extremely watered-down version of the Pelé Law in 1998—so watered down, in its final version, that Pelé withdrew his name. It was a bitter and public defeat. In 2001, however, Pelé and Teixeira called a truce and shook hands, agreeing to work together. It is for this, perhaps more than anything else, that Pelé is criticized in today's Brazil. Sports journalist José Trajano called it "the biggest stab in the back that those of us fighting for ethics in sport could receive," adding, "Pelé has let us all down. . . . He has sold his soul to the devil."[40] Kfouri wrote: "In Brazil there is still the ideology of '*rouba mas faz*'—it's OK to steal if you get things done. In football this is stretched to its most far-reaching consequences. Everything is forgotten in the light of victory."[41]

The Unity of Garrincha and Pelé

Garrincha and Pelé became known as the "golden partnership": the tragic and the corporate, coming together. As long as they were on the field at the same time, the Brazilian national team never lost a match. It was also profoundly significant for the country that Pelé was of Afro-Brazilian and Garrincha of Afro-Indigenous heritage. Under their young leadership, Brazil became the first multiracial team to win the World Cup. If Garrincha is the Wren or the Angel with Bent Legs—miraculous but vulnerable, celestial but delicate—then Pelé's other nickname reflects the distance he has created between himself and the masses: he is the "King." Journalist Alex Bellos puts it perfectly:

> There was no player as amateur in spirit as Garrincha. . . . Pelé, on the other hand, was unmitigatedly professional. . . . Whereas Garrincha indulged in most of the vices available to him, Pelé always behaved as a model player. He led a self-imposed ascetic life, concentrating on training and self-improvement. . . . Pelé had an

athlete's perfect body. Garrincha looked like he should not be able to walk straight. When Garrincha was still stuffing his wages into a fruit bowl, Pelé had registered his name as a trademark, employed a manager, invested money in business projects and advertised [international brands].[42]

After winning the 1958 World Cup in Sweden, the teenaged Pelé returned to São Paulo, where he was feted with a parade and given a luxury automobile. He refused to drive the car because he did not yet have a license. He told the crowd that he was grateful for the outpouring of love, but he had to go train for the upcoming season. Garrincha, on the other hand, returned to Pau Grande and drank a World Cup–sized amount of alcohol with his oldest friends. This would be a familiar compare-and-contrast throughout both of their lives. As Bellos summed up quite nicely: "Garrincha demonstrated, quite spectacularly, that there is no safety net in Brazilian society— while Pelé, unlike almost all his peers, found a career beyond football. Garrincha only ever thought of the short term. Pelé was—and is— always making plans. Garrincha argued with the establishment. Pelé *became* the establishment."[43]

While Pelé has become Brazil's symbol of individual success (and of using soccer to achieve that success), Garrincha symbolizes playing just for the sheer love of playing. Garrincha and Pelé: one amateur, improvised, creative; the other professional, regimented, formal, market-based—both of them fighting for the soul and the direction of their nation, long after hanging up their cleats. But perhaps the best way to understand their difference in the eyes of the country is to see how they are both immortalized at the Maracanã. The visitors' locker room is called "Pelé." Home is known as "Garrincha."

The Wisdom of Sócrates

Both of these soccer legends evoke the arguments another Brazilian soccer legend, Sócrates, was making about the changing nature of the game before his death in 2011. But before I relay Sócrates's critique of the homogenization of Brazil's beautiful game in the twenty-first century, it is worth establishing just who this man was and why we should take his words to heart.

Sócrates Brasileiro Sampaio de Souza Vieira de Oliveira was the captain of Brazil's 1982 World Cup squad, a team that did not finish first but whose players' style was so beloved that they are remembered with more affection, arguably, than any of the country's many World Cup victors. The masterful midfielder died from an intestinal infection at fifty-seven, but not before leaving a legacy that showcases the immensely powerful political echo of the sport in Brazil's history. Sócrates was a rare athlete whose outsized personality and effervescent humanity transcended the game. His interests, talents, and achievements were, frankly, staggering. He was a medical doctor, a musician, an author, a news columnist, a political activist, and a TV pundit. And somewhere in all of this, he managed not only to lead what may have been the most artful team ever to grace the pitch, but also, using his pulpit as a soccer star, to fearlessly challenge the military dictatorship that had ruled Brazil for decades.[44]

Alongside the 1982 Brazilian midfield of Zico, Falcao, Cerezo, and Éder, Sócrates exhibited a combination of technical prowess, deadly goal-scoring ability, and blissful creativity that has never been matched. If ever the uninhibited joy of play has merged seamlessly with raw competitive dominance, it was in the squad that Sócrates led to the World Cup semifinals in Spain. Sócrates approached soccer with the same intensity and lack of restraint he brought to every aspect of his life. He drank, he smoked, and—perhaps most daringly—he played without shin guards. His impetuosity as a player and a person was embodied in his signature move on the field: the blind heel pass. Sócrates became a full-time professional player almost as an afterthought, signing with Corinthians at the relatively advanced age of twenty-four. And unlike so many of his fellow players, let alone top-level professional athletes, he refused to check his politics at the door.

Unlike the great Pelé, Sócrates never made financial or political peace with Brazil's dictatorship. In fact, with his medical expertise, his flowing hair and full beard, and his politics of political resistance, he had less in common with Pelé than with Che Guevara. That is not hyperbole. Sócrates may be the only professional athlete ever to have organized a socialist cell among his fellow players. He helped to build Corinthians, a club team from São Paulo, on a radical political foundation. Under his leadership, cheering for Corinthians or even wearing their colors became a focal point for national discontent with Brazil's military dictatorship.[45]

The military, as we saw in the previous chapter, had ruled Brazil since 1964, when it overthrew left-wing president João Goulart. Throughout the 1970s, it had used soccer as a way to showcase national pride. By the early 1980s, as the dictatorship was beginning to strain under the weight of mass repression and economic stagnation, Sócrates and his teammate Wladimir were not only playing for Corinthians, but turning their team into the *time do povo*—the "people's team"— to demonstrate the power of democracy. With the blessing of club president Waldemar Pires, the players established a democratic process to govern all team decisions. As Sócrates explained, "Everyone at the club had the same right to vote—the person who looked after the kit and the club president, all their votes had the same weight." The players decided what time they would eat lunch, challenged strict rules that locked players in their hotel rooms for up to forty-eight hours before a match, and printed political slogans on their uniforms.[46]

In this way, one of South America's most popular teams became a beacon of hope not just to Brazilians but across a continent then stuffed to the rafters with US-backed dictators. In a country where a wrong word could have authorities knocking at your door, Sócrates was as bold as those national colors. On his way to 297 appearances and 172 goals for Corinthians, he was one of the most popular figures in the country and thus nearly unassailable, even by the military rulers. As he put it: "I'm struggling for freedom, for respect for human beings, for equality, for ample and unrestricted discussions, for a professional democratization of unforeseen limits, and all of this as a soccer player, preserving the ludicrous, and the joyous and pleasurable nature of this activity."[47]

The tragedy of Sócrates's death in 2011 lies both in his age—just fifty-seven—and in its timing. As the World Cup and Olympics thunder toward Brazil, his would have been a critical voice against the way these international sporting carnivals run roughshod over local communities for the benefit of the elite. When asked by the *Guardian* earlier in 2011 if the coming World Cup would help the poor of Brazil, Sócrates replied, "There will be lots of public money disappearing into people's pockets. Stadiums will be built and they will stay there for the rest of their lives without anyone using them. It's all about money. What we need to do is keep up public pressure for improvements in infrastructure, transport, sewerage, but I reckon it will be difficult."[48] But Sócrates, true to form in this interview, didn't confine his commentary to soccer: "What needs to change here is the focus on development. We need to prioritise the human being. Sadly, in the globalised world, people don't think about individuals as much as they think about money, the economy, etc."[49]

In another interview near the end of his life, he tried to analyze why the sport in Brazil had made that journey from joy to fear; from a uniquely Brazilian rhythm to the more regimented style that has begun to redefine the sport.[50] He began with the big picture, then worked his way down. He started by discussing the death of public space. "We've become an urban country," he said. "Before, there were no limits for playing—you could play on the streets or wherever. Now it's difficult to find space." The price for this—and this will sound very familiar to basketball fans in the United States—is that the game does not develop organically or through improvisation, but instead through highly structured league play from the youngest ages. As Sócrates put it, if you are playing the sport in a serious way and have any kind of athletic gifts, you will be "involved some kind of standardization."[51] He also spoke about how even the most innocent-looking soccer contests have been regimented: "The barefooted tykes kicking footballs on Rio's beaches are not doing so at liberty—they are members of *escolinhas*, Beach Soccer training clubs. . . . In São Paulo, children do not learn to play on patches of common land—because there is no common land anymore. . . . The freedom that let Brazilians reinvent the game decades ago is long gone." He then put a stunning exclamation point on the project:

> For many years soccer has been played in different styles, expressions of the personality of each people, and the preservation of that diversity is more necessary today than ever before. These are days of obligatory uniformity in soccer and everything else. Never has the world been so unequal in the opportunities it offers and so equalizing in the habits it imposes: in this end of the century world, whoever doesn't die of hunger dies of boredom. . . . Soccer is now mass-produced, and it comes out colder than a freezer and as merciless as a meat-grinder. It's a soccer for robots.[52]

These days, if you want to find creativity in Brazilian soccer, you'd be much better off looking at an area of Brazil's soccer world that has actually benefited from segregation and neglect—because no one has regimented its players with lessons about how they have to play. These are the women of Brazil.

Women and Soccer in Brazil

Can you imagine your son coming home with his girlfriend saying: "She's the defender for Bangu"? No way, huh.
        —Former Brazilian national coach João Saldanha[53]

Individual women and all-female teams were playing soccer in São Paulo and Rio by the beginning of the twentieth century. In the 1940s, during the early years of the Vargas dictatorship, historian Fábio Franzini has identified as many as forty teams in Rio alone. Then came Article 54 of Vargas's National Sports Council's decree of April 14, 1941, stating that "women will not be allowed to practice sports incompatible with the conditions of their nature, and for this reason, the National Sports Council should issue the necessary instructions to sports entities in the country."[54] Although women did break these laws and organize their own games throughout the following decades, the ban stood for a generation. Even in the 1970s, when an international women's movement was changing the relationship between women and sports, "Brazil reinforced the exclusion of women . . . [which] excluded them from a greater collective and a broad spectrum of social practices. Incapable of symbolically representing the nation, they were not only passive, silent and submissive, but also second-class citizens. To keep them from playing soccer was to exclude them from full participation in the nation."[55] As Roberto DaMatta noted, "In Brazil, soccer has a strong gender demarcation that makes it a masculine domain *par excellence*. It is a sport that contains all of the various elements that are traditionally used to define masculinity: conflict, physical confrontation, guts, dominance, control and endurance."

By law, women's soccer was banned in Brazil from 1941 until 1979. (Some sources even put that latter date at 1981.) Even when the ban was finally lifted, the National Sports Council implemented a series of rules to diminish both women's abilities and their accomplishments, such as requiring breast shields and shorter game times. The São Paulo Soccer Federation maintained that "feminine" appearance and beauty would be prerequisites for making the team. Its president, Eduardo Farah, said, "We have to try to combine the image of soccer and femininity."[56] Renato Duprat, another of Brazil's charming soccer bureaucrats, sniffed, "No one plays here with short hair. It's in the regulations."[57] This shows that homophobia is also strongly intertwined with gender norms; like in the United States, it's difficult to separate where homophobia ends and sexism begins when discussing women's sports. Even with the growth of these highly repressive local leagues, it took until 1994 for a countrywide championship tournament of women players to be held. The 1996 Olympics and the international success of the US women's team finally spurred a measure of national interest, investment, and respect. Despite its relatively new history, the Brazilian national women's team won the silver medal at the 2004 Olympics, made it to the final of the Women's World Cup in 2007, and even beat the powerful US women's team 4 to 0 in the semifinal. Shortly after placing second in the 2007 World Cup, the Brazilian women's team faxed a letter to the CBF, signed by all twenty-one of its players, demanding greater support for the women's game. The widespread prejudice against women's soccer in Brazil did not truly crack, however, until the national team won the Pan American Games, held in Brazil in July 2007. Only then did the CBF announce that it intended to set up a women's professional league.

The new women's league is known as the Campeonato Brasileiro do Futebol Feminino. It is an annual Brazilian women's club football tournament, contested by twenty clubs. Like its counterpart in the United States, Brazilian women's club soccer has had a difficult time gaining a foothold, not to mention corporate sponsorship. Santos closed its women's football club, which had been the most successful in recent years, in early 2012 in order to fund the male players' payroll, which had ballooned in the club's effort to keep budding superstar Neymar from leaving for Europe. The last women's championship tournament was played in near-empty stadiums, with an average audience of just three hundred people per game. The media coverage it gets is pitiful: one study of the four leading Brazilian news magazines showed eleven articles about women's soccer over four years.

Women have been historically discouraged not only from playing but even from attending men's games. The implications of this are profound. If soccer attendance—being part of the multitude in the stands—is Brazil's great cultural unifier, what does it mean to shut women out of that space? Symbolic of this is that the soccer fan clubs, the *torcidas*, exclude women from membership. Then there are the very terms with which the very ball is discussed: as if it is a woman to love or to ravage, depending upon who's doing the talking. Even Eduardo Galeano does this in his book *Soccer in Sun and Shadow*: "The ball laughs, radiant, in the air. He brings her down, puts her to sleep, showers her with compliments, dances with her, and seeing such things never before seen his admirers pity their unborn grandchildren who will never see them."[58] This is beautiful writing. It is also a ball. Little thought is given to whether this kind of discourse could alienate young girls from either playing or feeling like there is a place for them in the sport.

There is a story of a woman player saying, back in 1984, "Today, when I came onto the field, I heard a guy say that I should be at a laundry sink, washing clothes. But I did not bother to reply to him, although I was angry. My reaction came later, with the ball at my feet." One player who has challenged sexist assumptions about the place of women in the sport and made the beautiful game her own is soccer superstar Marta Vieira da Silva. Marta is an absolute genius with the ball, her plays YouTube-friendly highlights the likes of which are often forbidden to the men in the new, regimented soccer. Marta was named FIFA World Player of the Year five consecutive times, between 2006 and 2010.[59] Yet even she has had to fight for every bit of respect, signing a protest letter with teammates that said simply, "We need help." During the 2007 Pan American Games, when she was twenty-one years old, she said, "I hope that our successes will change everything. I've gone through hell myself." But the hell continues.

Neither Lula nor Dilma, in all their crowing about the benefits of bringing the World Cup to Brazil, has said a word about how hosting the Cup could benefit women's soccer. Without a movement to demand it, it is difficult to see how women won't be left behind once the Cup is done.

The Neoliberal Game

The reckless abandon, improvisation, and joy associated with Brazilian *futebol* has always been reflected the stands as much as on the pitch. Whether through song, dance, or celebration, the passion and creativity of Brazilian fans have always been a part of the show. Brazilian soccer matches were the first sports games in the world to feature fireworks shows at halftime, which were first remarked upon as early as the 1940s. The practice of having every fan hold up a colored card, which the NFL now has fans do to send messages of support for the US armed forces, started in the stands of Brazil. Then there are the costumes. Covering the body in wildly vibrant colors has historically been a statement all its own. In a nation whose different cultures clang together on a daily basis, where economic class separates people with grand chasms, the stands have always been the place where commonalities could be found and a national identity forged.[60]

Soccer has also reflected the contradictions of a country at once plagued by violence and blessed by joy. As Bellos wrote, "Brazilians are a happy, creative, excessively friendly people, yet—because of the country's social problems—they live with levels of murder and violent crime almost equivalent to a country in civil war."[61] Today, however, the contradictions are being ironed out, as Brazil's elite prepare to sell its national identity and culture by the pound for an international audience. Nowhere is this more evident than in the transformation of the Maracanã (discussed in chapter 1).

It can also be seen in the exploitation of the players. In November 2013, several Brazilian teams took the field with their arms folded, vowing "drastic measures" if the Brazilian Football Confederation refused to alter their intense, nearly nonstop schedule. Players also demanded "more vacation time, longer preseasons, fewer games and a bigger voice in decision making."[62] Some kept their arms folded throughout the contests. In other games, players passed the ball from one end of the field to the other after the referees threatened to give them yellow cards. At one match, during the national anthem, players from both sides unfurled a banner in the middle of the pitch that read, "For a football that is better for everyone." As their organizing body, Common Sense Football Club, posted on its Facebook page: "If there are attempts to prevent players from expressing themselves in a peaceful way, drastic measures will be taken. We expect an official position followed by moves that will benefit Brazilian football."[63] They even threatened to wear clown noses on the pitch if changes were not forthcoming.

The protests are understandable, if you know the reality of life for a Brazilian pro soccer player. Top guns on the best teams earn salaries that compare favorably to those on many of the best teams in Europe, but the overwhelming majority work for poverty wages, with 90 percent earning less than fifty dollars a month.[64] For all its bread-and-butter demands, though, this protest was really about corruption and exploitation in the CBF. Not even Pelé, with all of his cultural capital, could defeat that. The normalization of corruption as just a part of the sport is also far too familiar a theme in Brazilian soccer. This corruption, magnified by the demands of the World Cup, was the catalyst for the 2013 protests.

The truth is that Brazilian soccer has been corporatized and privatized half to death. Fábio Menezes once said, "The best way to project yourself in Brazil is either to start a church or a football club. . . . People use football clubs to serve their own interests."[65] Teams exist to sell players to the next level, mirroring what we have seen in the Brazilian economy: just another market-based product. The soccer historian Bellos said that researching the commercialization of the sport reminded him "of the *latifundios* [the old slave-based plantation estates]. Brazil is the world's largest exporter of sugar, coffee *and* footballers. I began to see the country like a big estate where the agricultural product is *futebol*. The country is a sporting monoculture. And football mirrors the old hierarchies. The oligarchic powers are sustained by those at the bottom who, like the cane-cutters, live on almost nothing."[66]

The CBF is a private organization that has corruption in the marrow of its bones. From 1997 to 2000 its revenue quadrupled, but it still somehow did not manage to pay off its debts. The aforementioned Ricardo Teixeira and his friends at the top, however, voted themselves pay increases of more than 300 percent. As they were paid more, they spent less on developing and expanding soccer. In 2000 alone, this cartel spent sixteen million dollars on air travel, "enough for 1,663 first-class tickets from Rio to Australia."[67] Summing up the conclusions of a congressional investigation, Senator Álvaro Dias described the CBF as "a den of crime, revealing disorganization, anarchy, incompetence and dishonesty."[68] In 2012 Teixeira stepped down after a Swiss judge found that he and his former father-in-law had taken forty-one million dollars in bribes from different companies vying for exclusive World Cup marketing rights. Despite the stench that surrounds him, Teixeira has not served any time for his obvious and extensive corruption.

Neoliberalism is making Brazilian soccer as static as the European game from which it once joyfully emancipated itself. Brazilians rightfully recognize this as a tragedy. If soccer is not Brazilian, then what is Brazil? They fear that Brazil does not have the time or space to answer these questions with the World Cup and Olympics breathing down its collective neck. They fear that, like the tree in Shel Silverstein's *The Giving Tree*, which gave everything it had until it was just a stump to be sat upon, Brazil has given all it has to give and is now compelled to offer up its culture to the world to sit upon. What is most personal becomes the last commodity to offer up to the European powers that are coming to call.

CHAPTER 5

Killing Santa

Warped mentalities and cracked personalities seem to be everywhere and impossible to eliminate.

—Avery Brundage[1]

lived in Chile as a student in 1995, just after the end of Augusto Pinochet's dictatorship. That was where I first heard the term "shock treatment" as meaning something other than a drastic method of therapy. In Chile, "shock treatment" was what Pinochet and the Chicago School–trained economists under his command did to Chile's economy after they slaughtered, tortured, and exiled the thousands who could have stood in their way. As Chile's citizens saw political murals painted over, schools closed down, their neighbors disappeared, their soccer stadiums turned into internment camps, and their rivers literally red with blood, the "shock treatment" began. Workplace protections were gutted, tariffs removed, and the economy privatized within an inch of its life. More than a few veterans of the struggle against the dictatorship expressed gallows humor that they did not know what was worse: the shock treatment to the economy or the shock treatment they personally received at the hands of Pinochet's sadistic torture guards. This idea of catastrophe, in this case a military coup leading to economic shock reform, inspired Naomi Klein to write *The Shock Doctrine*. In this modern classic of political journalism, the Canadian journalist writes about the ways those in power across the globe exploit horrifying political crises and natural disasters. She explores how tragedies become opportunities for people in power to enact brutal neoliberal reforms and massive redevelopment projects, ones they could never get away with if their populations weren't in a fever shock of trauma and mourning. But what to do if you are a leader who wants to enact "shock reforms" but don't have the patience to wait for the next tsunami? Enter the games.

Global mega-events like the World Cup and Olympics have become incredibly effective tools for reorganizing an economy on neoliberal grounds. It is not that these events are not profitable. It is a question of who sees the money and who pays the price. (As 1968 Olympian John Carlos often says, "Do you know why they only have the Olympics every four years? It takes them four years to count the money.") But a high-octane money grab, festooned with flags and streamers, is just the tip of the iceberg. To understand what these events do to a country, we need to look at their history. In this chapter we'll examine the age-old underbelly of athletic mega-events and how they have been staged in decades past in order to understand what they have become.

For most of their respective histories, nationalism aside, the World Cup and Olympics—not to mention their ruling bodies, FIFA and the IOC—were profoundly different kinds of operations. The World Cup, a global soccer tournament, was launched a quarter of a century after FIFA began, as a method to codify the global rules of the game. It needed soccer fields, a modicum of security to crack the heads of the stray hooligans here and there, and—oh yes—a ball. The Olympics, even in its early decades, was always a much more pungent kettle of fish. Mass evictions, police repression, and economic boondoggles with no use beyond the Games themselves have always been a part of the Olympic operation. Since 9/11, however, both of these tournaments have started to seem like conjoined twins. Together they now resemble what soccer writer Simon Kuper called "the sort of common project that otherwise barely exists in modern societies."[2] Both demand of would-be host nations the latest in high-tech security and surveillance, infrastructure, and new stadiums. Both now also require people—and this privilege is reserved almost exclusively for the poor—to be forcibly moved from their homes to make way for it all. As FIFA president Sepp Blatter said during Brazil's nationwide protests in 2013, "Brazil asked to host the World Cup. We did not impose the World Cup on Brazil. They knew that to host a good World Cup they would naturally have to build stadiums. But we said that it was not just for the World Cup. . . . There are other constructions: highways, hotels, airports . . . items that are for the future. Not just for the World Cup."[3] Indeed. The official FIFA slogan should be "I was evicted for the World Cup and all I got was this lousy airport."

As former professional soccer player–turned–mega-event critic Jules Boykoff has written, both of these global mega-events fall under the heading of what could best be called "celebration capitalism." As Boykoff writes,

> Celebration capitalism is disaster capitalism's affable cousin. Both occur in states of exception that allow plucky politicos and their corporate pals to push policies they couldn't dream of during normal times. But while disaster capitalism eviscerates the state, celebration capitalism manipulates state actors as partners, pushing economics rooted in so-called public-private partnerships. All too often these partnerships are lopsided: the public pays and the private profits. In a bait and switch that's swaddled in bonhomie, the public takes the risks and private groups scoop up the rewards.[4]

Celebration capitalism also provides a "once-in-a-generation opportunity [for police and military forces] to multiply and militarize their weapons stocks, laminating another layer on to the surveillance state. The Games justify a security architecture to prevent terrorism, but that architecture can double to suppress or intimidate acts of political dissent."[5] This has certainly been my experience covering these mega-events over the last ten years, as chapter 6 will show in detail. What is important, however, is seeing the massive security operations, graft, and evictions not as add-ons to a healthy celebration of national pride but as tightly intertwined with one another, part of the same sporting shock doctrine. Countries don't want these mega-events in *spite* of the threats to public welfare, addled construction projects, and repression they bring, but *because* of them.

This can be seen most clearly by examining the history of the Olympic Games. Nationalism plus sports metastasized quickly into Barnum-esque spectacle—and host nations became the devil's workshop.

In the Beginning

In 1896, when the modern Olympic Games began, the world was undergoing cataclysmic, unprecedented changes. Imperial rivals like France, Britain, and the emerging United States were in the process of slicing and dicing the globe, from Cuba to the Congo to the Philippines. One of their most important tools in justifying this project was nationalism. As Indiana senator Albert Beveridge said in 1897, "American factories are making more than the American people can use; American soil is producing more than they can consume. Fate has written our policy for us; the trade of the world must and shall be ours."[6] In the period before World War I, it was fashionable among the upper echelons of Western society to believe that a globe constituted of hyperpatriotic, battle-ready societies was actually the secret to ending wars between nations. (Turns out this view was not entirely accurate.) When French aristocrat Pierre de Coubertin launched the first International Olympic Committee at the end of the nineteenth century, he and his cohort were at the heart of these conversations among the world's elite. The initial members of the IOC were five European nobles, two generals, and nine of Europe's leading industrialists. Between 1894 and the turn of the century Coubertin added ten more barons, princes, and counts. The Games allowed these leaders to use sports as an amphetamine to spur fevered nationalist frenzies and, according to Courbertin (a master rhetorician), the promotion of sports was "an indirect preparation for war. In sports all the same qualities flourish which serve for warfare: indifference towards one's well being, courage, readiness for the unforeseen. . . . The young sportsman is certainly better prepared for war than his untrained brothers."[7]

Critical to Coubertin's Olympic ideal was his belief in amateurism —no professional athletes allowed, only those playing for love. This was seen as a nod to Greek antiquity, which is so central to the Olympic ethos. The only problem with this is that all available evidence indicates that ancient Greek athletes were rewarded quite substantially for their efforts, according to Patrick Hruby, who has written extensively on the topic. I spoke with him and asked him to elaborate:

> Modern Olympic amateurism was a fraud, rooted in a willful misreading of ancient Olympic history. The sports-loving Greeks of classical antiquity would have scoffed at the snooty, classist Victorian Era notion that athletes shouldn't be compensated for their hard work and on-field achievements—after all, ancient Olympic winners received prize money, prime amphitheater seats, generous pensions and other goodies; according to historians, one Games winner even parlayed his victory into an Athenian senatorial seat. Indeed, the ancient Greeks didn't even have a word for "amateur." The closest term? *Idiotes*. Which really needs no translation.

This "amateurism" was actually a concept that arose at the end of the nineteenth century to make sports the province only of those wealthy enough to not worry about being paid: "Specifically, snooty British elites who enjoyed rowing, winning, and keeping the unwashed, day-laboring masses at arm's length."

When US colleges copied this notion of amateur sports (which still underpins university athletics today), their motivations had less to do with high-minded ideas about education and the creation of gentleman-athletes than about enforcing a social caste system: "Both in America and in England a gentleman might hire an ex-prizefighter, a golf trainer or a tennis teacher to coach his son and might even brush up his own game in a round with the professional," said Hruby. "But when it was over, the pro left by the service entrance and the gentleman went in to tea." Keeping the great unwashed from competing was in step with the IOC's origins among the sorts of reactionary aristocrats and international nobility. After the 1922 rise of fascist Italian dictator Benito Mussolini, when the ruling followers of fashion found fascism, the IOC became a place where even the more extreme forces of the far right could feel at home. It became the kind of place where a man like Avery Brundage could thrive.

Nazism, the Olympics, and the Birth of Hypernationalism

The dominant Olympic figure of the twentieth century was not Jesse Owens, Nadia Comăneci, or Mark Spitz. It was Avery Brundage. As IOC president, Brundage never failed to use his politics to sculpt who and what the Olympics would glorify. Born, raised, and educated in material comfort in Illinois, the man who came to be called "Slavery Avery" was an athlete who competed in the pentathlon and decathlon at the 1912 Olympics in Stockholm. He lost both events to the great Native American athlete Jim Thorpe. Thorpe was later stripped of his gold medals when it was discovered that he had earned fifty dollars playing semiprofessional baseball before competing, making him insufficiently amateur. Brundage was a ferocious defender of the "amateur ideal" and held throughout his career held the line that Thorpe had violated that sacred tenet. Speaking on the benefits of amateurism, he once said that "when colleges pay boys for playing football, they destroy many illusions; the spirit of loyalty, the satisfaction that comes from successful play, the fun of it, the amateur spirit. It is like killing Santa Claus."[8] Yet Avery Brundage was so feared and so isolated, it is easy to imagine him saying this and actually believing in Santa Claus, with his coterie of hangers-on and lickspittles fearful to correct him.

In 1934, as head of the United States Olympic Committee (then called the American Olympic Committee, or AOC), Brundage became the leading advocate for Hitler's Berlin to host the 1936 Games. When he met resistance to rewarding a country that seemed to be a brewing cauldron of bad news, he curtly rejected what he called "the politicization of sport," arguing, "The very foundation of the modern Olympic revival will be undermined if individual countries are allowed to restrict participation by reason of class, creed, or race."[9] (He said this despite a lifelong belief that apartheid countries such as South Africa and Rhodesia should be allowed to field all-white Olympic teams.) Yet a boycott movement was growing, insisting that the Olympics refuse to lend Hitler the cloak of their legitimacy. The uproar would not subside, so Brundage went to Germany himself to settle the question about whether Hitler and his Nazi party were as toxic as the boycotters said. He was given a very public and sublimely choreographed tour of Berlin, shared smiles and handshakes with Hitler for the cameras, and returned to the States with tales of a new Germany that treated Jews and other national minorities with exceptional care. When asked about the anti-Hitler rumblings, he dismissed them as the work of a "Jewish-Communist conspiracy." The boycott push failed narrowly, despite support from Walter White of the NAACP and the IOC's American representative, Ernest Lee Jahncke, after Brundage pleaded in an AOC pamphlet for sports to stay out of the "Jew-Nazi altercation." Most infamously, Brundage absolved himself of all moral responsibility when he said that organized amateur athletics "cannot, with good grace or propriety, interfere in the internal, political, religious or racial affairs of any country or group."[10] Of course, by bestowing the grace of the Games on the Third Reich, he was doing just that. He claimed to believe that the "Olympic movement" should stay apart from politics, but this false neutrality benefited a certain kind of politics. It also helped Brundage negotiate the internal politics of the IOC: his steadfast support of Hitler earned him the respect of its members. They brought him into their exclusive club—after voting to expel the antifascist Jahncke, the first expulsion in IOC history.

The Nazi regime did not share Brundage's belief in the apolitical virtues of the Olympic movement—or perhaps it is more accurate to say that the two shared a belief about what politics the Olympics should and should not glorify. Indeed, Brundage's canard that politics and sport resided in separate worlds was betrayed by the Nazis' own publications. "Athletes and sport are the preparatory school of the political will in the service of the state," Kurt Munch wrote in a Nazi-sanctioned book titled *Knowledge about Germany*. "Non-political, so-called neutral sportsmen are unthinkable in Hitler's state."[11] The Nazi party had nationalism honed to a razor's edge, so the change to host the Olympics fit its political outlook like a jackboot. Hitler's propaganda department added many of the trappings—the opening ceremonies, the marching athletes—that today are icons of the Games.

The first Olympic torch run was actually the brainchild of Dr. Carl Diem, Germany's chief organizer for the 1936 Games. He convinced Hitler's media chief, Joseph Goebbels, that 3,422 young Aryan runners should carry burning torches along the 3,422-kilometer route from the Temple of Hera on Mount Olympus to the stadium in Berlin.[12] The event would be captured by the regime's filmmaking prodigy, Leni Riefenstahl. Hitler's words were broadcast to the world live over radio before the inaugural torch lighting: "Sporting chivalrous contest helps knit the bonds of peace between nations. Therefore, may the Olympic flame never expire."[13] Not so different from the plea of former Olympic chief Jacques Rogge, who retired in 2013, that the torch be a symbol of "peace, harmony and global unity." The running of the torch, as Chris Bowlby wrote for BBC News, "was planned with immense care by the Nazi leadership to project the image of the Third Reich as a modern, economically dynamic state with growing international influence."[14] Diem, in organizing its first journey, made sure the Olympic torch was carried exclusively through areas of Europe where the Third Reich wanted to extend its reach. When the flame made its way through Vienna, it was accompanied by mammoth pro-Nazi demonstrations. Two years later, the Nazis annexed Austria to Germany.

The Games themselves at first seemed to justify critics' fears that the Olympics would provide legitimacy to the Nazi regime. To Hitler, the Berlin games were "a fascist fantasy come true."[15] Every ceremony was calculated to shower further glory on the Third Reich. The legendary sportswriter Grantland Rice, covering the Games, described a chilling scene:

> Just twenty-two years ago this day the world went to war. On the twenty-second anniversary of the outbreak of that great conflict I passed through more than 700,000 uniforms on my way to the Olympic Stadium—brown shirts, black guards, gray-green waves of regular army men and marines—seven massed military miles

rivaling the mobilization of August 1, 1914. The opening ceremonies of the eleventh Olympiad, with mile upon mile, wave upon
wave of a uniformed pageant, looked more like two world wars
than the Olympic Games.[16]

The Nazi pomp and circumstance so decried today served in fact as a
launching pad for the kind of over-the-top nationalism now associated
with the Olympics.

The Nazi Olympics also expanded the stark repression that was beginning to be associated with hosting the Olympics, particularly the idea
of "cleansing" cities for an international audience. On July 16, 1936,
Berlin police rounded up eight hundred Roma people living in the
Berlin streets and put them in an internment camp. Many other political
dissidents disappeared, herded onto some of the first trains to the so-
called work camps. After the undesirables were out of sight, Berlin was
scrubbed down. Richard Walther Darré, the German minister of food
and agriculture, issued a decree to local authorities throughout Germany:

> All anti-Semitic posters must be suppressed during the period of
> question. The fundamental attitude of the Government does not
> change, but Jews will be treated as correctly as Aryans at this time.
> . . . Houses on the main roads must be whitened, and even repainted
> if possible. Street lighting must be improved. Streets and squares
> must be cleaned. Agricultural workers in the fields must not take
> their meals near the roads, nor pass near the roads.[17]

When you see the shiny signage and slogans throughout Rio and consider the twenty thousand homes that have, as of this writing, already
been cleared out, you can see more continuity than change from the
Games of 1936.

There were no Olympics in 1940 or 1944 because of World War
II, and by 1948 Germany was no longer Hitler's. Yet when the
Olympics relaunched, the IOC decided to keep—and normalize—the
nationalist trappings of the Berlin Games. The Games kept the ceremony, but now, instead of fascist spectacle, it became Cold War athletic
pornography. Sports, instead of becoming a force for unity, stood in for

global thermonuclear war. It was this dynamic that prompted George Orwell to write his essay "The Sporting Spirit," in which he lacerated this sort of thinking:

> I am always amazed when I hear people saying that sport creates goodwill between the nations, and that if only the common peoples of the world could meet one another at football or cricket, they would have no inclination to meet on the battlefield. Even if one didn't know from concrete examples (the 1936 Olympic Games, for instance) that international sporting contests lead to orgies of hatred, one could deduce it from general principles. . . . As soon as the question of prestige arises, as soon as you feel that you and some larger unit will be disgraced if you lose, the most savage combative instincts are aroused.[18]

Brundage was the unquestioned leader of this "orgy of hatred," emerging from World War II as the unquestioned leader of the IOC. Although as late as 1941 he had been publicly praising the Reich, including at an "America First" rally in Madison Square Garden, this did nothing to slow his rise. He remained chief of the IOC until 1972.

Under Brundage, mass evictions and police crackdowns were the norm. He had nothing to say when thousands were displaced for the Tokyo Olympics in 1964. His silence was deafening when Mexican security forces slaughtered hundreds of students and workers protesting in the streets in advance of the 1968 Games in Mexico City. Anything was permissible as long as the Games ran on time. He became a symbol of establishment reaction so profound that when African Americans attempted to organize their own boycott of the Olympics in 1968, due primarily to Brundage's desire to readmit apartheid South Africa and Rhodesia, removing Brundage from the IOC's leadership was one of their primary demands. As 1968 Olympic bronze medalist and protestor John Carlos explained:

> Avery Brundage was standing to the right of all things right-wing. He came off like someone with money and power who couldn't or wouldn't hear what we were trying to say. I also felt like he was a puppet for others. He might've been the face of the IOC, but I

think there were a lot more mechanisms behind him to turn the wheel, so to speak. In other words, he had a lot of support behind the things that he was saying. He was just a figurehead, but he was doing so much harm. He was the voice for apartheid South Africa and what was then known as Rhodesia. He wasn't an honest broker for the darker nations of the world. He had to go.[19]

Brundage didn't go just yet, but Carlos and his fellow medalist Tommie Smith created an iconic Olympic image of a different sort on the medal stand, when they raised their fists high in a salute to symbolize their commitment to human rights inside and outside the sports world.

Brundage is perhaps most notorious for his decisions surrounding the 1972 Summer Olympics in Munich, Germany. On September 5, a Palestinian group called Black September took eleven Israeli athletes hostage. Brundage insisted the Olympics continue while negotiations were taking place for their release. After all of the athletes were killed during a botched rescue attempt, Brundage announced that the Games would proceed as planned. Only a massive amount of pressure convinced the IOC to halt competition for a single day, instead holding a memorial service for eighty thousand spectators and three thousand athletes in the Olympic Stadium. When Brundage spoke, he shocked observers by pointedly making no reference at all to the slain athletes, instead praising the strength of the Olympic movement and stating that "the Games must go on." This position was also endorsed by the Israeli government, but not everyone agreed; several countries left in protest. As one Dutch athlete put it, "You give a party and someone is killed at the party, you don't continue the party, you go home. That's what I'm doing."[20]

In a subsequent speech, Brundage spoke of his steadfast belief that Rhodesia, despite its apartheid policies, should never be excluded from the Games. He then stated that the massacre of the Israeli athletes and the exclusion of the Rhodesian team were crimes of equal weight. Clearly, after standing astride the Olympics for most of the century, Brundage was becoming a liability. But when the IOC finally put him out to pasture, it settled on a replacement who differed from "Slavery Avery" only on the question of his all-time favorite fascist.

Don Juan Antonio

In 1980, the IOC named its new head: Spain's Don Juan Antonio Samaranch, a proud fascist of many years' standing. Born in 1920 in Barcelona, the son of a wealthy factory owner, Samaranch knew with an early clarity what side he was on. In 1936, when General Francisco Franco's fascists fought the Spanish Republicans during the Spanish Civil War, the teenage Juan Antonio was already a proud, active fascist street fighter and strikebreaker. Up until the dictator's death in 1975, Samaranch was still proclaiming himself "one hundred percent Francoist."[21]

Samaranch was also a sportsman who believed in the Brundage ideal of the Olympics as celebration of nationalism, amateurism, and power. He wrote letters to Brundage, "eulogizing in one of them the American's 'intelligence, laboriousness and love for [the] Olympic idea' and in another promising, 'I will entirely devote myself to go with your personality and prominent work.'"[22] Journalist Andrew Jennings notes that

> three decades of devotion to fascism had taught Samaranch a peculiar language. All the institutions in Spain—the monarchy, politics, the church, industry and its workers—were forced into slavish obedience; the dictator and his mouthpieces called it "sacred unity." This has been one of Samaranch's contributions to Olympic jargon. He calls frequently for the "unity" of the Olympic movement and hails the "sacred unity" of the committee, the international sports barons and the national Olympic committees around the world; all of course under his leadership.[23]

Samaranch's commitment to the Victorian ideal of amateurism, however, only went so far, especially when it got in the way of corporate sponsorships. It was he who ushered in the modern era, allowing athletes to accept endorsements, play professionally when not representing their countries, and at least somewhat benefit from their talents. In other words, if Brundage had lived to see the day, he would have known that it was his protégé Samaranch who killed Santa Claus. Far from destroying the Olympics, however, this made the Games swifter, higher, stronger, and more collectively profitable than ever: the spectacle of NBA players and other professionals competing in the Olympics was ratings gold. Samaranch also brought in corporate underwriters to fund the Games, making them a lucrative proposition for potential host countries hoping to "brand" themselves as well as for corporations hoping to burnish their images. The main sponsors the IOC has brought on board include the likes of Dow Chemical, British Petroleum, and McDonald's: the companies most in need of an Olympic absolution.

The IOC's love for Samaranch is why, in a stunner, Spain finished ahead of Chicago and second to only Brazil in the competition to host the 2016 Games. This was intended precisely as a tribute to Don Juan Antonio, who had fallen ill (he passed away in 2010). Samaranch was the midwife of "celebration capitalism" and a conjurer of shock doctrines. His fingerprints, even more than Brundage's, are on everything I have witnessed over the last ten years.

The way Samaranch reshaped the Olympics served a blueprint for the World Cup to transform from a sleepy rule-making body to a Cold War nationalist frenzy to nationalism as commercial branding. In the United States during the 1996 Atlanta Games, this last came complete with red, white, and blue commemorative mousepads—made, of course, in China.

FIFA and the World Cup

FIFA was founded with far more humble aspirations than Coubertin's IOC. On May 21, 1904, in Paris, the growth of international athletic competitions compelled representatives from different European countries to create a governing body that agreed to play by a set of uniform regulations. It was initially conceived as simply a rule-making body. Because it was founded in Paris, the organization took its acronym, FIFA, from the French: Fédération Internationale de Football Association. What began as an effort to make sure that tackling and the use of hands would not be seen as legitimate parts of the sport morphed over time into one of the most corrupt, scandal-plagued pits of infamy in the history of sports.[24]

Though FIFA called itself a "global governing body," it initially only oversaw countries in Western Europe. The first non-European country to join was South Africa in 1909, followed by the most European of South American countries, Argentina and Chile. The United States did not join until 1912. Brazil, a nation whose love and innovation with the soccer ball was already becoming folklore, was not asked to join until 1930.

Unlike the IOC, FIFA is not only in charge of its famed tournament but also of the international workings of soccer in between tournaments. Its influence is as profound as its wealth. The exact numbers are unknown, but its former president, the highly corrupt João Havelange, did brag in 1993 that FIFA's bottom line was larger than that of the world's biggest company at the time, General Motors. The roots of this wealth are not only in soccer's popularity. It comes as a result of selling every stitch of clothing on a player's body for ads and of mercilessly breaking any players who dare speak about organizing a union. In Forbes's 2012 list of the highest-paid athletes, only four of the top forty played soccer—even though it is the most lucrative sport on earth.[25]

FIFA has always seen its profits as being linked to its ability to own the product, and it sees its "product" as not only the game but the players themselves. FIFA's leaders have never worshipped a political ideology as fervently as their desire for money and for control over the beautiful game. In 1956, FIFA suspended Hungarian players who formed a rogue team after the USSR overran their country with tanks.[26] In 1958, as Algeria fought for independence, Algerian players formed their own team, including some who left cushy professional playing jobs in France to be part of the effort. Not only did FIFA blacklist those players and ban the team, it also suspended Morocco for having the temerity to play them in a match.[27]

It was in 1958, during all of this political tumult, that the World Cup was first televised to a global audience. It was—not coincidentally—also in the 1950s that FIFA first started selling entire sections of its uniforms to international corporations to advertise their brands.

Players did not joyously accept their new role as walking advertise-ments for FIFA's corporate partners. Obdulio Varela, captain of the Uruguayan national team that won the 1950 World Cup, refused, say-ing, "They used to drag us blacks around by rings in our noses. Those days are gone."[28]

In 1974, when Havelange ascended to the leadership of FIFA, this corporate domination took full root. "I have come to sell a product called football," he said upon assuming control.[29] Havelange was a Brazilian plutocrat who made his fortune in financial speculation, with a sideline in weapons sales. He made a point of telling one member of the media that the part of soccer he loved most was not the beauty, the grace, or even the winning. It was, he said, "the discipline." He loved the discipline and loved those who shared his fetish for order and cor-porate rule. In 1980, he convinced Adidas to underwrite the campaign of one of his dear friends to head the IOC. Adidas was skittish because of this person's controversial past, but did so on Havelange's encour-agement. That was Don Juan Antonio Samaranch.[30] Havelange also picked his own successor, Sepp Blatter, who has maintained the Have-lange way through corruption scandal after corruption scandal, rank sexism, and, above all else, a desire for "order" over justice. As an in-ternational uproar brewed after Israel jailed and even killed Palestinian soccer players in 2012, Blatter made sure that the under-twenty-one European tournament would be played as planned in Israel. This at-traction to authoritarian rule and order at all costs can be seen in recent revelations that several World Cup tournaments were in fact fixed to aid fascist and military dictatorships.[31]

The directors of FIFA were inspired to start a World Cup by the 1924 Olympic finals, which drew sixty thousand spectators for the final between Uruguay and Switzerland. The idea was received enthusiasti-cally in South America and most of Europe. (Interestingly, the English, thinking the tournament beneath them, did not vie for the Cup until 1950.)[32] Soccer has a contradictory political history, as we have seen: one that has both aided dictators and provided support and organiza-tion for movements against dictatorship. The history of FIFA, founded in 1930, is less complicated than that of the sport it purports to cele-brate. It has time and again sided decisively with authoritarian rule.

This longstanding attraction to authoritarian environments has had a decisive effect on the beloved World Cup from its first tournament. In 1934, the fascist dictator Benito "Il Duce" Mussolini made sure the referees knew that the tournament was Italy's—and Italy's alone—to win. In a 2013 presentation at an academic conference partially spon-sored by FIFA, Italian researcher Marco Impiglia showed that Italy's 1934 World Cup victory and Argentina's 1978 title were both altered, if not outright fixed, by the bloody dictators in power in the two coun-tries. Impiglia presented research showing that a series of decisions by referees either connected to or fearful of Mussolini was decisive in the outcome.[33] "It's the same old story: Sport and politics are brothers and sometimes sport is under the other brother," he told the Associated Press.[34] Mussolini actually did not like soccer—he thought it was "un-manly"—but he saw its potential power as a pump for political propa-ganda. Il Duce eventually came to view the tournament as a way to create the "myth of a new Italy," a use Impiglia describes as "political abuse": "It was a questionable win and it raised many doubts at the time."[35] Inside Italy, such doubts were whispered in furtive tones. *Il Popolo d'Italia*—Mussolini's government newspaper—described only the "vision of harmony, discipline, order, and courage" displayed by the national team. In 1938, Italy won again. Before the final, the team re-ceived a three-word telegram from Il Duce. It read: "Win or die." They did win, then marched in military uniforms at a procession presided over by Mussolini.[36]

Forty-four years later, the situation was similar. The host country was Argentina, led by its dictator, General Jorge Videla. Before the tournament began, Videla pinned a medal on the chest of a beaming Havelange. Standing next door to a structure the dictator had used as his torture and death chamber, Havelange said, "At last the world can see the true face of Argentina."[37] But Videla wanted more. He wanted Argentina to raise the cup. As the tournament progressed, his dreams appeared to have been dashed. Argentina needed to defeat Peru by at least four goals in the semifinals. They won 6 to 0 in a widely recognized farce, described at the conference as "notorious." After the match, Videla embraced the team and used star player Mario Kempes in much the same way Brazil's General Medici had used Pelé on campaign posters in 1970.[38]

In 2012, former Peruvian senator Genaro Ledesma confirmed that this triumph was a sham. The Peru result had indeed been brokered by the dictatorships of the two countries. Ledesma, now eighty-two, was an opposition leader in 1978. He testified under oath in a Peruvian court that Videla said he would not follow through on a deal with the Peruvian government to imprison and torture its political prisoners illegally unless Peru agreed to lose the semifinals by enough goals to ensure that Argentina would make the finals. "Videla needed to win the World Cup to cleanse Argentina's bad image around the world," testified Ledesma. "So he only accepted the group if Peru allowed the Argentine national team to triumph."[39] Latin American historian Ranaan Rein confirms that "there is in fact no question about it. It not only stains the military regime but it also stains the national team, and they had a great national team. In many ways, they deserved to win the World Cup."[40] After the 1978 World Cup ended, one of the military strongmen who made it possible, Admiral Carlos Lacoste, was named vice president of FIFA.

As shocking as these revelations are, even more gobsmacking was FIFA's reaction. At the conference itself, this bombshell garnered only a shrug from FIFA secretary general Jérôme Valcke, who acknowledged that "working with democratically elected governments can complicate organizing tournaments that require billions of dollars of investment in stadiums, airports, roads and hotels."[41] FIFA went on to prove that this mindset was not a relic of history with its decision to host the coming 2018 Cup in Putin's Russia, where the 2014 Sochi Olympics were created on a foundation of cronyism, corruption, and waste, and in 2022 in Qatar, an absolute monarchy already facing international outrage for using slave labor in building its World Cup stadiums. It's the FIFA way.

Here is the Michael Jackson statue, found in Favela Santa Marta in the heart of Rio. Jackson filmed the video for his protest song "They Don't Care about Us" partially in the favela.

Protest graffiti against the coming World Cup. I thought that the World Cup would be greeted with open arms and the Olympics would become the focal point of protest. Murals like this were an early indication that I was wrong.

Here is a huge billboard showcasing for passersby what the Olympic construction will look like when completed. The favelas are wiped out in the photos.

A sign in Vila Autódromo, a favela leading one of the most public Olympic fights. The slogan, translated, is "A Rio without forced removals."

This is Ana, a resident of Vila Autódromo, telling us that even without legs, she will fight to stay.

This is a mural with the Portuguese word for "freedom" replacing the familiar slogan of "Order and Progress."

This is Armando, explaining with passion and grace why he refuses to leave his home in Vila Autódromo.

Former professional soccer player, author, and activist Christopher Gaffney, showing how he feels about wholesale renovation of the sacred soccer space that is Maracanã Stadium.

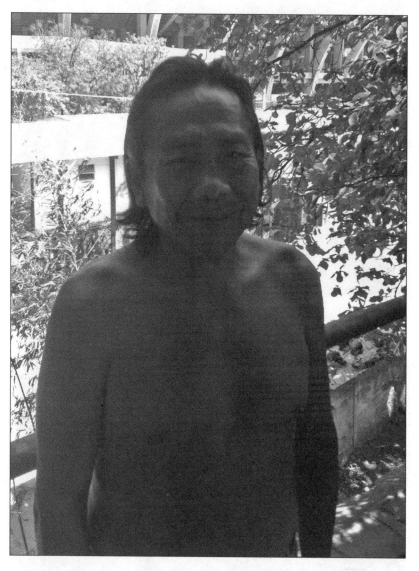

Carlos Tukano in the now-demolished Indigenous Cultural Center. The Maracanã is in the background.

As we arrived in Brazil, a national university strike had just ended in defeat. The Workers' Party won. The workers lost. This is a banner that no one took down.

Another billboard heralding what Providência will look like without the favela that bears its name. The massive sign is like a threat hanging over the entire community.

This is Glorinha. She recently heard that the government would be evicting her. "Like it or not, I have to go. I've been displaced. I have no place," she says. "My dream is not to leave here, for sure. But orders are orders. They gave us orders to leave. . . . I don't want to fight, I just want to be somewhere safe."

A view of how steep the favelas can be. Many of the homes are built at creative angles to match the hills.

Mauricio Hora, award-winning photographer and son of one of Providência's first drug traffickers. His perspective was invaluable.

More political mural art. The pig is a rather universal symbol.

At the Museum of the Slaves, built on top of a mass burial ground, you can see the bones through the glass in the floor.

Me inside the Maracanã, walking among the construction and destruction. It was enraging to see this temple of soccer history get its guts torn out.

Protesters gather in the streets of Divinópolis in June 2013. Photo by Fernando H. C. Oliveira.

CHAPTER 6

Neoliberal Trojan Horses and Sporting Shock Doctrines

Our defeat was always implicit in the victory of others; our wealth has always generated our poverty by nourishing the prosperity of others—the empires and their native overseers. In the colonial and neocolonial alchemy, gold changes into scrap metal and food into poison.

—Eduardo Galeano[1]

W hen all you have is a hammer, everything looks like a nail. When you are the IOC and FIFA, every country, no matter how unique, is subject to the same sets of expectations. These organizations have proven, particularly in recent years, their relentless intention to hammer any peg, no matter how square, into the round holes they require—which means infrastructure, displacement, security, corporate branding on anything that stands still, and of course billions upon billions of dollars in state spending. This is particularly the case in the post–9/11 period where terrorism fears—both real and imagined—have provided a pretext for security details that resemble occupying armies. Any look at sporting mega-events over the previous ten years confirms this. It is difficult to imagine countries more different than Greece, Canada, South Africa, Russia, China, and the United Kingdom. Yet the demands—and the dangers—are eerily similar.

Greece 2004[2]

The 2004 Athens Olympics were supposed to recall the antiquity and grandeur of the original, ancient Olympic Games. Instead they were a harsh reflection of the violent new realities we have reaped in the twenty-first century. These Games were the first held after the attacks of 9/11; under orders from the IOC, the Greek authorities were more than prepared. Greece's politicians overrode their own constitution by allowing fifty thousand Israeli, British, and US Special Forces troops to patrol the streets, their job to monitor not only external but also internal threats. Anger had been running particularly hot in Greece, for reasons that never made it onto the sports broadcasts. Amnesty International estimated that forty construction workers died in workplace accidents while building Olympic facilities.[3] The new center-right government of Kostas Karamanlis, terrified of international embarrassment for its less-than-modern infrastructure, turned the screws to finish the facilities on time by any means necessary.[4]

In the last push of round-the-clock preparation alone, thirteen laborers were killed making Athens, in the words of one Olympic official, "habitable for a global audience."[5] As Andreas Zazopoulos, head of the Greek Construction Workers' Union, said, "We have paid for the Olympic Games in blood."[6] Five hundred people, amid an atmosphere of tremendous repression, rallied on behalf of the dead and placed olive wreaths on thirteen crosses planted in the earth outside Greece's parliament. City authorities also spent the final days before the Games "rounding up homeless people, drug addicts, and the mentally ill requiring that psychiatric hospitals lock them up. Also affected by Athens Olympic clean-up [were] refugees and asylum seekers, some of whom [were] targeted for detention and deportation in the days leading up to the Games."[7] Inmates of six prisons protested against the government's decision, justified in the name of security, to stop authorizing parole while the Olympics were in town. A Greek organization with the name Revolutionary Struggle also began setting bombs in uninhabited buildings. After blowing up an empty police station, the group released the following statement: "With regard to the Olympic Games, we say that Greece's transformation into a fortress, NATO's involvement, the presence and activities of foreign intelligence units show clearly that [the Olympics] are not a festival like Games organizers say, but it's a war."[8]

The true crisis of the Olympic Games in Greece was in the costs. For six years, Greece had been mired in an epic debt crisis, one that is still ongoing today. Amid the stories of general strikes, growing fascist movements, and the evisceration of working-class living standards, what gets discussed far less is the role that the Olympics played in aggravating that crisis. When Athens "won" the Games in 1997, city leaders and the IOC estimated the cost to Greece at $1.3 billion. By the time the detailed planning was done, the price had jumped to $5.3 billion. By the time the Games were over, Greece had spent some $14.2 billion, pushing the country's budget deficit to record levels. Then IOC chairman Jacques Rogge said, "At Athens the legacy will be a new airport, new metro, new suburban train—this is a legacy the Greeks will be proud of."[9] The actual lasting legacy can be seen where some of city's homeless find shelter: they squat in dilapidated, unusable Olympic structures.[10]

Beijing 2008[11]

Not since Marco Polo has anyone traveled so far up China's Silk Road with such amoral élan. But there was Jacques Rogge, not only president of the IOC but also, incidentally, a knight of the court of King Leopold's Belgium and a three-time Olympian in the grand sport of yachting, standing astride Beijing at the close of the 2008 Olympic Games. In front of a stunning ninety thousand people at the closing ceremony, he said, "Tonight, we come to the end of sixteen glorious days which we will cherish forever. Through these Games, the world learned more about China, and China learned more about the world."[12]

But what did the world really learn? From the ratings-rich coverage alone, not all that much. We learned that China is remarkably beautiful, Michael Phelps can really swim, and Usain Bolt is truly quite fast. Oh, and there are cute pandas. We can't forget about the pandas. The amount of China that remained hidden from view was not lost on some members of the media. Veteran *Washington Post* sports columnist Thomas Boswell wrote from Beijing, "In all my decades at the *Post*, this is the first event I've covered at which I was certain that the main point of the exercise was to co-opt the Western media, including NBC, with a splendidly pretty, sparsely attended, completely controlled sports event inside a quasi-military compound. We had little alternative but to be a conduit for happy-Olympics, progressive-China propaganda. I suspect it worked."[13]

We should applaud Boswell for his honesty, but it is hard not to feel contempt for the aside that journalists "had little alternative" but to dance the infomercial shuffle. Boswell and the press made a choice the moment they stepped on China's soil. They chose not to seek out any of the almost two million people evicted from their homes to make way for Olympic facilities. They chose not to report on the Chinese citizens who tried to register to enter the cordoned-off "protest zones" only to find themselves in police custody. They chose not to report on the foreign nationals held in Chinese prisons for daring to protest. (According to the Associated Press, the US Embassy pleaded with China to free protestors, gently suggesting that China could stand to show "greater tolerance and openness.") They chose not to report on the Tibetan citizens removed from their service jobs by state law for the duration of the Games. They chose not to ask what forty-two billion dollars, the price tag of the Games, could have meant to earthquake-ravaged Sichuan.

They chose to not point out the bizarre hypocrisy of seeing Michael Phelps—with full media fanfare—taking a group of Chinese children to their first meal at McDonald's (an Olympic sponsor). (Even though Phelps famously eats twelve thousand calories a day during training, I can't imagine much of it comes from Mickey

D's.) They chose not to ask why George W. Bush was the first US president to attend the Olympics on foreign soil or why the State Department, in April 2013, took China off its list of nations that commit human rights violations. They chose not to ask whether it was a conflict of interest for General Electric, which owned NBC at the time, to be one of the primary sponsors of the Games as well as the supplier of much of their high-tech security apparatus, including three hundred thousand closed-circuit cameras. All indications are that these cameras remained in place once the world turned its attention elsewhere.[14]

They chose not to ask (and keep asking) why the Games were held in Beijing in the first place, considering that Rogge and Beijing organizing committee head Liu Qi both promised that the Olympics would come alongside significant improvements in human rights.[15] As Sophie Richardson of Human Rights Watch said:

> The reality is that the Chinese government's hosting of the Games has been a catalyst for abuses, leading to massive forced evictions, a surge in the arrest, detention and harassment of critics, repeated violations of media freedom, and increased political repression. Not a single world leader who attended the Games or members of the IOC seized the opportunity to challenge the Chinese government's behavior in any meaningful way.[16]

The legacy of the Beijing Games is China's dominance in winning more gold medals than the United States, the aquatic dominance of Michael Phelps, and the blistering triumph of Usain Bolt. But we should also remember the ravaging of a country sacrificed at the altar of commercialism and "market penetration." And we should recall a mainstream press, derelict in its duty, telling us they had "little alternative" but to turn this *shandeh* into a globalization infomercial.

Liu Qi called the Olympics "a grand celebration of sport, of peace and friendship." Not quite. Instead it was a powerful demonstration of the way the elephants of the East and West can link trunks and happily trample the grass.

Vancouver 2010[17]

My lasting memory from the Vancouver 2010 Winter Olympics will always be that the Vancouver Olympic Committee was forced to import snow—on the public dime—to make sure that the Games could proceed as planned. This use of tax dollars was just the icing on the cake for angry Vancouver residents. Unlike the snow, that anger still simmers years after the fact.

When I arrived in Vancouver several weeks before the start of the Games, the first thing I noticed was the frowns. The IOC had leased every sign and billboard in town to broadcast Olympic joy, but they couldn't pay the local populace to crack a smile. It's clear that the 2010 Winter Games had darkened the mood in the bucolic coastal city; the vibe was decidedly overcast. Even the customs police officer checking my passport started grumbling about "five-thousand-dollar hockey tickets."

Polls released on my first day in Vancouver backed up my initial impression. Only 50 percent of residents in British Columbia thought that the Olympics were a positive thing, and 69 percent said too much money was being spent on the Games.[18] "The most striking thing in the poll is that as the Olympics get closer, British Columbians are less likely to see the Games as having a positive impact," said Hamish Marshall, research director for the polling firm Angus Reid. "Conventional wisdom was that as we got closer to the Olympics, people here would get more excited and more supportive."[19] If the global recession hadn't smacked into planning efforts the previous year, with corporate sponsors fleeing for the hills, maybe the Vancouver Olympic Committee would have found itself on more solid ground with residents. But public bailouts of Olympic projects are hard to swallow when people see their own jobs and social safety net slashed. In fact, on my first day in Vancouver, a local newspaper ran a story about the need to import snow—alongside another piece about funds for physical education being cut. It does not take a media studies degree to see these two articles side by side and fume.

I spoke to Charles, a bus driver, whose good cheer diminished when I asked him about the Games. "I just can't believe I wanted this a year ago," he said. "I voted for it in the plebiscite. But now, yes. I'm disillusioned." This disillusionment grew as the financial burden of the Games was increasingly revealed. The original cost estimate was $660 million in public money. At the time of my visit, it was admitted to be six billion dollars and steadily climbing. An early economic impact statement forecast that the Games could bring in ten billion dollars—but then PriceWaterhouseCoopers released its own study showing that the total economic gain would be more like one billion dollars. In addition, the Olympic Village came in a hundred million dollars over budget and had to be bailed out by the city. As for security, the estimated cost was $175 million. At that point, it was already clear that any economic gain would be swallowed by cost overruns.

These budget overruns coincided with drastic cuts to city services. On my first day in town, the cover of the local paper blared cheery news about the Games above the fold, with a headline announcing the imminent layoff of eight hundred teachers much further down the page. As a staunch Olympic supporter, a sports reporter from the *Globe and Mail*, said to me, "The optics of cuts in city services alongside Olympic cost overruns are, to put it mildly, not good." But to Vancouver residents—particularly those living in the Downtown Eastside neighborhood, the most impoverished area in all of Canada—these weren't just public-relations gaffes. Carol Martin, who works in the blighted neighborhood, made this clear: "The Bid Committee promised that not a single person would be displaced due to the Games, but there are now three thousand homeless people sleeping on Vancouver's streets—and these people are facing increased police harassment as they try to clean the streets in the lead-up to the Games." When I explored the backstreets of Downtown Eastside, I found police congregated on every corner, trying to hem in a palpable anger. Anti-Olympic posters plastered the neighborhood, creating an alternative universe to the cheery 2010 Games displays by the airport. The Vancouver Olympic Committee tried to quell the crackling vibe by dispersing tickets to second-tier Olympic events like the luge. It wasn't working.

Officials were feeling the anger—and the independent media, frighteningly, was paying the price. In November 2009, *Democracy Now!*'s Amy Goodman was held while trying to cross the border for reasons that had nothing to do with the Olympic Games. In an interview with CBC News, Goodman recalled that the border agent

> made it clear by saying, "What about the Olympics?" And I said, "You mean when President Obama went to Copenhagen to push for the Olympics in Chicago?" He said, "No. I am talking about the Olympics here in 2010." I said, "Oh, I hadn't thought of that." He said, "You're saying you're not talking about the Olympics?" He was clearly incredulous that I wasn't going to be talking about the Olympics. He didn't believe me.[20]

Derrick O'Keefe, co-chair of the Canadian Peace Alliance, said to me, "It's pretty unlikely that the harassment of a well-known and respected journalist like Amy Goodman . . . was the initiative of one overzealous, bad-apple Canadian border guard. This looks like a clear sign of the chill that the IOC and the Games' local corporate boosters want to put out against any potential dissent." Harsha Walia, member of No One Is Illegal and the Olympic Resistance Network, confirmed when we spoke that such treatment has become standard practice:

> In the lead-up to the 2010 Vancouver Olympic Games, we have witnessed and been subjected to an increasingly fortified police state, including intimidation and harassment of activists by security and intelligence forces as part of an unparalleled one-billion-dollar security and surveillance network. In contravention of basic rights, police have stated their plans to set up checkpoints, search people without cause, and erect security exclusion zones.

The Canadian government was leveling public housing, stifling civil liberties, and harassing local activists. The last thing it wanted was someone like Amy Goodman telling the world.

For those with just a passing knowledge of our northern neighbors, this must all seem quite shocking. When we think of human rights abuses and suppression of dissent, Canada is hardly the first place that comes to mind. But Canada has its own history of cracking down on peaceful protestors, as anyone who attended the 2001 demonstrations in Quebec against the FTAA trade agreement will attest. But the people of Downtown Eastside and beyond developed a different outlet for their Olympic angst: a full-scale protest to welcome the athletes, tourists, and foreign dignitaries. Vancouver residents put out an open call for a week of anti-Games actions, organizing demonstrations on issues ranging from homelessness to Indigenous rights. Protestors from London and Russia, sites of the next two Olympics, joined in. Tellingly, polls showed that 40 percent of British Columbia residents supported the aims of the protestors, compared to just 13 percent across the rest of Canada. Harsha Walia said to me, "We are seeing increasing resistance across the country as it becomes more visible how these Games are a big fraud."

The Games also coincided with the largest and longest-standing annual march in Vancouver: the February 14 Memorial Women's March, which calls attention every Valentine's Day to the hundreds of missing and murdered women (particularly Indigenous women) in British Columbia. The Vancouver Olympic Committee asked the Memorial March organizing committee if they would change the route of the march for the Olympic Games. Stella August, one of the organizers with the Downtown Eastside Power of Women Group, told me that wouldn't happen: "We are warriors. We have been doing this for nineteen years and we aren't going to bow down to the Olympics."

But it's not just the Olympics. All international sporting events tend to act as neoliberal Trojan horses, preying on our love of sports to enforce a series of policies that would in any other situation be roundly rejected. Nowhere have I seen this more clearly than in South Africa in 2010, before that country's historic turn as host of the most popular tournament on earth.

South Africa 2010[21]

If you stepped off a plane in Johannesburg International Airport in 2010, the first image you would have seen was a mammoth soccer ball hanging from the ceiling. It read, "Let's Go! WORLD CUP!" If you swiveled your head, you would see that every sponsor from Coca-Cola to Anheuser-Busch had joined the party and branded its own banners with the FIFA seal. When your head dipped down, you would see another, less sponsored universe. Even inside this state-of-the-art airport, men from the ages of sixteen to sixty would ask if they could shine your shoes, carry your bags, or even walk you to a cab. It's the informal economy fighting for breath under the smothering cloak of official sponsorship.

Welcome to South Africa, a place of jagged contrasts: rich and poor, black and white, immigrant and everyone else, the dispossessed and the self-possessed fighting for elbow room. The old system of racist apartheid, as many are quick to point out, has been supplanted with "economic apartheid," a reality visible throughout the country if you choose to see it. It is not uncommon, but always entirely tragic, to hear black South Africans reflect on how some parts of their lives were easier under apartheid. Under apartheid there was a welfare state. There was employment. There was massive state intervention in the economy. The white minority in power made these investments to stave off inevitable social unrest. Today, it's a free-marketeer's paradise. These are the normal conditions, the normal contrasts. But the 2010 World Cup took these contrasts and inflated them to the bursting point.

The lead-up to the World Cup in South Africa could best be dubbed "*Invictus* in reverse." For those who haven't had the pleasure, the film *Invictus* dramatizes how Nelson Mandela used sports, particularly the nearly all-white sport of rugby, to unite the country after the fall of apartheid. The World Cup, in contrast, provoked efforts to camouflage every conflict and present the image of a united nation to the world. As Danny Jordaan, the World Cup's lead South African organizer, said, "People will see we are African. We are world-class."[22] Note that the concern was with what the world would see, not what South Africans would see. What South Africans saw, as one young man told me, was that "football is looting our country."

The contrasts became conflicts because the South African government, at the behest of FIFA, was determined to put on a good show no matter the social cost. Thousands were displaced, forced from their homes into makeshift, tin-roofed shantytowns, to make way for stadiums and ensure that tourists could avoid unseemly scenes of poverty. The United Nations even issued a complaint on behalf of the twenty thousand people removed from the Joe Slovo settlement in Cape Town, which World Cup organizers called an "eyesore." The homeless were packed into guarded settlements hundreds of miles from the action. Johannesburg councilor Sipho Masigo justified their removal by saying, "Homelessness and begging are big problems in the city. You have to clean your house before you have guests. There is nothing wrong with that."[23]

There was also a heavy crackdown on those who make their living selling goods by the stadiums. Authorities told Regina Twala, who has been vending outside soccer matches for almost forty years, that she and others must remain at least one kilometer from the stadiums at all times. "They say they do not want us here," Twala told the *Sunday Independent*. "They do not want us near the stadium and we have to close the whole place."[24]

To make matters worse, FIFA pushed the South African government to announce that it would arrest any vendors who tried to sell products emblazoned with the words "World Cup" or even the year, 2010. One young woman whose mother works in a clothing factory told me of the factory manager looking on hurriedly to make sure that "2010" didn't find its way onto any of the labels. In addition, local beers, soft drinks, and fast foods not branded with the FIFA label could not be sold in close proximity to the stadiums. A once-vibrant landscape of small shops selling locally made, artisanal goods and food became dotted with the fast-food chains common in any American suburb. The areas around soccer stadiums started to resemble descriptions of the Green Zone in Iraq: an unreal, transplanted, homogeneous landscape. Samson, a trader in Durban, said to me, "This is the way we have always done business by the stadium. Who makes the laws now? FIFA?"

Samson was only referencing the threats toward vendors, but his criticism was an equally valid description of the series of legal ordinances

South Africa passed to prepare for the tournament. Declaring the World Cup a "protected event," the government, in line with FIFA requirements, passed bylaws that put in writing "where people may drive and park their cars, where they may and may not trade or advertise, and where they may walk their dogs." These laws also made clear that beggars or even those caught using foul language (presumably off the field of play) could be subject to arrest.

Then there were the assassinations. In a story that made international news but gained next to no notice in the United States, two people were assassinated for "whistleblowing" on suspected corruption in the construction of the $150-million Mbombela Stadium. The *Sunday World* newspaper obtained a hit list with twenty names, including two journalists and numerous political leaders. Accusations swirled that the list was linked to the ruling African National Congress (ANC), which the ANC has denied in somewhat bizarre terms. "The ANC wants to reiterate its condemnation of any murder of any person, no matter what the motive may be," said ANC spokesperson Paul Mbenyane.[25] It's never a good sign when you have to make clear to the public that you are staunchly opposed to murder.

To add to this shadow of political violence, an extremist right-wing white-supremacist organization, the Suidlanders, was found to be stockpiling arms in advance of the tournament. After the April 2010 murder of white-supremacist leader Eugene Terreblanche, the Suidlanders held meetings around the country and encouraged people to boycott the World Cup in solidarity with their cause. "The time has come for people to realise they cannot be on the sideline any longer and everybody's participation is needed to defend the last bastion of a true Christian nation against total annihilation," read the statement on their website. While the Suidlanders committed no violence during the World Cup, the fear factor enhanced the ANC's efforts to create a security state.

All of this—displacements, crackdowns on informal trade, the rumblings of a terrorist white minority, even accusations of state-sponsored assassinations—echoed the days of apartheid. Responsibility for this state of affairs falls firmly on the shoulders of FIFA, but also on the ANC. After all, South Africa's turn hosting the World Cup was meant to bolster both "brands." I saw this firsthand when I took a private tour of the breathtaking $457 million Moses Mabhida Stadium in Durban, South Africa. I left the stadium utterly stunned, for both better and worse.

Named after the late, legendary leader of the South African Communist Party, the stadium is a stylistic masterpiece. The eggshell-white facility is visible for miles, its milky waves rising from the earth in sharp contrast with the dusty urban environs that surround it. The open roof has a graceful, slender arc connecting one side of the stadium to the other. The arc itself is a wonder: it starts as one clean curve, then splits into two separate stretches of white. This is an homage to the postapartheid South African flag, whose stripes symbolize "the convergence of diverse elements within South African society, taking the road ahead in unity."[26] Well-heeled adrenaline junkies can even go to the top of the arc and bungee-swing across the pitch. Unity is now a thrill-ride for the benefactors of the postapartheid regime.

On one side of the stadium, behind the goal, is a completely open vista that majestically welcomes the Durban skyline into the stadium. But the true engineering achievement of Moses Mabhida Stadium is its bleachers. They angle up with such subtlety that the effect is of a saucer instead of a bowl. Each of the seventy-four thousand seats has a picture-perfect sightline on the action, whether you are in the nosebleeds or the corporate boxes. The seats themselves are painted in rich colors: the first level is royal blue to represent the ocean, the middle one is green to signify the land, and the top is brown, as a sportswriter said to me, "so it looks full on television." (Sure enough, filling the stadium—and all the new stadiums—in the two years since the World Cup has been a quixotic effort.) The most striking color in the stadium is not in the bleachers, though. It's the grass, which is a green so bright it hurts the eyes, as if every blade were painstakingly colored with a magic marker. The shade was achieved with the aid of near-infinite gallons of crystal-clear water, which I saw constantly irrigating the field.

I raise the issue of the stadium's incomparable beauty because South African politicians in support of the World Cup accused detractors of what they called "Afro-pessimism." They alleged that critics lacked faith that South Africa could host an event of this magnitude. They held up the steady stream of racist invective in the European press about the "looming disaster of the South African World Cup" to implicate any critics, no matter their motives. If the World Cup "lost," they argued, then Africa would also lose. But this argument was aimed at squelching dissent, not challenging European prejudice. When a country already dotted with perfectly usable stadiums spends approximately six billion dollars on new facilities, that's an unconscionable squandering of resources no matter the continent. The situation grows even more egregious when you learn that 48 percent of South Africans live on less than 322 rand (about 42 dollars) a month.[27]

At the stadium, it became clear that the health of the grass took precedence over the health of South Africa's poor. In townships across the country, lack of access to water spurs regular protests. As Simon Magagula, who lives in a mud house near one of the new stadiums, said to the *New York Times*, "We've been promised a better life, but look how we live. If you pour water into a glass, you can see things moving inside."[28] To see an architectural marvel like Moses Mabhida Stadium in a country where so many lack access to basic, affordable shelter is to witness politicians' interests colliding with those of the citizens they've been elected to serve. And to see such a stadium named in honor of Moses Mabhida, who symbolizes the struggle against poverty for millions of South Africans, is to stare at irony in at its most lurid form.

As the price and FIFA's demands grew more onerous, many South Africans had second thoughts. Zayn Nabbi, a sports correspondent for South Africa's E Television, gave me a stadium tour. He said, "We were all so caught up in the love story of winning the World Cup—the romance of it all—we didn't grasp or we weren't told the repercussions. We all got caught up in the spin. I put myself in that category certainly.

The hangover when this is all done will be brutal, man." Youth activist Peter drew a similar conclusion: "The World Cup is like a marvelous party, but what happens the next day when we're hung over and the bill comes due?"

But the hangover started before the party ended, as these stark contrasts provoked fierce, wholly predictable resistance. In a normal month, South Africa has more protests per capita than any nation on earth. During the World Cup crackdown, the numbers skyrocketed. More than seventy thousand workers took part in strikes connected to World Cup projects, with twenty-six strikes between 2007 and 2010. A woman named Lebo said to me, "We have learned in South Africa that unless we burn tires, unless we fight police, unless we are willing to return violence on violence, we will never be heard." Patrick Bond of the Center for Civil Society in Durban commented to me that protests should be expected: "Anytime you have three billion people watching, that's called leverage."

The struggles on display put the concept of *ubuntu* to the ultimate test. *Ubuntu* is a treasured Bantu term roughly translated as "unity." But "unity" doesn't quite do it justice. Nobel Prize–winning Liberian peace activist Leymah Gbowee defined it as meaning "I am what I am because of who we all are."[29] During South Africa's decades-long struggle against apartheid, *ubuntu* meant unity of purpose among the country's black majority against brutal oppression. It meant asserting humanity in the face of an inhuman system.

The sacred word resurfaced, unsurprisingly, amid South Africa's lead-up to the 2010 FIFA World Cup. This time, though, *ubuntu* was used quite differently in speeches and rallies held by the ruling ANC. It still meant unity, but now its use was cheapened to pep talks. It was also used against people who dared ask uncomfortable questions. As Saleh, a youth activist in Johannesburg, said to me, "If someone stood up at a [council meeting] and said, 'Why are we spending so much on stadiums? Why are we giving the police so many powers?' we were told that we were violating the spirit of *ubuntu*." Although the *ubuntu* soured far sooner than anyone could have predicted, the 2010 World

Cup was without question a major sporting success for South Africa. The gleaming fields opened on schedule, new airports welcomed scores of visitors, and with cameras ready to catch it, disparate groups of South Africans who usually self-segregate exulted together in public. But now the party's over. The country was subsequently hit with massive strikes involving 1.3 million public-sector workers, including teachers, civil-service workers, and health workers. The public-sector strike was particularly shocking, for South Africans and international observers alike. When striking workers marched through a police line while sounding the World Cup's iconic *vuvuzela*, they were assaulted with rubber bullets.[30]

The strikes, as well as the rapid-fire erosion of the World Cup's *ubuntu*, speak to a serious political crisis facing South Africa's scandal-plagued president, Jacob Zuma. They also reveal deep fissures between the ANC government and its base of support. The ANC has benefited greatly from its reputation as the freedom fighters who led South Africa's struggle against apartheid. But in today's South Africa, sixteen years after the end of apartheid, 1.9 million people (15 percent of the total population) live in shacks. More than half of eighteen- to twenty-five-year-olds are unemployed, with unofficial numbers likely much higher. Rates of rape and violent crime keep climbing. Meanwhile, the top twenty paid directors at companies listed on the Johannesburg Stock Exchange make 1,728 times the average income of a South African worker. And on August 16, 2012, South African security forces killed forty-four people, the majority of whom were striking mineworkers, in what has become known as the Marikana massacre. This was the most deadly act by the South African state since the darkest days of apartheid.

For a nation forged in a struggle against injustice, this situation is intolerable. The ANC depends on its tripartite alliance with the South African Communist Party and the Congress of South African Trade Unions (COSATU), which is behind the recent strikes. If you're a part of the new black middle class, one of the "Black Diamonds," as they're known, you probably have a positive view of the party. If you live in the townships or are a young member of COSATU and your existence has been defined by economic apartheid, it's not enough. Indeed, the ANC now finds itself in direct conflict with the very unions that traditionally comprised its spine.

A resurrection of *ubuntu* is surely on the agenda in South Africa. But it's an *ubuntu* that could leave the ANC out in the cold—that could well take form *against* the ANC—as South Africa's youth and workers demand economic justice and strive to reclaim their country.

There is a scene in *Invictus* where Morgan Freeman's Mandela says, alluding to the famous poem, "I thank whatever gods may be for my unconquerable soul. I am the master of my fate." Indeed, the people of South Africa consider themselves unconquerable, whether they face apartheid, FIFA, or their current government. By insisting on the notion of sports as an apolitical space, we do a great disservice to those facing the realities of "event sports." When athletic mega-events like the Olympics and World Cup come to town, people face very real police abuses, displacement, and onerous taxation. Media outlets do their best not to discuss these issues so as not to ruin the big party—but if we don't talk about them, Brazil will continue paying a terrible price.

In the poem "Invictus," from which Mandela took so much inspiration, William Ernest Henley writes,

Beyond this place of wrath and tears
Looms but the Horror of the shade,
And yet the menace of the years
Finds, and shall find, me unafraid.[31]

It's a poem about taking control of our own destinies, no matter the obstacles. Sporting mega-events shape the economic, political, and personal destinies of masses of people, with zero accountability for the trail of displacement, disruption, and destruction they leave behind. Brazilians are already showing themselves to be "unafraid" as they attempt to master their fate. They will remind the world that the party has a price.

London 2012[32]

Forty-eight thousand security forces. Thirteen thousand five hundred troops. Surface-to-air missiles stationed on top of residential apartment buildings.[33] A sonic weapon that disperses crowds by creating "head-splitting pain." Unmanned drones peering down from the skies.[34] A safe zone cordoned off by an eleven-mile electrified fence, ringed with trained agents and fifty-five teams of attack dogs.[35]

One would be forgiven for thinking that these were the counterinsurgency tactics used by US army bases in Iraq and Afghanistan, or perhaps the military methods taught to third-world despots at the Western Hemisphere Institute for Security and Economic Cooperation (formerly the School of the Americas) in Fort Benning, Georgia. But instead of being used in a war zone or theater of occupation, this was in fact the very visible security apparatus created in London for the 2012 Summer Olympics.[36]

London already had the most street cameras per capita of any city on earth, and for the seven years since the terror attacks of July 7, 2005, its political leaders have spared no expense to monitor their own citizens. But its Olympic operation went above and beyond anything ever before seen when a Western democracy has hosted the Games. Not even China in 2008 used drone planes or ringed the proceedings with a massive, high-voltage fence. But there was London, preparing a counterinsurgency and parking an aircraft carrier right in the Thames. There was London, adding "scanners, biometric ID cards, number-plate and facial-recognition CCTV systems, disease tracking systems, new police control centres and checkpoints."[37] Stephen Graham at the *Guardian* referred to the entire state of affairs as "Lockdown London": "the UK's biggest mobilisation of military and security forces since the second world war." He is not exaggerating in the slightest. The number of troops exceeded the number of forces the UK ever had on the ground in Afghanistan.[38]

What was striking about this wasn't just the costs or the incredible invasions of privacy. It was the powers given to police under the 2006 "London Olympic Games Act," which empowered not only the army and police but also private mercenaries to deal with "security issues" using physical force. These "security issues" were broadly defined to include everything from "terrorism" to peaceful protestors to people selling bootleg Olympic products on the streets and any corporate presence that didn't have the Olympic seal of approval. For help with the last part, "brand protection teams" were set loose around the city. These teams also operated inside Olympic venues to make sure no one would "wear clothes or accessories with commercial messages other than the manufacturers" who are official sponsors.[39] The security operation also meant street harassment of young people—that will sound familiar to readers in the United States. As the *Guardian* reported, police were given "powers to move on anyone considered to be engaged in antisocial behaviour, whether they are hanging around the train station, begging, soliciting, loitering in hoodies or deemed in any way to be causing a nuisance."[40]

Not to shock anyone, but there are no signs that any of the security apparatus has been dismantled since the Olympics were staged. Local police forces were given an inordinate number of new toys and the boxes have been opened, the receipts tossed away. London has been left with a high-tech police force, terrible debt, higher taxes, and a camera around every corner. The total cost to Londoners ran about fifteen billion dollars.[41] The ones who left this party enriched were those in the private security industry, which touted "the peace" as its personal accomplishment—encouraging more of the global 1 percent to seek more guards, more walls, and more separation from the great unwashed.

There is no reason the Olympics have to be this way. There is no reason that an international celebration of sports—particularly sports more diverse than our typical US high-carb diet of football, baseball, basketball, and more football—can't take place without drones and aircraft carriers. There is no reason athletes from across the globe can't join together and showcase their physical potential. But the Olympics aren't about sports any more than the Iraq war was about democracy. The Olympics are not about athletes. And they're definitely not about bringing together the "community of nations." They are a neoliberal

Trojan horse aimed at bringing in business and rolling back the most basic civil liberties.

Sochi 2014[42]

It was Josef Stalin who uttered the demonic (though possibly apocryphal) truism that, when it comes to the human attention span, "One death is a tragedy but a million is a statistic." Stalin's political descendant, Russian Federation president Vladimir Putin, is now proving that this applies to the world of sports and corruption. New England Patriots owner Robert Kraft set the sports press on fire in 2013 when he revealed that, in 2005, Putin stole his Super Bowl ring. This was caught on camera and generated a lot of laughs: the video shows Putin trying it on at a press event and then walking out of the room as a slack-jawed Kraft looked on. The Patriots organization played it off as an intentional gift. But Kraft later revealed that it was a straight theft, with the comically alpha-male Putin icily looking at Kraft and saying, "I can kill someone with this ring." Then, in Kraft's words, "I put my hand out and he put it in his pocket, and three KGB guys got around him and walked out."[43]

The intervention of George W. Bush, the man who once said he had "looked into Putin's soul" and seen a great person, stopped Kraft from pursuing the matter. "I really didn't [want to]. I had an emotional tie to the ring, it has my name on it," Kraft said. "I don't want to see it on eBay. There was a pause on the other end of the line, and the voice repeated, 'It would really be in the best interest if you meant to give the ring as a present.'"[44] It's a great, punchy story, and I don't blame sports reporters for flocking to it like a seagull to a dead hermit crab. It also fits with a US foreign policy narrative that makes Putin look only slightly more rational than Bill O'Reilly. But when the story broke, it was galling that this snapshot of Putin's character got so much attention while a massive thirty-billion-dollar sports-related theft goes undiscussed.

I'm referring, of course, to the 2014 Winter Olympics, which were held in the subtropical region of Sochi. According to a report issued by Russian opposition leaders in May, businessmen and officials close to

President Putin stole up to thirty billion dollars from funds intended for Olympic preparations.[44] This pushed the cost of the Winter Games, historically far less expensive than the Summer Games, to more than fifty billion dollars. As Andrew Jennings, the most important Olympic investigative reporter we have, said to me, "Original cost projections had them costing twelve [billion dollars]. That fifty-billion-dollar price tag would make them the most expensive ever"—more expensive even than the 2008 pre-recession spectacle in Beijing. "The Games have always been a money spinner for the cheerleaders in the shadows. Beijing remains impenetrable but is likely to have been little less corrupt than Putin's Mafia state," Jennings added. "Mafia state" may sound extreme, but these Winter Games will go down in history as perhaps the most audacious act of embezzlement in human history.

The costs were not accrued because of security concerns, although there were thirty thousand soldiers on the ground and an unprecedented amount of surveillance. The bill is a result of some of the most brazen cronyism imaginable.[46] Industrialists Arkady and Boris Rotenberg have been Vladimir Putin's friends since childhood. They received twenty-one government contracts worth seven billion dollars—more than the entire cost of the 2010 Olympics in Vancouver. Meanwhile, a thirty-one-mile railway from the Olympic Village to the mountains cost a staggering $8.7 billion. Russian *Esquire* estimated that, for that price, the tracks could "have been paved entirely with a centimeter-thick coating of beluga caviar."[47] As Russian opposition leaders Boris Nemtsov and Leonid Martynyuk wrote,

> Only oligarchs and companies close to Putin got rich. The absence of fair competition [and the presence of] cronyism . . . have led to a sharp increase in the costs and to the poor quality of the work to prepare for the Games. . . . The fact is that almost everything that is related to the cost problems and abuses in preparation for the Olympic Games was carefully concealed and continues to be covered up by the authorities.[48]

Even worse was the shoulder-shrugging of the IOC. Jean-Claude Killy, the French Alpine star who now heads the IOC's coordinating commission for the Sochi Games, sounded fatalistic about the corruption in the Russian city on the Black Sea. "I don't recall an Olympics without corruption," Killy said. "It's not an excuse, obviously, and I'm very sorry about it, but there might be corruption in this country, there was corruption before. I hope we find ways around that."[49]

The IOC also chose to turn a blind eye to a series of laws aimed at criminalizing the LGBTQ community in Russia. Putin and his government have set about criminalizing every aspect of gay life. In 2013, the Russian Duma (parliament) voted 436 to 0 in favor of banning "propaganda for non-traditional sexual relations." This law is so broad that it threatens prison time for anyone who acknowledges the mere existence of LGBTQ people in any public forum: the Internet, a classroom, or even a street corner. Putin also signed a law banning the adoption of Russian children not only by gay couples, but by any single people or unmarried couples who reside in a country where marriage equality is on the books. And he still wasn't done. He also approved legislation that hands out two-week jail sentences to any tourist *suspected* of being gay. (Four Dutch tourists were in fact recently arrested for "suspicion of promoting homosexuality to children."[50]) Many see this spate of legislation as connected to a string of brutal beatings and several grisly murders.[51] The government doesn't track antigay hate crimes, but in one poll, 15 percent of LGBTQ people in Russia said they had been physically assaulted for their sexual orientation in the past ten months.[52] Some lawmakers also threatened "homosexuality-promoting" Olympic athletes with arrest. This led to hasty pronouncements by Putin himself that "the Games will be held in full accordance with the Olympic Charter—without any discrimination for any reason."[53] Putin also banned demonstrations for the sixty-day period leading up to the Games. During the Games themselves, demonstrations could only take place in a pen seven and half miles away from the site. As for the IOC, it said nothing, except that politics should not be a part of the discussion and that athletes would be punished if they so much as painted their fingernails in rainbow hues. The Olympics provided cover and legitimacy for Putin, in a way that actor and LGBTQ activist Harvey Fierstein called a disturbing echo of the 1936 Berlin Games.[54]

But the problems run even deeper. In Sochi itself, thousands of families have been forcibly displaced. According to Human Rights Watch, the village of Akhshtyr, which has 49 homes and a population of 102, has been without water for a year because of Olympics-related construction. This isn't an Olympics—it's a scene from *Goodfellas*. It also isn't something any sports fan with a conscience should support. As for Putin, he can keep the ring.

Qatar 2022

FIFA's construction operation in Qatar, site of the 2022 World Cup, makes Brazil's look positively benign. *Guardian* reporter Pete Pattisson, doing the kind of journalism that sometimes seems extinct, has written a series of articles about Qatar's stadium-building policies, which have already resulted in the deaths of dozens of Nepalese migrant laborers. Unlike other Olympic-sized projects with a body count, the deaths are not primarily a result of workplace accidents, but of heart failure—healthy young men having heart attacks:

> This summer, Nepalese workers died at a rate of almost one a day in Qatar, many of them young men who had sudden heart attacks. The investigation found evidence to suggest that thousands of Nepalese, who make up the single largest group of labourers in Qatar, face exploitation and abuses that amount to modern-day slavery, as defined by the International Labour Organisation, during a building binge paving the way for 2022.[55]

The charge of "slavery" that many Nepalese workers are bringing forth results from the fact that their pay is being withheld to keep them from fleeing the labor camps in the night. Food and water have also been rationed as a way to compel them to work for free. After a day in the scorching sun, they sleep in filth, twelve to a room.

Pattisson quotes one Nepalese migrant employed at the Lusail City development, a $45 billion city being constructed from the ground up, which will include the ninety-thousand-seat stadium for the World

Cup final. "We'd like to leave, but the company won't let us," he says. "I'm angry about how this company is treating us, but we're helpless. I regret coming here, but what to do? We were compelled to come just to make a living, but we've had no luck."[56]

In normal times, more than 90 percent of workers in Qatar are immigrants, with 40 percent coming from Nepal. But these are not normal times. There has been a massive push for migrant workers. Qatar aims to spend more than a hundred billion dollars on stadiums and infrastructure for the World Cup, part of a broader effort to re-make and "modernize" the emirate. A hundred thousand workers have already come from Nepal, one of the poorest nations on earth, and as many as 1.5 million will need to be recruited to get the job done. Thousands more will die if action is not taken.[57] I spoke with Jules Boykoff, author of *Celebration Capitalism and the Olympic Games* and a former professional soccer player. He said, "Sports mega-events like the World Cup are upbeat shakedowns with appalling human costs. This is trickle-up economics that magnifies the widening chasm be-tween the happy-faced promises of mega-event boosters and on-the-ground reality for the rest of us."[58]

The issue is clearly not soccer. The issue isn't even having a global tournament like the World Cup. It is the way these mega-events are linked to massive development projects used as neoliberal Trojan horses to push through policies that would stun the most hardened of cynics: a shock doctrine of sports. The people of Brazil, demanding "FIFA-quality hospitals and schools," are showing the world a way to envision how we can emerge from this brutal cycle. The Nepalese mi-grant workers, just by having the courage to come forward, are doing the same.

Everything I have seen in this world of "celebration capitalism" and "neoliberal Trojan horses" makes me extremely anxious about how host-ing the World Cup and Olympics, like a back-to-back one-two punch, will affect Brazil over the next two years. All of the most viral germ cul-tures in World Cup and Olympic planning—police brutality, evictions, real-estate grabs, the negation of public space, corruption—are already boils on Brazil's body politic. Activists, political reformers, and ordinary citizens have been working for generations to lance these boils. The World Cup and Olympics are instead causing them to spread, grow, and mutate until you cannot tell where the mega-event planning ends and the Brazilian state begins. In so many ways, landing the Olympics was the perfect coda to Lula's peculiar brand of politics.

Brazil's greatest hope lies in resistance—not after the fact, when the bill comes due, but now, while the sporting shock doctrine is still being implemented. In the next chapter, we'll look at how that resistance is growing in Brazil's favelas.

CHAPTER 7
Target Favelas

Where opulence is most opulent . . . misery is most miserable.
                                            —Eduardo Galeano[1]

Bruce Springsteen once wrote a song called "Mansion on the Hill." Its image of the wealthy living on high, lording their homes and their status over the unwashed masses in makeshift shacks, rings as true in the United States today as it did in the distant past. If you live in California and just say you live in "the Hills," people know, thanks to a mass culture that glorifies and bathes itself in excess, that this means status, wealth, and security. Maybe the wealthy have always taken comfort in that symbolism, or maybe they're just fighting a primitive fear of being wiped away in a biblical flood, but a better quality of life has always been inextricably linked with living in a state of elevation. The wealthy live on the hills while the poor eke out a living in their shadows, gazing upward in wonder and envy.

In Brazil, this state of affairs has historically been turned on its head. The wealthy of the great city of Rio have always lived at the bottom of the hill, safe from mudslides thanks to an environmental preservation policy at the turn of the twentieth century that declared the hillsides public land. In an effort to settle close to jobs in what was then Brazil's capital city, and with no large-scale affordable housing policy to assist them, people occupied these poorly protected hillside spaces, moving quickly into the higher-up areas. These communities of the poor are, of course, known as favelas.

All favelas share a common history as squatter settlements developed autonomously over the course of decades by Brazil's working poor and unemployed, with minimal or no government support, thanks to very stringent squatters' rights laws.[2] Today they range widely in size, from countless small communities to places like Rocinha, a favela in Rio that is home to about 150,000 people. Favelas also contain a wide range of income levels and employment statuses, as well as churches, schools, and small businesses. Many if not most favela houses, contrary to stereotypes, are solidly built with materials not commonly associated with slums. Most favela homes have electricity and running water; a sizable percentage have Internet access as well. In one recent study of six favelas, 31 percent of homes had computers and Internet access. Yes, as we will see, there is tremendous variance in the standard of living in the favelas, from stable working-class homes to extremely precarious living situations. But to venture into a favela is to see with your own eyes that people devote an unbelievable amount of care to their individual homes, often with the help of neighbors, to make them uniquely theirs—places where they are proud to raise their families.

The Scramble for Rio

With the advent of the World Cup and Olympics, however, Rio has become ground zero for a speculative real-estate boom that would make the San Francisco Bay area blush. The real-estate tycoons and construction magnates are looking up to the hills and envisioning that land developed: a Rio without favelas. Normally, Brazil's stringent laws would prevent this from happening. But the World Cup and Olympics have created "states of exception"—think eminent domain on steroids—that allow politicians to declare settled laws obsolete. Using any possible pretext—drugs, crime, environmental hazards—they can state that, with so many foreign visitors and heads of state coming to the country, they have an obligation to *higienizar* (clean out) the favelas to make the nation "safe" for the World Cup. This new reality, in which people's homes become fair game, has massive implications for residents across the country—but particularly in Rio. Inequality actually worsened in Rio under Lula, though it improved in many parts of the country. In 2011, Brazil's statistical agency, the IBGE (Instituto Brasileiro de Geografia e Estatística), released the findings from its 2010 census, which stated that 22.03 percent of the 6,323,037 residents of Rio de Janeiro live in favelas—what the report refers to as "substandard" and irregular housing communities. Although the city's total population grew only 3.4 percent, the favela population has grown by 27.7 percent over the last decade.[3]

In 2014, even though the official line is that race is "not an issue" in Brazil, the descendants of slaves not only make up more than half of the nation's population but also are the largest group in the favelas. Brazilians of African descent live shorter lives, make less money, have more difficulty finding employment, and are more likely to be among the ten thousand people killed by police over the course of the last decade. As Bryan McCann writes,

> Black favela residents have faced particular hurdles in achieving civil rights, and persistent racism does explain part of the stigma against favela residents. . . . Black residents were inevitably concentrated more heavily in the substandard, precarious urban spaces effectively reserved for those without full rights: Rio's favelas. Furthermore, their blackness reinforced dominant understandings of these as zones beneath the protections of law and guarantees of citizenship.[4]

The difference with the United States, and this is immediately visible upon walking the favela streets, is that the favelas aren't segregated: there is no "black favela," "white favela," or "Indian favela." Intermarriage is very frequent, and 30 percent of households in today's Brazil are multiracial. Yet racism is so persistent that it is not uncommon to hear complaints about "too many" people of African descent on the public beaches or in the malls. This has led to organizing campaigns where groups of black Brazilians numbering in the hundreds walk as one into malls, their very visibility a statement of protest.

The favelas are perhaps best known, and most notorious, for their history of poverty and violence—mostly in the minds of those who have never set foot inside these communities. My own experience in the favelas is that they feel far more open and friendly than many of Rio's wealthier neighborhoods, which are defined by gated communities and a militarized police force. This experience is not uncommon. According to one poll, 79 percent of people who had heard of Brazil's favelas—but had never actually set foot inside them—had a negative view of them. However, 72 percent of people who had actually visited the favelas came away with positive feelings. Count me among the 79 percent who had a negative view, equating favela with "slum," before I was able to see them for myself—and among the 72 percent who turned around after experiencing them for myself. My negative views were formed by a concern that some have romanticized the poverty in which people have historically been forced to live. Having reported from the townships of South Africa and the south of Chile, I know that poverty in the Global South is nothing anyone should paint in pretty colors. The favelas of Rio, however, are a different and very specific kind of community.

When you walk up a hill into a favela, you are entering a different world. Of course, it depends on the favela, but the contrast is more than a hillside community on top of wealth. It's the difference between an open community, where people are generally friendly, hanging out on stoops, and ready to talk, and a sidewalk where people are rushing to work, eyes straight ahead, clutching their bags. I spoke with Theresa Williamson, a city planner and executive director of Catalytic Communities, a nonprofit that works with communities in Rio's favelas to distribute real images of their lives and to challenge the myths used to justify residents' expropriation. She said,

> You need to start, first of all, by exploding the connection between the favelas and criminality. At the height of the drug-trafficking explosion last decade, the drug trade and attendant realities were practiced in less than 50 percent of favelas. Even in those communities, we are talking about less than 2 percent of residents directly involved. Obviously the community has connections

indirectly. There's a lot of money flowing because of drug trafficking, so indirectly a lot of people benefit, you could say. But most
of those people don't want that. That's not their choice. It's the
money that's flowing in their community. No one mentions that
the reason favelas exist in the first place is because there's no history of affordable housing.

In the twentieth century, after the 1888 abolition of slavery, "squatting,"
or building on unused land without authorization, was most city
dwellers' only option in a land dominated by oligarchs. To this day,
Brazil has some of the world's most extreme concentration of land
ownership; until the late 1980s its land inequality was the worst in the
world. Some individual Brazilian families own swaths of land bigger
than some European countries. Brazil is also one of the most urbanized
societies in the world, with a higher percentage of the population living
in the cities than we have in the United States, and it went through
this process of urbanization earlier than the United States did.

Indeed, the idea of "squatting" assumes that land has always been
private property—but for most of human history, people have simply
built homes where they could. As Gisela, who lives in Vila Autódromo,
put it to me, "There is this assumption that we're squatters. We joke
among ourselves, every one of our ancestors squatted. They didn't buy
it, it's a process. People have to find a way to survive." Or as Theresa
Williamson put it: "The assumption internationally, but in Brazil especially, is that these are unknowable, dangerous, precarious communities. All of these negative assumptions ignore huge [positive] qualities
in these neighborhoods."

The most derisive, stereotypical ideas about the favelas exist within
Brazil itself. In my visits, I've found that middle-class Brazilians take
pride in having never gone up the elevators, tramways, or stairs into
these communities. They take pride in their families' historic blindness
to the favelas whose entrances lie mere yards from some of the city's
central thoroughfares. They discuss the favelas, especially incidents of
violence—the more lurid the better—with their eyes wide and a shake
of their heads. But they do not reckon with their reality. To be clear, I

do not want to seem like I am in any way underselling the very real poverty there. But the same questions that plague the rest of Brazil—education, health care, employment—are the questions for the people of the favelas.

One thing that was immediately obvious when I visited the favelas was the amount of care, personal ownership, and dedication that residents put into developing their own small spaces. They invest every cent they earn into their homes and often do the construction themselves, in collectives. People in the neighborhood gather to build, setting aside a Saturday to help a neighbor put on a roof or put up walls. "I've personally watched a community form from scratch and watched how they took an area that was wetlands—it was full of water—and literally filled it in with construction debris," said Theresa. "They put stakes in the water. It was just amazing. And they do it collectively, and then they put up tables where they serve food in the evening and they have a community toilet for everybody in the beginning . . . but literally within a few months, they were putting in plumbing. Squatting and building on land can be seen as far more effective than finding a place to rent."

This sentiment is shared by many others, she added:

> Every story is different. What they all have is a very strong feeling of attachment and association with that house that they built. . . . Sometimes you have a whole plot and you'll have three houses on the plot for three separate families. Within the community you have subcommunities, microcommunities of families, and they interact with each other . . . [and] provide each other with support: a mother has kids who need daycare and there's no daycare anywhere, so the other mother will take the kids. Every single inch is embedded with memory. It's not like a building that went up, and you bought an apartment. . . . The whole space around you is embedded with memory . . . of the blood, sweat and tears that went into it, of the sacrifices that went into it, of the different people who helped build it, of the family—that somebody died here, somebody lived there, somebody was born here and somebody got sick there. You have all these layers of memory, and it's simply not the case for the Brazilian middle class, there's very little recognition.

When you consider everything that families put into building the favelas, it makes the land grab all the more repugnant. It also explains why alongside these evictions have also come mass movements and organization against them. The World Cup, even though it is a smaller, less expensive operation than the Olympics, is actually a greater danger to these communities precisely because, as mentioned, it reaches out, octopus-like, with tentacles in cities and towns all over the country.

I visited several favelas on day trips organized by Catalytic Communities. What I saw was that from the Favela do Metrô, next to Rio's legendary Maracanã Stadium, all the way to favelas distant from the mega-event action, everyone feels under threat. You can sense it—or you can just open your eyes and see it. At Favela do Metrô, hundreds of families found themselves living on the rubble of their former homes with nowhere to go after a merciless round of demolitions by Brazilian authorities. The *Guardian* reported that "redbrick shacks have been cracked open by earth-diggers. Streets are covered in a thick carpet of rubble, litter and twisted metal. By night, crack addicts squat in abandoned shacks, filling sitting rooms with empty bottles, filthy mattresses and crack pipes improvised from plastic cups. The stench of human excrement hangs in the air."[5] This may be accurate, but let's be clear: the squalor moved in largely after the people were pushed out. These conditions are the *result* of the evictions, not a reason to carry them out. They did not exist until *after* the residents were forced to leave their homes.

One favela resident, Eomar Freitas, said, "It looks like you are in Iraq or Libya. I don't have any neighbors left. It's a ghost town." The reasons for this are a mystery to nobody. He said, "The World Cup is on its way and they want this area. I think it is inhumane."[6] In response, the Rio housing authority said that it was offering favela dwellers "dignity." Dignity, translated, means newly built government housing where families are asked to live in a place roughly the size of a supermax prison cell. Maybe something was lost in translation. Or perhaps a bureaucrat's conception of "dignity" is becoming homeless so your neighborhood can serve as—literally—a parking lot for wealthy soccer fans. By bulldozing homes before giving families the chance to find new housing or be "relocated," the government is flagrantly violating basic human rights. Amnesty International, the UN, and even the IOC—fearful of the damage to its "brand"—have raised concerns, although the IOC and FIFA certainly haven't said anything about *stopping* it. And there is more "dignity" on the way. According to Julio Cesar Condaque, an activist opposed to leveling the favelas, the worst-case scenario is that "between, now and the 2014 World Cup, 1.5 million families will be removed from their homes across the whole of Brazil."[7]

Christopher Gaffney said to me, "It's like a freefall into a neoliberal paradise. We are living in cities planned by PR firms and brought into existence by an authoritarian state in conjunction with their corporate partners." There are, in fact, some favelas from which people want to be relocated. Generally this is because the area in question is affected by mudslides or the housing is just too precarious for people to continue living there. As Theresa Williamson said to me,

> The city went through and made a list of people who wanted to be relocated because they were at risk of dying in a landslide. And [in 2011] there was a report in *O Globo* that only 15 percent of the families who had asked for relocation had actually been relocated. . . . And yet, all these families who have built all these houses that are consolidated or functional, or that simply help them meet their needs and progress along their paths, are the ones who are being relocated.

Perhaps reflecting the decentralized, heterodox nature of Brazil, perhaps reflecting conscious strategy, every favela that has faced expulsion has been treated differently. In some communities there is compensation. In other communities there is none. In some favelas, people are placed into public housing two hours away, far from jobs, family, community, and where they have lived and led their lives. In others, they are placed in makeshift projects at the bottom of the hill, their beautiful—and highly valued—vistas of the city expropriated. One resident, Marcelo, told me he was forced to keep his child out of school "for a year" because their World Cup eviction took place after the start of the school semester. Other families just set about keeping their children in school by commuting with them more than two hours each way. It's the same with jobs: if you work seasonal, nonunionized, "flexible" jobs, as many working-class Brazilians do, the distance to work is a killer. Within every favela, there are jobs uniquely created and self-organized specifically for that community. There is one man from Favela do Metrô whose job was to pick up tin from the businesses around the stadium and take it in to get recycled. Now that he has been displaced, that work requires a two-hour trip on public transportation, which he cannot afford.

The real-estate and construction magnates' dream of totally removing the favelas from Rio cannot be disconnected from the goals of hosting the Olympics and the finals of the World Cup: a full-scale effort by the city to rebrand itself as a global city. After decades of the world associating Rio de Janeiro with crime, kidnapping, and poor governance, Brazil thinks that the time is ripe to turn Rio into the kind of tourist site and foreign investment hub it has always dreamed of being. Destroying the favelas is a part of that, but there is little discussion of what would actually be lost if the favelas are uprooted. "The favelas are critical to the cultural and social life of Rio," says Williamson:

> Their proximity to the center of city life is very rare in any urban center in the world, even as urban planners around the world today charge themselves with the difficult task of creating centrally located, affordable housing. In Rio, the central nature of the favelas to the city's history, its culture, its image, makes them a critical component of this city's identity.... If we value these communities and create policies to support them and their development based on recognizing their qualities and participatory engagement to address their challenges, then there's a legacy we could be proud of. But all trends point in the opposite direction. This is a human rights issue. We are currently at risk of losing a great deal of culture and history as we lose the favelas. There is memory embedded in every brick, and you can imagine how such a loss will impact people emotionally whose ancestors have invested so much.

If there is a kernel of hope for the favelas in the context of the World Cup and the Olympics, it is the number of foreign journalists who will make their way to Rio—which provides an opportunity to introduce them to a different perception of favelas than the stereotype of lurid places that require a bulletproof vest to enter. News organizations like the BBC and the *Guardian* will set up permanent base camps in Rio for the duration of both events. Given the stranglehold of the IOC and its exclusive broadcast partners over the actual content of the Olympics, all those journalists are going to have to cover something. Expect a great many special reports on these communities. As favela residents themselves have learned, their number-one tool in fighting expulsion has been the use of cell-phone cameras, the Internet, and social media to bring the demolitions and police incursions to the view of the world. They need to do this because the main media organization in Brazil, Globo, has no love for the favelas, even instructing its reporters to arrive only with an armored car and a bulletproof vest, regardless of the nature of the favela they are visiting.

Visibility is the favela residents' greatest ally. It is for that reason above all others that I was welcomed so warmly when I entered the favelas to talk to people about the possibility of expulsion. This was particularly true in Vila Autódromo.

Struggling Against Eviction in Vila Autódromo

If you want to see what the 2016 Olympics are going to do to Rio de Janeiro, go to Vila Autódromo, a community named for the Formula 1 racetrack built next to it.

Vila Autódromo, located adjacent to the Olympic Park, was slated for a mass eviction. Ideas about what to do with the land ranged from luxury housing to a parking lot but in 2013 a movement of citizens fought back and prevented the eviction—though recent developments have once again rendered the favela's future unclear. The Association of Residents, Fishermen, and Friends of Vila Autódromo (AMPAVA) declared in August 2013, "After years of resistance and struggle, Vila Autódromo achieved a commitment from the mayor: Vila Autódromo and its residents will not be removed."[8] Even more importantly, any efforts to demolish homes would now have to be approved by a residential assembly made up of people from Vila Autódromo. That being said, the mayor and the land developers have not given up and the situation remains uncertain.

Located on the banks of beautiful Lake Jacarepaguá, this community sits on land the city's real-estate speculators have long lusted after. To understand why Vila Autódromo has become a target, you first need to travel there—and when you do that, it becomes increasingly obvious why Rio's urban developers have spent twenty years pining for its destruction. Unlike Rio's South Zone favelas, Vila Autódromo is not situated upon a hill above the city. Finding it means driving through an area that resembles the sprawling, sparkling, pricey end of Miami Beach. I had thought of Rio as an old city with character—but that's not this area, known as Barra da Tijuca, one of the fastest-growing middle- and upper-income parts of the city. Although Barra represents only 4.7 percent of the city's population and 13 percent of the total area of Rio, it is responsible for 30 percent of all taxes collected in the city. But its similarities to Miami lie not just in the bombastic, bright signage and the "newness" of it all. Just as South Beach was once wetlands and now represents some of the most expensive real estate on the planet, this part of Rio has also only been developed in the last thirty years. It has traversed the trajectory of real-estate speculators' dreams: from swamp to beachfront property. I tell a Brazilian friend who has spent time in the United States about the Miami vibe. He says to me, "This is Miami. It looks like Miami. It smells like Miami. It has the real-estate speculation of Miami. People are on the beach. It is this car-dependent, closed-condominium, socially isolated, upper-middle-class landscape. And the mayor's political base comes from here, from the real-estate speculators and large construction firms."

I venture there by Rio bus, zooming down a central highway at a breakneck speed that makes me look around to see if Keanu Reeves and Sandra Bullock are hanging out somewhere in the back. It becomes evident how the highway itself, a relatively new construction project, has created a massive physical divide between the beachfront development and the rest of the city further inland. As we disembark and head toward Vila Autódromo, we walk by a large replica of the Statue of Liberty in a mall called New York City Center. As a New Yorker by birth, seeing the city identified with a mall amid sprawl provides me no end of distress. Now I am reminded of the higher end parts of Northern Virginia, with strip malls and streets so wide you need to drive to get from one side of the street to the other. As one of my guides says to me, "People on the other side of the lagoon see Vila Autódromo and they see an eyesore. But people here, as well as sympathizers, look at the pollution, development, the high rises, and see a different kind of eyesore."

Once we get past the Great Mall of New York, we finally arrive at Vila Autódromo. There is a large billboard right by the entrance of the favela that displays the city's plans for the entire area. It takes some serious examination, but sure enough, the area currently occupied by Vila Autódromo appears to be designated as a future parking lot. At the top of the billboard, in blaring blue letters, is a simple phrase: *País rico é país sem pobreza* ("a rich country is a country without poverty"). A governmental commitment to "ending poverty" is something we haven't seen in the United States since the Lyndon Johnson administration. The irony of such a slogan right next to an open plan to turn people's homes—and all the wealth they've put into those homes—into parking lots speaks for itself.

When we arrive, our first impression is that Vila Autódromo is a peaceful, beautiful community, and that is exactly why it is in danger. It is too beautiful. The land on one side of Vila Autódromo faces the Formula 1 track, but the other side rests right on the aforementioned Lake Jacarepaguá, which looks like it was plucked from a postcard. According to many residents, developers and real-estate speculators drive through often, salivating at the thought of taking it over. The Olympics provide the pretext and the construction magnates provide the bulldozers. Like an army standing at the border, there are rows of luxury condominiums across the lake.

The residents of Vila Autódromo have fought judges, politicians, and developers for their survival for more than twenty years: the first mass eviction was ordered all the way back in 1992, when Rio hosted the Earth Summit. In 2007, Rio hosted the Pan Am Games and the bulldozers again came calling. In 2009, before the confetti had even completed its journey to the ground after Rio was awarded the 2016 Games, Rio mayor Eduardo Paes had announced that Vila Autódromo would be razed to the ground. In his estimation, the community was "too close to the security perimeter for the Olympics."[9] Yet while Mayor Paes was raising security fears (as if the tight-knit Vila Autódromo would become the site of a terror cell), real-estate developers were in the process of building high-rise apartment buildings even closer to the security perimeter. Apparently it never occurred to the mayor what message this was sending about who was considered a security threat and why.

The people of Vila Autódromo knew that they were in an "organize or die" situation. At the time of my visit their most pressing objective was, very simply, to avoid joining the twenty-six communities already wiped off the map—and get their story to as vast an audience as humanly possible. I saw a community desperate to have its voices heard. Not only did the residents organize conventional protests, they also engaged and worked with a range of volunteer partners to develop an alternative community development plan. They wanted to show that the Olympic Park could be built without their displacement and that their homes should not be flattened and paved just so the Olympic Park can, for two weeks, have adequate parking.

The entrance to Vila Autódromo stands awkwardly at the western edge of the dusty racetrack's parking lot. Eight hundred to a thousand families live here, wedged into a sliver of land between the racetrack and the highway. We are there on a Sunday, so many people are at home. Families and groups of friends are out walking in the dusty road. Others are out working on their houses. People lounge in front of their homes as radios play. Kids play soccer with balls made from rolled-up socks.

There is a building with a corrugated roof, removed somewhat from the road, emblazoned with a large hand-painted sign that announces it as the Community Association. It resembles a ramshackle schoolhouse. The building is divided into two small rooms divided by sheets of plywood. There is a makeshift bookshelf, with an assortment of law books as well as classics like *Don Quixote* and *King Arthur and the Knights of the Round Table*. Inside is one of the Community Association's directors, Jane Nascimento. Jane is not tall, but she conveys reservoirs of strength, with a presence that belies her size. Her curly hair is cropped close to her head. We chat with her in the entrance and she is casual and amicable, in jeans and a V-neck sweater, leaning against the doorframe. I ask her how the community feels about the coming Olympics, and she floors us by telling a story—in very straightforward, matter-of-fact language—about two elderly residents who died from worry that they would be evicted. "Everything was put into their homes. The thought of being moved and leaving it all behind was too much."

At the back of the neighborhood association headquarters are a chalkboard and roughly twenty mismatched chairs. This was, remarkably, the planning area for the actions that brought Rio's Olympic-industrial complex to its knees. The back of the room is stacked with maps and diagrams: plans and counterplans for Vila Autódromo. Theresa and Jane show us a diagram: the Plano Popular for the Olympic site. Jane tells us it was developed by residents, in conjunction with architecture and planning students and faculty from Federal Fluminense University and the Federal University of Rio de Janeiro. This plan would maintain the community in its current location.

Then she turns the table on us and asks if she can film me as I ask her questions. This matters because part of how Vila Autódromo and many other favelas are saving themselves is by using social media. They are posting as much as they can online about the movement and their supporters, as well as publicly documenting every time they see the police, the military, or the developers sniffing around their homes. Jane describes herself as "a major social media person." To lead a community movement in 2013, you have to be, since social media has become the favelas' lifeline to the outside world. "We want people to know that we are alive," she says. "We feel that our community should be known. We want to document it all somehow. We are trying, using videos, using photos, using the Internet, using social media."

Then we walk the streets. The amount of care people put into their individual homes, as well as the homes of their neighbors and friends, is immediately visible. There are a number of small, narrow, slightly lopsided homes adorned with intricately constructed fences and decorations. A few families have self-paved driveways for cars, fences and gates for their driveways, and even second-floor balconies where people sit to look out onto the street. All of the homes in Vila Autódromo have electricity and running water, and there are old-fashioned lampposts with streetlights. There is even trash collection twice a week. At one corner, there is a striking red stucco house decked out with carefully tended plants. This is not every home—there is clearly a kind of economic diversity in Vila Autódromo. In its very cramped quarters, some narrow rowhouses are incredibly well kept, with small satellite dishes and fresh coats of paint, while others are in absolute disrepair.

What is also noticeable on this scorching hot Sunday is that soccer is being played around almost every corner. We see five young boys playing on a rutted dirt pitch. As we talk, the ball bounces around on the uneven ground and flies back and forth through the air. Interestingly, though there is also a small soccer field, it sits empty while children play in the streets. Later on this scorching day, the shirtless kids run to the front of the building to take deep drinks from a hose and splash each other with water. As we walk, Jane Nascimento keeps up a running commentary, in her soft voice, about everything we are seeing. It's true: every brick has a story. Something about seeing the children, however, causes her voice to rise and her body language to become more visibly animated. She tells us,

> What really hurt was that the mayor made it clear that impacting us was an open, stated objective of the plan. We were the target. He wanted to get rid of us. The disrespect—not even speaking to

us, just stating it as an objective. But every day since, we have grown as individuals and as a community. This community has a history of fighting against evictions. This is nothing new for us. So we got together and we decided to organize and to fight. People in the favelas often don't know that they have rights. We try to inform them of that. When they learn that they have housing rights, they get very excited. It creates a sense of indignation—especially among the youth. It is true that this long fight has pushed some people to want to give up. They are tired. They want to move. They are not happy. Our job in the Community Association is to make sure people know why we are fighting. No one can be forced to resist, but people also need to know that resistance is an option.

Jane says that their other job is to cut through the lies local officials spin about the "benefits" of taking the mayor's deal and moving to government housing. "There's a lot of uncertainty around the promised public housing," she says. "Some people see it and say 'this is better than what I have now,' but there are a lot of hidden expenses that people don't know about. There are service fees, taxes, and moving costs that they are not told about before they sign the deal. I think that people who move usually don't understand this and won't end up staying because of it. And the city doesn't have a plan for what happens then." Then she says something very stark, but true: "Only the social mobilization has prevented people from being removed at gunpoint." She makes it very clear that any repression will be met with resistance. She is also sober about the fact that exposure, social media, and trying to shame the government into doing the right thing will only get them so far:

> Even with TV cameras and media, it doesn't mean that city officials wouldn't be violent with us. The evicted communities are often evicted with tear gas while TV cameras are rolling. It doesn't stop it. The reason they treat us this way is because of this view that they promote that sees all favela residents as criminals. That's how they see us, and they respond according to that. We recently went to deliver our Plano Popular to the mayor, and they closed the gates on us as if we were some kind of threat. . . . We waited for four hours outside the mayor's office, and finally he met with us, for one hour. When he arrived, he showed up with eight police officers by his

side. . . . It was a meeting that produced nothing. He accused us of being there as a political stunt to impact the mayoral elections. He belittled the university people who came with us. He finally promised us another meeting—in forty-five days. We were outraged.

The mayor then spoke about the meeting in the press, denouncing the urban planners who devised the alternative plan for Vila Autódromo as "hypocrites, demagogues, and imbeciles" who "don't know the city" while pointedly not saying anything negative about the residents themselves. This "divide and conquer" strategy simply did not work. Despite his best efforts, Vila Autódromo became a symbol of resistance. Jane Nascimento tells us with terrific pride that researchers and leaders from other favelas have come to Vila Autódromo to study how they built a community of resistance. One lesson from Vila Autódromo, she says, is the openness of their work: they have welcomed "outsiders" coming in to work with them on building a resistance, unlike many other communities that have closed themselves off or turned inward and treated outsiders with suspicion.

I ask Jane what motivates her to do this kind of work. She replies that the stories of friends who have been forcibly moved by the government are so heartbreaking, she is committed to seeing as few of them happen as possible. She tells a story about her friend Rita, who had to relocate from her home in Colônia Juliano Moreira. Rita was promised that moving would be an orderly process—and it was, until the government came and trashed her house. They arrived in a very aggressive fashion and threw everything she owned into the back of a truck, which the state-sponsored movers then dumped on the ground upon arriving at her new home. Rita's livelihood was growing plants, herbs and other assorted home remedies, but all of her seedlings were destroyed.[10]

There is a ten-foot-high masonry wall across the street from the neighborhood association. The wall blocks the noise from the racetrack, just on the other side. In front of the wall is a small playground. Several girls are playing on a swing set. Painted on the wall is a mural, part of which is a large Brazilian flag—except where the usual slogan, "Order and Progress," would be, only one word is inscribed: *Liberdade.* The church is probably the most modern-looking building in the community and it gleams with care. The stucco is freshly painted and its immense wooden doors are adorned with carvings and sconces that were hand-made by people in the community. Making our way through the narrow dirt streets, we come upon a group of people gathered in the shade of a leafy tree. A middle-aged man is squatting on the ground, working on an old refrigerator motor. Next to him is a very old woman in a wheel-chair. Her name is Ana Paula. She has no legs and just a few teeth left in her mouth. She looks as old as time, but is sharp as a tack and beau-tiful in plastic jeweled bracelets and a collared blue dress with a floral pattern. I ask Ana Paula for her thoughts about the drama in her com-munity. She says, "I love living here. I think it is the best place there is. I like everything about it. When I arrived there were only two houses here—mine and one other. I came to look after someone's property. But the woman whose property I was looking after, she decided she didn't want the property at all. So I just stayed." She has a great deal of pride in Brazil, she tells us, and thinks that the Olympics will be a great deal for Rio as long as she does not have to move. This is the rub in other discussions: people love the thought of hosting the Games. They are proud of their communities; the idea that an international audience will see what they have created is a source of joy. The idea, however, that they would be physically removed, like unsightly imperfections air-brushed out of a *Vogue* photo shoot, is painful.

Behind Ana Paula is a small canal. The smell of sewage wafts up from its stagnant water. Just on the other side is the highway. A group of five or six young children, boys and girls, are playing around us in the street, without fear or the hovering, worried parents who haunt the playgrounds of the United States. There is a baby in a diaper stag-gering around on newly walking legs. A boy rolls a ball toward him and the baby, who can barely waddle, kicks it back with authority. We walk around to a point where a small triangle of land juts into the la-goon. From here we have a sweeping view across the water to the ex-panse of fancy high-rise apartment buildings. It feels like they're staring at us. Jane says the real-estate developers want to turn this into a place similar to Lagoa, a picturesque neighborhood near Ipanema where people can walk or bicycle around the lagoon. "Obviously this community is a threat to that." Just behind us, a group of young men and women are blasting *funk* (or *funk carioca*) music—sort of a Brazilian version of reggaetón.

I am quickly understanding why people in Vila Autódromo are fighting so hard to stay. This becomes obvious to me when we meet a man in his sixties named Armando. Armando really wants to show us his house. "You are about to see the most beautiful house in the world," he says. Armando is a diesel mechanic. His wife, Vilma, is a seamstress. He built their home from scratch. He says that he has lived here for twenty years, adding to and upgrading the house little by little. Now it is two stories high with plumbing, electricity, and his sweat and handiwork in every square inch. The fixtures, the tile, even a lamp wire stretched tightly so it hangs behind a framed picture of his son and gorgeous twin grandchildren, bear the marks of toil and love. In the back of the house they have a kitchen that is larger than the living room, as well as a washing machine and dryer. The interior of Armando's home quickly becomes an amusement park/jungle gym for a group of children: these are the grandkids. They set up a tent in the middle of the tiled floor of the living room, so two couches and a television surround it. Armando tells us with great joy that they come over every Sunday. It is difficult to even hear him speak over their shouting and playing. At one point they even break out into song. You would have to really love children to endure it. Armando looks thrilled.

Armando and his wife Vilma actively attend the neighborhood association's public meetings. "There are many bigger powers involved in the Olympics that we don't control," he says, referring to thirsty local developers, whom he thinks are manipulating the "cleansing" of Rio. Armando's adult son, whom everyone refers to as Armandinho ("Young Armando") is also extremely easy to talk to. I ask him about the Olympics. He says, "When we heard they were coming to Rio, we thought it would be great for the city. We really had no idea about the changes that would happen here. They are supposed to be games. I don't see why hosting them means my father has to lose his home." He tells us that younger people in Vila Autódromo are more "realistic" in their thinking than some of the older folks, like Jane and his father. Armandinho and his family live in another community a fifteen-minute bus ride away, precisely so he won't have to engage in a constant series of fights just to have a home and raise his family. He is wearing a T-shirt with a large photo of his two sons on it. Below the photo are the Portuguese words: "Papa, thank you for sharing the best moments of my life with me."

"Moving the community is bad, of course," he says. "But this is more than just a housing issue. The environmental impact of all of this development is bad too. It is bad for our local environment and the planet." He harkens back to Rio's hosting of the Pan American Games in 2007. "They didn't leave any positive impact for the people who live in Rio," he says. "The worst part was seeing these huge amounts of money getting spent, with none of it benefiting the locals. They built all of these arenas that weren't even used after the Games."

The senior Armando overhears us and, as his toddler grandchildren play underfoot, expresses his frustration: "We are fighting for our right to survive here. Our right to live. Do you know how many years I've worked my butt off to build this house? I did it for my kids and for my grandkids so we would have a place to live and be a family, so days like today we could all have space to be together."

The Olympic preparations have put these "slums" in the crosshairs of city officials, President Dilma Rousseff, and the IOC, but to enter a favela like Vila Autódromo is to see a place that could teach the powers that be a few things about civilization. Again, I don't want to romanticize the poverty and very real day-to-day struggles to survive many in Vila Autódromo face. But I saw a community where people keep their doors open and children play joyously in the streets. It's a place where people like Armando build and develop their homes over decades to fit their changing families. I ask him if there is anything anyone can do to help. He replies, "Just let people know that we're here . . . and we don't want to leave." As we leave, we see a shirtless man leaning out from the balcony, just watching the street. We ask him the same thing we've been asking everyone: what do you think about the Olympics? He says, "I don't really care. I do hope they think we are going to leave quietly. That will make it all the more satisfying when they see that we are not going anywhere. I am excited for the World Cup. Most of all, I don't like the idea of being pushed around."

Developments in early 2014 have once again thrown Vila Autódromo's future into question, despite the benefit of publicity. In response to the unprecedented level of resistance in Vila Autódromo, the Brazilian political authorities engaged in an aggressive effort to simply buy everyone out. Residents who are choosing to leave are receiving what are being called the first market-rate compensation offers in favela history. Those accepting buyouts are also being forced to move only one kilometer away—not across the city, as with many other favela removals—which will be easier on schoolchildren and residents who use public transportation to commute to work. As of this writing, there are sixty families fully committed to staying no matter what—and the bulldozers are warming up, ready to demolish the space. The fight is not over, but the forces allied against Vila Autódromo are showing their commitment to using both carrots and sticks in order to achieve their goals. Whatever happens, though, the people here have shown the world that resistance matters—and their courage is an inspiration.

The Port, Providência, and Maurício Hora

Later that week I receive a tour of one of the most aggressively developed parts of Rio, the port, and the favela that sits above it, known as Morro da Providência. This would not be an ordinary tour. We were to be shown around by one of Rio's great photographers, a man who also happened to grow up in Providência: Maurício Hora. Maurício has been taking photos of Providência for more than twenty years. He is also the son of a man who was one of Rio's most powerful drug traffickers in the 1960s and 1970s. He is a stocky, intense-looking man with intelligent eyes and a short-cropped goatee. He's dressed in a striped V-neck shirt, with glasses hanging from his collar. Maurício is exceptionally friendly but also deliberate in his speech. There is no excess verbiage.

The base of Providência is just two blocks from Rio's central train station. As with several of the other favelas we have visited, we can see the construction of a massive new cable between the station and the base of the hill. Grey steel beams project out of the ground behind a corrugated metal construction fence, creating a cacophonous, dusty welcome. Two construction workers are on an aerial lift, welding something at the top of a squat, octagonal concrete pillar. A backhoe roughly the size of Trenton, New Jersey, moves the earth behind them. Maurício informs us that this construction site was once an open space and public square, the most important one in the neighborhood. The street at the base of the hill is bustling, with sprays of industrial dirt turning all of Brazil's typically bright colors into a shade of grey. Plaster is cracking and paint chipping. This neighborhood has been targeted for Olympic-sized change. And there, at the end of the street, Providência rises up in front of us, a photogenic favela on a steep hillside.

Providência was Rio's first favela. It was originally known as Morro da Favela, which is why all of these communities now go by this name. It was first settled by veterans of the 1897 Canudos war who were promised housing in Rio. They waited for homes that were never built; finally, they began building their own. By the 1910s, it had become known as one of Rio's most violent places. Recently there has been a turnaround, although not without a cost.

Before we ascend up into Providência, we stop at the base of the hill to walk through a street market. Each stall looks like it just came out of an IKEA box, with uniform red-and-white signs and black lettering. The market's perimeter is constructed from concrete and steel that looks significantly less grey than the surroundings. Maurício confirms that, yes, it has been newly constructed. It's not just the market. Several steps away is a new pedestrian bridge over the street where cars buzz into a tunnel underneath Providência's hill. Maurício tells us that the story of evictions carried out today echoes that of a hundred years prior, when squatters in a tenement building were removed from the same location where the market is now. Many of the market stalls are empty or closed, and foot traffic is minimal.

We ask a merchant selling shirts and jackets how business is going. "Slow, if not stopped," he responds. "This is not a strategic spot for a market. They built it here just to have an excuse to take our stalls away from the Central Station." Business-wise, the old location was much better, he says. Then the UPP, the favelas' "pacifying police," entered Providência for the purpose of "cleaning it out." That same day, there was a suspicious fire in the old marketplace. The merchant explains, his voice rising, that the whole market burned. There was a fire station less than a kilometer away, yet it took the fire engine forty-five minutes to arrive. He says he was not at the market when the fire started, but received a call shortly after it started that his stall and those of his friends were going up in smoke. Though he tells us he was "six kilometers away," he arrived at the market half an hour before the fire trucks made it onto the scene. The merchant and Maurício both indicate—as if it is obvious, as if insulted to even have to articulate it—that the fire was a deliberate act of arson, aimed at burning the vendors out so they would have no choice but to move into the new market.

The merchant, whose name is Henrique, is wearing brown leather shoes and clean blue jeans, with a red Nextel clipped to his belt. As he talks with us he leans against his stall. This stretch of the market is located on a ramp sloping gently upward from the street. Henrique informs us that he recently spent two years unemployed, selling odds and ends on street corners. Now, in his stall, next to a credit-card machine, he proudly displays his official vendor's license. He is hopeful that there must be some kind of master plan to grow the area, provide him with a steady stream of customers, and finally give his new credit-card machine a workout. "I am certain that the city government will not leave us stranded," he says. "They will do something." Henrique is excited about the Olympics because he sees redevelopment as being linked to more customers. If the redevelopment just means endless construction, with the dirt and noise driving people away, he knows that he could be facing disaster.

After we part ways with Henrique, Maurício leads us up the first set of steps ascending Providência's hill. As we walk up the steep incline in heat nearing a hundred degrees, Maurício keeps up a steady patter about his home. He tells us that during the dictatorship, people from favelas were often picked up by the police for loitering, even if they were working selling wares on streets around the city. This gave them a criminal record—which made future legal (and extralegal) discrimination against them easier. With a record, getting a normal job becomes that much more difficult. We tell him that there are similar criminal justice strategies in the United States; we find a warped kind of solidarity in discussing whether the current US prison system is worse than the Brazilian dictatorship. Then the conversation takes a turn to the personal. "That's how my father got into drug trafficking," Maurício explains. "He had a mark on his record and during the dictatorship it was the only way he saw to make a living."

As we ascend the steps, we reach a small landing where the sidewalk levels out for about ten yards before another set of stairs begins. There is a small, rubble-strewn area set back from the sidewalk. Maurício informs us that five families had been living here, piled together on this tiny patch of ground. "It was awful," Maurício says of their living situation. "It was very precarious." Then they were all evicted. Now there are patches of debris and burned garbage on the abandoned site.

We climb more stairs. A small drainage ditch runs down the hill next to us, smelling like raw sewage. Up ahead, we see a group of typically close-packed favela houses, some with satellite TV dishes mounted on their outside walls. Here the houses are brightly painted and have numbers on their doors. These are the contradictions of favela living: satellite televisions next to an open ditch carrying raw sewage. We walk by an open window and inside I can see a forty-two-inch flat-screen TV hanging on the wall. Once again we hear that sound so familiar in the Rio of 2012: jackhammers, construction noise, and the clinking of metal on brick. Ahead there will surely be a construction site, the first construction we will have seen in a favela that was not the people doing the work for themselves. This set of stairs ends in a cobblestone road. It winds around a sharp bend as it climbs up ahead of us.

Maurício tells us of a big eviction fight recently. There was an open community space up in the favela where groups could come to play sports or have cookouts and outdoor gatherings. After a great deal of protest, it was destroyed to build a stop for the new tram and a concrete waiting area. Sure enough, a large concrete tram pillar rises up ahead: the source of that jackhammer symphony we were hearing. Its conductors are dozens of very official-looking construction workers in matching hard-hats and blue overalls. They even have several steel cranes. I never do find out just how they got them up the hill, but seeing cranes on the landing of a favela is impressive. (They were all painted bright yellow—festive destruction!) The city received a great deal of flak for destroying the original public space, and its solution speaks volumes about the logic of Rio's developers. They have now evicted a group of families from their homes in order to build a new covered field to replace the lost community space. This eviction-to-eviction cycle is a reminder that controlling construction, brick, and mortar in pre-Olympic Rio means power.

The Olympic developers are destroying more than old homes. To our left stands a series of old houses, one of them bearing the date 1884. Maurício tells us that the favela dates from 1897, but some of the buildings closer to the base are older. About seventy million dollars will be spent around Providência in what is being called "World Cup and Olympic modernization." Most of that money will be spent on a cable car, even though most favelados will not use it. Why are they building it, then? Maurício's answer is as logical as it is distressing: "A lot of people get a lot of money from public works projects. It looks good for the city, too—even though it's not good for the community. This cable car is not for the residents. It makes the city look clean, without the image of favelas and poverty. It's for the tourists. Meanwhile the construction in and around Providência will push people to leave even if they are not [forcibly] evicted."

I ask him if he thinks that there is actually a plan to have a Rio without favelas. He doesn't hesitate: "Absolutely." Then he explains how this process has deeper roots than just pre-Olympic opportunism:

The first part of the process is giving people title—formalizing the land as a marketable commodity owned by one individual rather than controlled informally by the community. Land value goes up—many people will sell or be tempted to sell—not to people in the community because almost nobody here has enough money to buy. So, eventually, much if not all of the land in the favela will be sold to people from outside the favela, people who have more money. It's a business opportunity for developers and by extension the government. They don't think micro, on the scale of people's lives. They only think macro.

Maurício sounds like an economist, but he is speaking from direct experience. This process has already begun in Providência. We soon will see evidence of this for ourselves.

We stop and talk to an older woman seated on a stoop in front of a group of buildings. She has short-cropped grey hair and is wearing earrings and a black tank top. She is seventy-one years old, born and raised in Providência. Her name is Doralice, but she goes by Glorinha. She recently heard that the government would be evicting her. "Like it or not, I have to go. I've been displaced. I have no place," she says. "My dream is not to leave here, for sure. But orders are orders. They gave us orders to leave. . . . I don't want to fight, I just want to be somewhere safe." Glorinha—and this says more about her spirit than the reality of the situation—tells us that she considers herself one of the lucky ones, because her new home will be an apartment down by the train station at the bottom of the hill. She feels fortunate that at least she is not being moved miles from friends and family, as others she knows have been. I ask her if she believes that all of the men in matching hardhats, all of the cranes, all the rubble will yield something positive for Providência in the end. She smiles, shrugs her shoulders, and says, "I won't know if it's good or bad until I've seen the end of it. All I've seen so far is lots of holes in the street." Then she gets much more serious: "I've heard reports of unsafely built public housing. Here we make our homes safe. I don't want to be somewhere made by [the housing authority] that isn't safe. I don't want to end up on the street, but I've got children, grandchildren, great grandchildren."

Maurício tells us that, while different kinds of projects and objectives around the World Cup and Olympics are leading to the evictions, the end result in Providência will be the displacement of eight hundred homes, roughly one-third of the community. "There's no reason they couldn't build new houses on the hill for those they're displacing. Look at this new tram station. Its foundation is formed from solid granite. If they can build a giant tram, they could also build a large apartment building up here." We part ways with Glorinha and crouch through a small doorway that leads into a steep, narrow staircase wedged in between two buildings. Sunlight streams onto our faces from above. This is one of the many favela alleyways and shortcuts in which you can easily get lost without a guide. The staircase cuts up the hillside and at the top we meet the road again, after it has rounded the bend on its gentle climb up. Below, the road was paved. Here, it's mostly dirt and gravel.

After we reach the top and take in the remarkable view of the port, Maurício speaks about the drug trade, which was the pretext for Providência's "pacification" and now its gentrification. "It's important to understand drug trafficking in Rio," he says. "The violence that happened in Providência was not infighting over territory between rival gangs. The fighting that occurred here was between the traffickers and the police. The police would come here, up this road here"—he points uphill about a hundred yards, where the road dead-ends into a wide concrete staircase that continues upward—"and they would shoot at the stairs. There could be normal people here going about their business, children, women, a person on crutches—the police wouldn't even see that. They'd just shoot, as long as there were traffickers nearby. It was very dangerous and caused a lot of havoc in the community." Sure enough, bullet holes still dot the areas where Maurício says the shootings took place. In Rio, one of the most expensive cities on earth, police make the equivalent of slightly over a thousand dollars a month. That is a recipe for corruption and violence. Because of this, when the UPP came to Providência, Maurício tells us people were actually relieved because "they protected us from the regular police."

As we walk the narrow roads, we see VW Kombi vans, a shuttle service, speeding up and down the hills at breakneck speeds, spewing exhaust. Across the street, two young boys sit outside a small café playing Galaga, a classic arcade game from the 1980s I remember pouring whole allowances' worth of quarters into. A couple of construction workers walk down the hill while I show the kids my Galaga skills. One of them carries a jackhammer slung over his shoulder. Maurício pulls me away and continues on the theme of the police. Before the UPP, it was common practice for the police to extort bribes from residents who ran businesses in the community. "The police would make the place more dangerous so that they could make money getting paid off to provide 'security' for businesses.'" He describes how deeply entrenched this system was—and still is—in much of Rio. Money flows upward: from the small business owners to the crooked cops they pay off for protection, from those cops to their battalion commanders, and from the battalion commanders to the state deputies who oversee the police force. This is the darker side of the "Brazilian cost," and it hasn't gone anywhere.

We approach the wide staircase. Off to the right, several thick concrete pillars rise from the ground. This area is packed with construction workers and machinery. Maurício informs us that this was the community's public square before the city took it over for the cable-car project. He tells us stories, pointing to different rock-strewn spots where a barbecue or a game had taken place. Now the square is gone, soon to be replaced by the top station of the cable car. On the corner adjacent to the work zone is a café with an open doorway. Inside a group of men sit drinking sodas and talking loudly. Their voices echo out onto the street corner.

We make our way up the wide concrete staircase. Maurício points out even more bullet holes in and around the stairs, evidence of past battles between police and drug traffickers. Some holes are in the metal railings on either side of the staircase and others are still in the houses that line the way. As he talks, two more blue-overall-clad construction workers walk around the corner, also with sledgehammers resting on their shoulders. There is an odd tension as we wait for them to pass. We learn that, remarkably, the cable car is not the only disruptive project underway in Providência. Just beyond where the cable car ends, at the base of the wide central staircase, the city is planning to build a new funicular tram to go the rest of the way up the hillside. We see evidence of its construction—there, a pile of rubble sits where there used to be a house. In fact, according to Maurício, everyone in the homes on the left side of the staircase will be evicted to build the tram.

Then he tells a story that will stay with me long after the Olympic confetti has been swept away. Maurício tells us that, originally, the city wanted to evict the residents of all of the houses on both sides of the staircase. When development plans for the city came out in the wake of the World Cup and the Olympics announcement, the city ruled that all of the houses on the left side of the staircase were "unsafe" and thus needed to be cleared. Shortly thereafter, a plan came out showing a tram to be built along the right side of the staircase—meaning those houses would also be demolished. It took ferocious community resistance to beat back the real-estate developers and keep what they had. Maurício and others from the community protested to the city, asking why they couldn't just build the tram on the left side of the stairs, where they were going to evict people anyway. The city responded as coldly as it had to Jane Nascimento in Vila Autódromo: "We have our plan, so save your breath." What happened next is a beautiful example of art as resistance. Maurício took photos of all the residents who lived in the houses on the right side of the stairs—the side that would be unnecessarily evicted to build the tram. He had them blown up larger than life, then wheat-pasted them on the sides of the houses lining the stairs. It was a massive public art display that humanized the cost of demolishing all these homes. A public rally was called in Providência to highlight the city's intransigence and neglect of the community's wishes. The photo installation became a viral story on social media and eventually in Brazil's corporate press. Finally, the city relented and decided to change its plan—only the precarious homes on the left side of the staircase would be evicted after all. The tram could be built in their place; those living on the other side of the stairs would be able to keep their homes. It was a small but important example of the kinds of concessions the city government could be forced to make.

About halfway up the stairs, we meet an older woman who knows Maurício. She stands in the doorway to her house, which is slated for eviction. Seven people live here. She is the head of her household and is still negotiating with the government over where they will relocate her family. The apartment they are offering, she says, is only forty square meters. Alongside the staircase, we see one of the makeshift engineering feats that allow communities like Providência to exist: an old cast-iron water main with literally dozens of "unofficial" (read: illegal) taps in it, each branching off into a smaller PVC pipe that snakes its way into the densely packed homes. Maurício tells me that each tap in the main probably feeds about thirty homes. This type of utility rigging has historically brought power, water, and other services to favelas all across Brazil, in violation of existing building codes and the mores of private property. Like the rest of the favelas, these utility hookups reflect nothing but the work, skills, and creativity of community members in meeting their needs.

After we reach the top of the stairs, we make a beeline down the pathway to a larger building painted bright yellow. This is Maurício's community arts center, called Favelarte. Favelarte provides basic education to community youth, with a special focus on the visual arts. Inside are a library, study center, and rooms where tutors run after-school programs in literacy, math, and the arts. Maurício describes their film screenings, poetry readings, and other activities. "When we first started," he explains, "we put in this library. But we soon realized that most kids coming to us didn't know how to read. So we put in the reading room upstairs, where there is someone who can help teach them to read." The story of Maurício's school is emblematic of Rio's breakneck real-estate appreciation. He bought the building in 2009 for around twelve thousand dollars. Eighteen months later, when development plans for Providência got under way, the government offered to buy the building from him for thirty-two thousand dollars. He rejected the offer. Now, he says, the building is valued at seventy thousand dollars, an appreciation of nearly 500 percent in just over three years' time.

The rising real-estate values at the top of Providência shed light on something else: the evictions of most families at its very pinnacle. These are the people who would ostensibly be served by the tram. So why evict them? According to the oft-repeated statements of city officials, it is because these homes are built in a "precarious fashion" and reside in a "risk area." In other words, they are in danger of being damaged or destroyed by landslides. However, the last landslide here was in 1968. Most community residents don't accept that these homes are at any kind of risk. They believe that rising property values are a far greater danger to their homes than mudslides. I am told that, just on the other side of the hill, several homes have already been bought up by a wealthy Brazilian who is building a large mansion nearby.

Maurício points out another factor that we cannot see from our vantage point at the top of Providência: viewed from the rapidly developing port area and downtown, the hill where we stand is an important element of the Rio skyline. Atop Providência sits a beautiful old white chapel, just a few hundred yards from Maurício's house. However, the chapel is currently surrounded by homes that block views of it from below, down the hillside. "If you take these houses down," Maurício says, "the favela is no longer visible from the city below. The city wants to fix up this historic chapel and make this a scenic view from below." It is part of a massive and multifaceted process of "sanitizing" the city, displacing residents and destroying history and culture, in order to make Rio more palatable for tourists and the wealthy—that is, to make it more marketable.

Maurício takes us down the other side of the hill; it is a harrowing experience. We walk along a path that is now being widened, underpinned, and made into a road. He describes it as the path the drug gangs used to take their victims to execute them. They would blindfold people, walk them down this path, shoot them, and then dump their bodies over the cliff, he says.

Further down, Maurício stops at a little yellow-painted corner where the path branches out in two different directions. We are among extremely tightly packed buildings now. "This spot is where my father's drug trafficking operation started," Maurício says. He tells us about the drug ring run by his father and his father's cousin. As far as he knows, it was the first drug trafficking ring in all of Rio. At first all they sold was marijuana. Then in 1965, cocaine came in, brought in by a guy who worked for the Brazilian Air Force. The 1970s were when violence between competing traffickers became particularly brutal, he says. In addition to competing over turf, the state turned a blind eye to some traffickers if in return they agreed to police the favelas. Another journalist on the tour comments,

> There is a very deliberate attempt to unlock value that's been long trapped in Rio de Janeiro because of violence. The drug trafficking during the last generation has kept the lid on real estate prices in Rio and other Brazilian cities, and this UPP program is a way of releasing that value into the national and international market without any break whatsoever. And that's why the pacification programs are being financed by people like Eike Batista, Brazil's wealthiest man. . . . He sees it as an investment that will generate immediate and spectacular returns.

Maurício doesn't say much more. He feels like he has said enough. If we don't see it by now, there simply is not much more he can say.

When we return to the offices of Catalytic Communities, I listen to the words of Marcos Alvito, with whom I spoke on my first day. After seeing Vila Autódromo and Providência, I hear new meaning in his words: "The mega-event preparations are about sweeping the human surplus out of sight by the thousands upon thousands. Rio de Janeiro's magical urban developers conjure away the spectacle of the poverty the system produces. Soon only the mastications of prosperity, but not its excrement, will be seen in these cities, where the wealth created by all of Brazil is squandered."

"FIFA-Quality Schools"

As far as I'm concerned, the explosion of indignation in Brazil is justified. In its thirst for justice, it is similar to other demonstrations that in recent years have shaken many countries in many parts of the world. Brazilians, who are the most soccer-mad of all, have decided not to allow their sport to be used any more as an excuse for humiliating the many and enriching the few. The fiesta of soccer, a feast for the legs that play and the eyes that watch, is much more than a big business run by overlords from Switzerland. The most popular sport in the world wants to serve the people who embrace it. That is a fire police violence will never put out.

—Eduardo Galeano[1]

The Resistance

The streets of Brazil erupted in 2013 as a million people took to the streets in the first mass demonstrations the country had seen since the dictatorship. Every major city, and even several small towns, saw people in the streets, bravely facing tear gas, violence, and intimidation. The protests coincided with the Confederations Cup, a top-shelf international soccer tournament viewed as a precursor to the almighty World Cup. Everywhere a publicly funded stadium grew from the ground, it became a focal point for protest. Without any formal leadership or traditional social movement organizations, people were

205

protesting everything: corruption, the priorities of government, the ways the "Brazilian cost" had become a millstone hanging from their necks. Journalist Wright Thompson outlined their anger:

> The billions spent on World Cup stadiums sparked June's outrage over corruption. A law which requires local governments to balance their budgets was suspended for cities hosting soccer matches, clearing the way for huge public spending which allegedly lined the pockets of politicians. In Cuiabá, five public works projects were begun on the same day. None of them will be finished in time for the tournament. Three different government websites claim to offer transparency over the World Cup spending, which is a dramatic change from the past in Brazil, when no transparency existed at all. The problem is that the sites all have different sets of numbers for the same projects. It's all fiction. Nobody can really say what is being spent.[2]

The article, published in *ESPN: The Magazine*, as mainstream a sports publication as we have in the United States, warned darkly that "anger may consume the World Cup."

In every city, protestors adapted their tactics based on the needs, ideas, and particular political traditions of that place. This led to wildly different assessments and characterizations of both the political character and the aim of the masses in the streets. Yet some slogans did shine through, reflecting that the protestors were extremely aware that the whole world was watching. One slogan within the protests was "The Giant Awakens." They were of course drawing attention to themselves, the Brazilian masses. It was also a cheeky reference to a Fiat ad meant to hype the World Cup.[3]

What was particularly interesting about these protests was that they made all the sense in the world, given the current set of frustrations throughout the country, and yet everyone was stunned. When I traveled to Brazil, most people in the community of social movements agreed that these sports extravaganzas would leave behind major collateral damage. Everyone agreed that the spending priorities for stadiums, security, and all attendant infrastructure were monstrous, given the health and education needs of the Brazilian people. Everyone agreed that the deficits incurred would be balanced on the backs of workers and the poor. What people disagreed upon was whether anybody would do anything about it.

Most argued that the country had become too apathetic. After six years of economic growth, which followed thirty years of stagnation, military dictatorship, and the occasional spike of hyperinflation, people were either too content or apathetic to protest. The ruling Workers' Party was generally popular; most expected that as soon as the countdown to the World Cup actually began, all restiveness over the disruption would be washed away in a sea of green, yellow, and blue flags. Others argued that statistics showing rising wealth and general quiescence actually masked a much deeper discontent. Brazil was simmering, and the lid could stay on the pot for only so long.

The pot, in 2013, officially boiled over. After the demonstrations, I spoke to Maria Oliveira, a young labor activist. She said, "We are often hamstrung in Brazil by the fact that it is so diverse and so vast that no one thinks anyone has anything in common with anyone else on a national level. But the arrival of the mega-events, which was supposed to unify and nationalize support for the government, has instead unified and nationalized dissent." Brazil's financial capital, mighty São Paulo, the world's third-largest city, was brought to a standstill. In Brazil's political capital, Brasília, protestors occupied the roof of the National Congress building.[4] In Rio, thousands marched on the legendary Maracanã Stadium at the start of the Confederations Cup. As fans cheered inside, police gassed and beat protestors outside.[5] While sports journalists recorded the action on the field, reporters in the streets were shot with rubber bullets—they were targeted even after identifying themselves as members of the press.[6]

This protest eruption has been referred to as the "salad uprising" because a journalist was arrested on charges of having vinegar in his backpack. (Vinegar can be used to ward off the worst effects of tear gas.) After his arrest, people began openly carrying vinegar out of solidarity—and, given the expansive use of tear gas, out of practicality.[7] Numerous factors drove people into the streets, but what crystallized all discontent was a twenty-cent fare hike for public transportation. The country was investing billions in tourist-centric infrastructure and paying for it by fleecing workers on their daily commutes. It was too much. Chris Gaffney emailed me:

> Big shit happening [in] downtown Rio tonight, with cars set on fire around the state legislature and attempted invasions of the building that were repelled from inside. News of police using live ammunition as well. It is of course linked to the spending for the mega-events, but also reflects a larger dissatisfaction with the state of the country. The government is corrupt, the police incompetent, the roads and services and schools and healthcare atrocious . . . and this [is the state of services] for the middle class! . . . People are realizing that the 50 billion spent on the mega events is going into the pockets of FIFA, the IOC, and the corrupt construction firms, etc. This latest little insult, hiking the fares by twenty cents, was just enough to get people out on the streets during the Copa. This is truly historical and inspiring. I didn't think the Brazilians had it in them, and I don't think they [thought they] did either. But they do and it's massive.[8]

The activists of the Movimento Passe Livre (Free Fare Movement), after protesting fare hikes for more than a decade and winning concessions with little publicity, suddenly found themselves with a mass audience. They were savvy enough to link their struggle with spending priorities for the mega-events. Reports from the ground were that demonstrators were holding up posters that read "We don't need the World Cup" and "We need money for hospitals and education." The slogan that has really gone down in the history books, though, was a reference to Sepp Blatter, the slithering head of FIFA. Blatter is infamous for always insisting with the regularity of a metronome, no matter the host country, that the old stadiums are simply not good enough and that the country must build "FIFA-quality stadiums." Now people were holding up signs saying, "We need FIFA-quality schools" and "We need FIFA-quality hospitals."

The protests caused a head-on collision between the people of Brazil and the sport that reputedly defines their country, their culture, and their way of life. One massive demonstration gathered outside a luxury hotel in Fortaleza, where the Brazilian national soccer team was staying, with signs that read, "FIFA, give us our money back!" and "We want health and education. World Cup out!" A protestor in São Paulo named Camila was quoted in the international press as saying, "We shouldn't be spending public money on stadiums. We don't want the Cup. We want education, hospitals, a better life for our children."[9]

The right wing was also present in the streets, as Yuseph Katiya, who lives in the conservative city of Curitiba, pointed out to me. One of the loosely organized groups in the streets was a formation called Acorda Brasil (Wake Up Brazil). As Katiya wrote on his extremely informative Facebook wall:

> This is a mixed bag and difficult to describe, and I think is poten-
> tially dangerous. These are middle-class people that share some of
> the concerns of the World Cup/Olympic protesters and the Free
> Fare Movement people, but their beef is mainly with government
> corruption. Suddenly, the right-wing press here is supporting the
> protests but they are more likely to blame politician salaries on the
> country's problems. I don't think they care about rising transporta-
> tion costs, let alone how it might impact low-income Brazilians.[10]

Nevertheless, the protests gained energy and found voice among the Brazilian diaspora throughout the world. More than three hundred people marched in New York City. One sign read:

> Olympics: $33 billion.
>
> World Cup: $26 billion.
>
> Minimum Wage: $674 [about US $320 a month].
>
> Do you still think it's about 20 cents [the price of the bus fare
> hike]?[11]

Protests were also reported in France, Ireland, and Canada, among others. This wasn't a movement against sports. It was a movement against the use of sports as a neoliberal Trojan horse. It was a move-ment against sports as a cudgel of austerity.

This must have made Sepp Blatter, President Rousseff, and Pelé incredibly nervous, because they all went public with the same disciplined message to the nation: "For the love of God, don't blame the World Cup for our current mass upheaval." Dilma said in a nationally televised address:

> Brazil, the only country to have participated in every World Cup and a five-time world champion, has always been very well received everywhere. We must give our friends the same generous welcome we have received from them—with respect, love and joy. This is how we must treat our guests. Football and sport are symbols of peace and peaceful coexistence among peoples.[12]

Blatter, displaying his renowned empathy, was even more blunt: "I can understand that people are not happy, but they should not use football to make their demands heard. . . . When the ball starts to roll, people will understand!"[13] Pelé, meanwhile, had to backtrack dramatically after saying, "Let's forget all this commotion happening in Brazil, all these protests, and let's remember how the Brazilian squad is our country and our blood." Another Brazilian soccer hero, Ronaldo, said in response to critiques of stadium spending, "You can't hold a World Cup with hospitals."[14] In sharp contrast to this was national-team star Neymar, who said, in an epic statement,

> I've always had faith that it wouldn't be necessary to get to this point, of having to take over the streets, to demand for better transportation, health, education and safety—these are all government's obligations. My parents worked really hard to offer me and my sister a good quality life. Today, thanks to the success that fans have afforded me, it might seem like a lot of demagogy from me—but it isn't—raising the flag of the protests that are happening in Brazil. But I am Brazilian and I love my country. I have family and friends who live in Brazil! That's why I want a Brazil that is fair and safe and healthier and more honest! The only way I have to represent Brazil is on the pitch, playing football and, starting today against Mexico, I'll get on the pitch inspired by this mobilisation.[15]

True to his word, Neymar was the star of the national team's next Confederations Cup match, a victory against Mexico.[16]

The Real President

What Dilma, Blatter, and Pelé are doing is basically begging the people of Brazil not to turn the 2014 World Cup into a symbol of what ails the country. What frightens them is that, clearly, people don't see the World Cup—not to mention the 2016 Olympics in Rio—as some sort of abstract, postmodern symbol of poor public services and high taxes but as an aggravator of social ills. It didn't help Dilma's argument that, after her statement, she deployed the National Force, Brazil's feared federal troops, outside soccer stadiums for the duration of the Confederations Cup.

And what about Lula? The wildly popular former leader, his cancer in remission, took to the leading newspapers with his own analysis of what was happening—but those looking for real insight would have to go elsewhere. It was an exercise in chutzpah. Lula wrote that he believed the "demonstrations are largely the result of social, economic and political successes. . . . We sharply reduced poverty and inequality. These are significant achievements, yet it is completely natural that young people, especially those who are obtaining things their parents never had, should desire more." He added that "even the Workers' Party, which I helped found and which has contributed so much to modernize and democratize politics in Brazil, needs profound renewal. It must recover its daily links with social movements and offer new solutions for new problems, and do both without treating young people paternalistically."[17] Given all that Lula did to engineer the separation of his party from the social movements, as we saw in chapter 3, such a statement beggars belief. But the coup de grace lies not in what is said, but in what is not said. Three words that did not make it into his piece were "World," "Cup," and "Olympics." (Perhaps he was just abiding by their copyright statutes.)

What none of the powers that be can say is that the World Cup, in their hands, is a tool of neoliberal plunder. Neoliberalism, at its core, is about transferring wealth out of the public social safety net and into the hands of private capital. As anyone who has ever relied on public services—little things like schools and hospitals—can understand, this agenda is wildly unpopular with much of the world. But the IMF wants it. The World Bank wants it. Local elites want it. And international capital wants it. So how do they make it happen? One way is to unleash the police to simply smash institutions of popular economic self-defense such as trade unions, general assemblies, and social movements. But that approach carries an attendant risk. As we've seen in Turkey, Brazil, and even New York City in the early days of the Occupy Wall Street movement, police repression can make demonstrations look sympathetic and even wildly attractive to people who are fed up but have no outlet for their frustration.

The Olympics, World Cup, and other mega-events have, over the last thirty years, provided something that couldn't be found at the end of a military-grade truncheon: the consent of the masses to neoliberal policy goals. The walled city of Troy is the social safety net, and the Trojan horse is the games people are initially proud to host—until the marauders of the free market descend from its hollowed-out stomach and start taking their pound of flesh. The countries change, but the scenario stays the same: a profit orgy and a tax haven for corporate sponsors and private security firms, obscene public spending on new stadiums, and then brutal cuts that fall on the backs of the poor when the party's over. But in Brazil, they're not waiting until the cameras are gone and the confetti has been swept away. People started protesting *in advance*— and that immediately made what they were doing historic. To find a similar scenario, you would have to go back to the 1968 mass protests in Mexico City before the Olympics, which ended in tragedy: the slaughter of hundreds of Mexican students and workers. (Remembering the horrors of what is known as "the massacre at Tlatelolco Square" is a way of ensuring that it won't happen again.)

The mass actions of the summer of 2013 exposed the neoliberal theft rooted in the planning and execution of the World Cup. No truer words were said during the protests than those of Romário: "FIFA is the real president of our country. FIFA comes to our country and imposes a state within a state. It's not going to pay taxes, it's going to come, install a circus without paying anything and take everything with it. They are taking the piss out of us with our money, the public's money. The money that has been spent on the [one] stadium could have been used to build 150,000 housing units."[18] The demonstrators swear they will return for the World Cup, but this is a great unknown—the problem with social explosions is that they're unpredictable. You can be assured, though, that Dilma will use military hardware, drone planes, and preemptive arrests to make sure that any protests are a blip on the international radar.

But something changed in 2013. The protests in Brazil were far more than an expression of extreme anger and disaffection. While polls of mass demonstrations should be taken with a grain of salt, one survey of demonstrators showed that 84 percent don't see themselves as part of any political formation.[19] The protests became a catch-all for every grievance under the sun, with World Cup and Olympic spending coming to symbolize an austerity economy beyond the reach of any semblance of democracy. This is both a strength and weakness. It's a strength because the Brazilian people are learning lessons in real time about democracy in the streets: São Paulo city officials even repealed the hated bus fare hike in an effort to quell demonstrators.[20] It also is a weakness, as reactionary forces enter the fray hoping to turn demonstrators against the Workers' Party government and make the protests about "government spending." It's a cheap, opportunistic effort to deflect attention away from the behind-the-scenes corporate feeding frenzy *in conjunction with the Workers' Party*. The right wing in Brazil has no problem with austerity; it just doesn't like who is administering it. But, as Theresa Williamson, who was among the throngs being tear-gassed, said to me, "It is about individual demands and frustrations that converge into a unified whole. This is a future-oriented movement. If a handful are trying to appropriate it you can bet the movement will get them out. If they don't, things will digress only to evolve in a few years into something even more substantial."

Whatever politics eventually carry the day, it is clear that masses of young people marched with the basic hope that their dreams for a more just and democratic nation would take concrete form. They were acting to reshape their country, with incredible bravery, amid tear gas, rubber bullets, and concussion grenades. They took the fight to the stadiums and forced those inside to feel the itch of wafting tear gas in their eyes, hear explosions in the distance, and see the reality of international sports in the age of neoliberalism. Sepp Blatter said, "When the ball starts to roll, people will understand." Indeed, they might. But as the smoke wafts into the Maracanã, they will understand something far different than what Blatter, FIFA, and Rousseff had in mind. They will understand that, in the twenty-first century, the World Cup arrives with a terrible price.

Juca Kfouri, a leading Brazilian commentator, said that the protests hold the possibility of waking the world up to the reality of Brazil, not just the Disney image marketed to tourists: "There is a false idea of Brazilian happiness that is based on a wrong assumption that Brazilians do not claim ownership," he said. "But next year, there will be big parties inside the stadiums and big protests outside."[21] When Romário was asked if he thought the demonstrations would return for the Cup, he said, "Not only do I think they will return, I think they should return. There will be a World Cup here next year, we know that. But this, these demonstrations, is the way you make politicians wake up." Then he laughed and said, "This is the way you make people think about whether or not they are going to rob you again tomorrow."[22]

The Nobodies

The nobodies: nobody's children, owners of nothing. The nobodies: the no ones, the nobodied, running like rabbits, dying through life, screwed every which way.

Who are not, but could be.
Who don't speak languages, but dialects.
Who don't have religions, but superstitions.

Who don't create art, but handicrafts.

Who don't have culture, but folklore.

Who are not human beings, but human resources.

Who do not have faces, but arms.

Who do not have names, but numbers.

Who do not appear in the history of the world, but in the police
blotter of the local paper.

The nobodies, who are not worth the bullet that kills them.

—Eduardo Galeano[23]

If you have made it this far, you may have noticed that I've started almost every chapter of this book with a quote by the great author Eduardo Galeano. If you have never had the privilege, please read Galeano's book *Soccer in Sun and Shadow*. It captures what I believe will be the most difficult part of seeing the destruction of Brazil over the next several years: the fact that many of us who are horrified at every eviction, every instance of police brutality, every community destroyed, will also be swept up in the energy, color, nationalism, and yes, joy of the World Cup and the Olympics. *Soccer in Sun and Shadow* attempts to square the beauty, adrenaline, and—heaven forbid—fun of sports with the ways it can be used to crush the very human spirit it purports to promote.

If we love Brazil, if we love its culture, play, dance, and energy, then we have to reckon with the fact that everything we love about it was created by the very "nobodies" who, in the eyes of FIFA and the IOC, "are not worth the bullet that kills them." If we love soccer and all sports—the creative mayhem amid structure, the improvisation amid order, the ability of players to discover new boundaries and a higher sense of confidence within themselves—then we also have to love every nobody we've ever played pickup ball with, every nobody who created the beauty of the "beautiful game," whatever we may feel that beautiful game to be. We also have to realize that the death of public space, the death of leisure time, the death of security, and the fostering of fear means the death of sports as well.

If we get swept up in the World Cup but forget the nobodies who are swept away, then we should not be surprised when FIFA or the IOC comes calling again in our own towns and we find ourselves branded nobodies. Galeano once said that he does not believe in charity—he believes in solidarity, because solidarity is horizontal and carries within it the understanding that we can learn from others. I would argue that it also implies that our collective destiny is tied up with every eviction, every surveillance camera, and every cracked skull on the road to the World Cup and Olympics. It is their World Cup. But it is our world.

Notes

Introduction

1. Adrian Grant, *Michael Jackson: Making History* (London: Omnibus Press, 1998). When this song is remembered, it's usually for its unfortunate use of anti-Semitic phrases like "Jew me" and "kike me" in the lyrics (which Jackson later changed and apologized for). Bigotry aside, that "They Don't Care about Us" has been forgotten is a damn shame.
2. Diana Jean Schemo, "Rio Frets as Michael Jackson Plans to Film Slum," *New York Times*, February 11, 1996, www.nytimes.com/1996/02/11/world/rio-frets-as-michael-jackson-plans-to-film-slum.html.
3. Ibid.
4. Ibid.
5. Larry Rohter, *Brazil on the Rise: The Story of a Country Transformed* (New York: Palgrave Macmillan, 2012).
6. Amnesty International, "Focus on Indigenous Peoples' Rights and Police Violence in Brazil," August 5, 2013, www.amnestyusa.org/news/news-item/focus-on-indigenous-peoples-rights-and-police-violence-in-brazil.
7. Wright Thompson, "Generation June," *ESPN: The Magazine*, December 5, 2013.

Chapter 1

1. Eduardo Galeano, *Open Veins of Latin America: Five Centuries of the Pilage of a Continent* (New York: Monthly Review Press, 1997), 248.
2. Rohter, *Brazil on the Rise*, 7.
3. *Economist*, "Brazil Takes Off," November 12, 2009, www.economist.com/node/14845197.

4. Ibid.

5. Silvia Salek, "Brazil: No Longer 'Country of the Future,'" BBC News, March 6, 2012, www.bbc.co.uk/news/business-17270649.

6. Rohter, *Brazil on the Rise*, 223.

7. *Economist*, "Has Brazil Blown It?" September 28, 2013, www.economist .com/news/leaders/21586833-stagnant-economy-bloated-state-and-mass -protests-mean-dilma-rousseff-must-change-course-has.

8. Gerard Aziakou, "Two Dead in Brazil World Cup Stadium Accident," Agence France-Presse, November 27, 2013, www.google.com/hostednews /afp/article/ALeqM5iu9pX6v9R3al0ALLHV8UlBVk6bzw?docId=5f7d23ce -5cf7-49c9-81b0-8158c56a85f1.

9. Jonathan Watts, "Two Killed as Crane Collapses at Brazilian World Cup Stadium," *Guardian*, November 27, 2013, www.theguardian.com/football /2013/nov/27/crane-collapse-corinthians-brazil-three-killed.

10. Ibid.

11. Ibid.

12. Sam Borden, "Romário, a World Cup Champion, Is Now a World Cup Dissenter," *New York Times*, October 15, 2013, www.nytimes.com/2013/10 /16/sports/soccer/romario-a-world-cup-champion-is-now-a-world-cup -dissenter.html?_r=0.

13. Reuters, "Construction Accident at Brazil World Cup Stadium Kills Two," November 27, 2013, http://uk.reuters.com/article/2013/11/27/uk-soccer -brazil-stadium-idUKBRE9AQ0UT20131127.

14. Ibid.

15. Ibid.

16. ESPN.com, "2014 World Cup Guide: Curitiba," December 2, 2013, http://espnfc.com/news/story/_/id/1584760/venue-guide-arena-da- baixada-curitiba-2014-world-cup-stadium-brazil?cc=5901.

17. Associated Press, "Labor Slaves, Prisoners Helping WC Prep," February 22, 2012, http://espn.go.com/sports/soccer/story/_/id/7600446/brazil -using-prisoners-labor-slaves-prep-2014-world-cup-venues.

18. Rob Walker, "Brazil World Cup Host City Natal Seethes at Cost," *Guardian*, November 28, 2013, www.theguardian.com/world/2013/nov/28 /brazil-world-cup-natal-cost.

19. Ibid.

20. Ibid.

21. Ibid.

22. David Biller, Christiana Sciaudone, and Taís Fuoco, "Singapore Changi, Odebrecht to Buy Rio Airport for $8.3 Billion," *Bloomberg News*, Novem-

ber 23, 2013, www.bloomberg.com/news/2013-11-22/singapore-munich
-operators-to-pay-9-1-bln-for-brazil-airports.html.

23. Walker, "Brazil World Cup Host City Natal Seethes."

24. Rohter, *Brazil on the Rise*, 225.

25. Borden, "Romário, a World Cup Champion."

26. Guilherme Cruz, "Brazil Running Out of Time to Get Things Done for World Cup 2014," *SB Nation*, December 4, 2013, www.sbnation.com /soccer/2013/12/4/5174850/world-cup-2014-brazil-stadiums.

27. Bryan McCann, *Hard Times in the Marvelous City: From Dictatorship to Democracy in the Favelas of Rio de Janeiro* (Durham, NC: Duke Press, 2014), 2.

28. Renato Cosentino, "Largo do Tanque: One More Summary Removal for the Rio Olympics," *Rio on Watch*, February 26, 2013, http://rioonwatch .org/?p=6980.

29. Rohter, *Brazil on the Rise*, 40.

30. Michael Kimmelman, "A Divided Rio de Janeiro, Overreaching for the World," *New York Times*, November 25, 2013, www.nytimes.com/2013 /11/26/world/americas/a-divided-rio-de-janeiro-overreaching-for-the -world.html.

31. For the sake of clarity, figures are given in US dollars.

32. Simon Romero and Taylor Barnes, "Police Storm Squatters at Rio Stadium Site," *New York Times*, March 22, 2013, www.nytimes.com/2013 /03/23/world/americas/brazilian-police-storm-indigenous-squatters-at -maracana.html.

33. World Wildlife Fund, "Amazon," 2014, http://worldwildlife.org/places /amazon.

34. Rohter, *Brazil on the Rise*, 221.

35. Rainforest Foundation, "25 Years: In Honor of Chico Mendes," December 20, 2013, www.rainforestfoundation.org/article/25-years-honor-chico-mendes.

36. Sam Borden, "Building a World Cup Stadium in the Amazon," *New York Times*, September 24, 2013, www.nytimes.com/2013/09/25/sports/soccer /in-building-world-cup-stadium-in-amazon-rain-is-just-one-challenge.html.

37. See Dave Zirin, "Soccer on Chile's Killing Field," *Los Angeles Times*, December 12, 2006, www.latimes.com/news/la-oe-zirin12dec12,0,4806850 .story#axzz2qrw776fX.

38. Anna Jean Kaiser, "Can Brazil Deliver on Safety for World Cup, Olympics?" *USA Today*, July 24, 2013, www.usatoday.com/story/sports/soccer/2013 /07/24/brazil-sports-security/2584905/.

39. Owen Gibson and Jonathan Watts, "Brazil Plans 'World Cup Courts,'"

Guardian, December 4, 2013, www.theguardian.com/football/2013/dec /04/brazil-world-cup-courts.

40. Travis Waldron, "As Attention Turns to World Cup, Brazil Ramps Up Security to Prepare for More Protests," *Think Progress*, December 4, 2013, http://thinkprogress.org/sports/2013/12/04/3020751/attention-turns -world-cup-brazil-ramps-security-prepare-protests.

41. A video of the massacre is online at *OVGuide*, "Watch Complexo Do Alemão Massacre Video," undated post, www.ovguide.com/complexo-do -alemao-massacre-9202a8c04000641f8000000006bbbbdf.

42. PBS, "Q&A with Professor Henry Louis Gates, Jr.," *Black in Latin America* website, 2011, www.pbs.org/wnet/black-in-latin-america/featured/qa -with-professor-henry-louis-gates-jr/164/.

Chapter 2

1. Quoted in Saleem Badat, *The Forgotten People: Political Banishment under Apartheid* (Leiden, Netherlands: Brill, 2013), xxvi.

2. E. Bradford Burns, *A History of Brazil*, 3rd ed. (New York: Columbia University Press, 1993), 1.

3. Ibid., 1.

4. Hans Staden, *Hans Staden's True History: An Account of Cannibal Captivity in Brazil*, ed. Neil L. Whitehead, trans. Michael Harbsmeier (Durham, NC: Duke University Press, 2008).

5. James Minahan, *Ethnic Groups of the Americas: An Encyclopedia* (Santa Barbara, CA: ABC-CLIO, 2013), 49.

6. Thomas E. Skidmore, *Brazil: Five Centuries of Change*, 2nd ed. (Oxford: Oxford University Press, 2009), 15.

7. James Holston, *The Modernist City: An Anthropological Critique of Brasília* (Chicago: University of Chicago Press, 1989), 16.

8. Galeano, *Open Veins of Latin America*, 47.

9. Kátia M. de Queirós Mattoso, Arthur Goldhammer, and Stuart Schwartz, *To Be a Slave in Brazil: 1550–1888* (New Brunswick, NJ: Rutgers University Press, 1987).

10. Stuart B. Schwartz, *Sugar Plantations in the Formation of Brazilian Society: Bahia, 1550–1835* (Cambridge: Cambridge University Press, 1986), 369.

11. *Atlanta Black Star*, "Afro-Brazilian Story II: Slavery, Identity and the Question of Racism," November 18, 2013, http://atlantablackstar.com /2013/11/18/afro-brazilian-story-ii-slavery-identity-question-racism.

12. Mattoso, Goldhammer, and Schwartz, *To Be a Slave in Brazil*, 10.

13. Skidmore, *Brazil*, 26.

14. Galeano, *Open Veins of Latin America*, 57.
15. PBS, "Q&A with Professor Henry Louis Gates, Jr."
16. Henry Louis Gates, *Black in Latin America* (New York: NYU Press, 2011), 43.
17. Mattoso, Goldhammer, and Schwartz, *To Be a Slave in Brazil*, 41.
18. Gloria Kaiser, "January 9, 1822: Fico—I Am Staying," *The World of the Habsburgs*, 2011, www.habsburger.net/en/chapter/january-9-1822-fico-i-am-staying.
19. Galeano, *Open Veins of Latin America*, 178.
20. Herbert S. Klein and Francisco Vidal, *Slavery in Brazil* (Cambridge: Cambridge University Press, 2009), chapter 5.
21. Skidmore, *Brazil*, 39.
22. Ibid., 39.
23. Rohter, *Brazil on the Rise*, 14.
24. Skidmore, *Brazil*, 18.
25. *Atlanta Black Star*, "Afro-Brazilian Story II."
26. Skidmore, *Brazil*, 69.
27. Antônio de Castro Alves, "O Navio Negreiro (Slave Ship)," 1880, available with English translation at AllPoetry.com, http://allpoetry.com/poem/8560731-O-Navio-Negreiro-Part-1.—With-English-Translation—wbr—by-Antonio-de-Castro-Alves.
28. Neill Macaulay, *Dom Pedro: The Struggle for Liberty in Brazil and Portugal, 1798–1834* (Durham, NC: Duke University Press, 1986), 147.
29. Skidmore, *Brazil*, 68.
30. Ibid., 70.
31. Manu Herbstein, *Ama: A Story of the Atlantic Slave Trade*, digital ed. (ereads.com, 2000).
32. Rohter, *Brazil on the Rise*, 22.
33. Boris Fausto and Arthur Brakel, *A Concise History of Brazil* (Cambridge: Cambridge University Press, 1999), 158.
34. Skidmore, *Brazil*, 77.
35. Ibid., 86.
36. Ibid., 87.
37. Richard Bourne, *Getúlio Vargas of Brazil, 1883–1954: Sphinx of the Pampas* (London: C. Knight, 1974), 195.
38. June Edith Hahner, *Emancipating the Female Sex: The Struggle for Women's Rights in Brazil* (Durham, NC: Duke University Press, 1990), xvi.
39. Louise Sherwood, "Brazilian World War II Workers Fight for Recognition," *BBC News*, August 8, 2010, www.bbc.co.uk/news/world-latin-america-10787714.

40. Skidmore, *Brazil*, 118.
41. Bourne, *Getúlio Vargas of Brazil*, 195.
42. Galeano, *Open Veins of Latin America*, 99.
43. Economist, "A Giant Stirs," June 10, 2004, www.economist.com/node /2752700.
44. Galeano, *Open Veins of Latin America*, 216.
45. David Goldblatt, *The Ball Is Round: A Global History of Soccer* (New York: Riverhead Books, 2008), 368.
46. *Encyclopaedia Britannica Online*, s.v. "Jânio da Silva Quadros," accessed February 2, 2014, www.britannica.com/EBchecked/topic/485946/Janio -da-Silva-Quadros.
47. Tanya Ogilvie-White and David Santoro, eds., *Nuclear Dragon: Disarmament Dynamics in the Twenty-First Century* (Athens: University of Georgia Press, 2012), 152.
48. Peter Kornbluh, ed., "Brazil Marks 40th Anniversary of Military Coup," National Security Archive, March 31, 2004, www2.gwu.edu/~nsarchiv /NSAEBB/NSAEBB118.
49. Ibid.
50. Galeano, *Open Veins of Latin America*, 155.
51. Ibid., 212.
52. Ibid., 212.
53. Ibid., 138.
54. Noam Chomsky and Edward S. Herman, *The Washington Connection and Third World Fascism* (Boston: South End Press, 1979), 48.
55. McCann, *Hard Times in the Marvelous City*, 5.
56. Skidmore, *Brazil*, 160.
57. Rohter, *Brazil on the Rise*, 143.
58. McCann, *Hard Times in the Marvelous City*, 5.
59. Paul Chevigny, *Edge of the Knife: Police Violence in the Americas* (New York: New Press, 1997), chapter 6.
60. McCann, *Hard Times in the Marvelous City*, 5.
61. Palash Ghosh, "Candelaria Church Massacre: Brazil Marks 20th Anniversary of Police Murders of Homeless Street Children," *International Business Times*, July 25, 2013, www.ibtimes.com/candelaria-church-massacre -brazil-marks-20th-anniversary-police-murders-homeless-street-children.
62. John Lyons, "As Crime Rattles Brazil, Killings by Police Turn Routine," *Wall Street Journal*, July 12, 2013, http://online.wsj.com/news/articles /SB10001424127887323836504578553643435119434.
63. Rohter, *Brazil on the Rise*, 142–45.

64. Ibid.
65. Kenneth Maxwell, "The Two Brazils," *Wilson Quarterly*, Winter 1999, www.wilsonquarterly.com/essays/two-brazils.
66. *Index Mundi*, "Brazil – Population below Poverty Line," 2010, www.indexmundi.com/g/g.aspx?c=br&v=69.
67. Kenneth Maxwell, *Naked Tropics: Essays on Empire and Other Rogues* (New York: Routledge, 2003), 254.

Chapter 3

1. Perry Anderson, "Lula's Brazil," *London Review of Books*, March 31, 2011, www.lrb.co.uk/v33/n07/perry-anderson/lulas-brazil.
2. Ibid.
3. Rohter, *Brazil on the Rise*, 140.
4. Ibid., 166.
5. Luis Fleischman, "Brazil's Tilt Towards Chavez and Iran," Center for Security Policy, October 8, 2009, www.centerforsecuritypolicy.org/2009/10/08/brazils-tilt-towards-chavez-and-iran-2.
6. Robert Minto, "Lula For World Bank," *Financial Times*, February 17, 2012, http://blogs.ft.com/beyond-brics/2012/02/17/guest-post-how-about-lula-for-world-bank.
7. Rohter, *Brazil on the Rise*, 275.
8. Ibid., 146.
9. Ibid., 153.
10. *Al Jazeera English*, "Lula Bids a Tearful Goodbye," December 30, 2010, www.aljazeera.com/news/americas/2010/12/2010123054815679161.html.
11. Anderson, "Lula's Brazil."
12. Ibid.
13. Ibid.
14. Ibid.
15. Ibid.
16. Ibid.
17. Ibid.
18. Ibid.
19. Tom Lewis, "What Change Will Lula Bring?" *International Socialist Review* 26 (November 2002), www.isreview.org/issues/26/Lula.shtml.
20. Daniel Bell, quoted in Naomi Klein, *The Shock Doctrine* (New York: Metropolitan Books, 2007), 51.
21. Klein, *Shock Doctrine*, 51.

22. Ibid., 15.
23. Ibid., 17.
24. Sarah LeBlanc Goff, "When Education Ceases to Be Public: The Privatization of the New Orleans School System after Hurricane Katrina," master's thesis, University of New Orleans, 2009.
25. Kevin Sullivan, "Brazil Brings Haiti a Joyful Respite," *Washington Post*, August 19, 2004.
26. Tom Phillips, "Brazil Announces Troop Pullout of Haiti," *Guardian*, September 30, 2011.
27. Mark Doyle, "Haiti Cholera Epidemic 'Most Likely' Started at UN Camp—Top Scientist," BBC News, October 22, 2012, www.bbc .co.uk/news/world-latin-america-20024400; *BBC News*, "Haiti Protestor Shot Dead by UN Peacekeepers," November 16, 2010, www.bbc .co.uk/news/world-latin-america-20024400.
28. Taylor Barnes, "Brazil's Bolsa Família: Welfare Model or Menace?" *Christian Science Monitor*, November 17, 2013.
29. Anderson, "Lula's Brazil."
30. Ibid.
31. Ibid.
32. Ibid.
33. Ibid.
34. Ibid.
35. Andre Soliani and Helder Marinho, "Brazil's Pre-Salt May Hold 25–100 Billion Barrels," *Bloomberg News*, September 29, 2009.
36. James Petras, "Don't Cry for Lula: The Politics of a Decaying Workers' Regime," blog post, July 30, 2005, http://petras.lahaine.org/?p=26.
37. Anderson, "Lula's Brazil."
38. Ibid.
39. Beth McLoughlin, "Rio Lawmaker Marcelo Freixo 'to Flee' Rio after Threats," BBC News, November 1, 2011, www.bbc.co.uk/news/world -latin-america-15466647.
40. Ibid.
41. Max Ajl, "Brazil: New Challenge from the Left?" North American Congress on Latin America website, February 23, 2009, http://nacla.org /news/brazil-new-challenge-left.
42. *The Dark Knight*, Warner Brothers, directed by Christopher Nolan, 2008.
43. Anderson, "Lula's Brazil."
44. *Economist*, "Has Brazil Blown It?"
45. *Economist*, "A Rough Ride for Rousseff," September 28, 2013, http://www

.economist.com/news/special-report/21586677-much-could-still-change
-year-next-election-rough-ride-rousseff.

46. Robert M. Levine, "Sport and Society: The Case of Brazilian *Futebol*," *Luso-Brazilian Review* 17, no. 2 (Winter 1980): 233–52.

47. Associated Press, "Reagan 'Burned' During Toast," December 2, 1982.

Chapter 4

1. Eduardo Galeano, *Soccer in Sun and Shadow* (New York: Nation Books, 2013), 31.

2. Alex Bellos, *Futebol: The Brazilian Way of Life* (London: Bloomsbury, 2009), 27–28.

3. Ibid.

4. BBC News, "Census Records Show Scot 'Started Football in Brazil,'" March 27, 2011, www.bbc.co.uk/news/uk-scotland-12874090.

5. Bellos, *Futebol,* 29.

6. Ibid.

7. Ibid.

8. Ibid., 32.

9. Ibid.

10. Ibid., 33.

11. Bellos, "On a Glorious Bender," *Guardian*, April 27, 2002, www.theguardian.com/football/2002/apr/27/sport.features.

12. Bellos, *Futebol,* 33.

13. Quoted in Bellos, *Futebol,* 40.

14. Bellos, *Futebol,* 34.

15. Ibid., 45.

16. Ibid.

17. Ibid., 54.

18. Ibid., 101.

19. Ibid., 56.

20. Ibid., 97.

21. Alex Bellos, "For 50 Years One Moment Has Haunted Brazil. Why?" *Guardian*, July 15, 2000, www.theguardian.com/football/2000/jul/15/newsstory.sport.

22. Quoted in Bellos, *Futebol,* 111.

23. Goldblatt, *Ball Is Round,* 370.

24. Ibid., 380.

25. Levine, "Sport and Society."

26. Ibid.

27. Ibid.

28. Goldblatt, *Ball Is Round*, 380.

29. Ibid., 391.

30. Ibid., 381.

31. Ibid., 391.

32. Quoted in Goldblatt, *Ball Is Round*, 394. On Medici's tenure see Associated Press, "Brazil's Former President Medici Dies," *Los Angeles Times*, October 10, 1985, http://articles.latimes.com/1985-10-10/news/mn-15636 _1_southern-brazil.

33. Quoted in Kevin Foster, "Dreaming of Pelé: Football and Society in England and Brazil in the 1950s and 1960s," *Football Studies* 6, no. 1 (2003).

34. Levine, "Sport and Society."

35. Ibid.

36. Callum Fox, "Seleção Legend Romário Slams 'Imbecile' Pelé," *Sambafoot*, April 28, 2013, www.sambafoot.com/en/news/46232_selecao_legend _romario_slams__imbecile__pele.html.

37. Goldblatt, *Ball Is Round*, 792.

38. Levine, "Sport and Society."

39. Richard Sandomir, "Turning Pelé's Appeal into Profit," *New York Times*, June 22, 2006, www.nytimes.com/2006/06/22/sports/22iht-wcpele .html?_r=0.

40. Todd Benson, "Brazilians Mock Pelé Appeal to End Protests," Reuters, June 20, 2013, http://uk.reuters.com/article/2013/06/20/uk-brazil-protests -pele-idUKBRE95J03O20130620.

41. Goldblatt, *Ball Is Round*, 792.

42. Bellos, *Futebol*, 112.

43. Ibid., 346.

44. Quoted in Bellos, *Futebol*, 346.

45. Quoted in Goldblatt, *Ball Is Round*, 794.

46. The following passage is adapted from Dave Zirin and Zach Zill, "The Death of Sócrates," *Nation*, December 12, 2011, www.thenation.com/article/165098 /death-socrates-celebrating-sportspolitics-soccer-legend.

47. Quoted in Goldblatt, *Ball Is Round*, 632.

48. Alex Bellos, "Sócrates: 'Everyone Who Comes to Brazil Falls in Love with Someone,'" *Guardian*, June 12, 2010, www.theguardian.com/theobserver /2010/jun/13/socrates-brazil-football-world-cup.

49. Ibid.

50. It must be noted that with the play of the great Neymar, many are saying

that Brazil is trending back toward the beautiful—although it is an open discussion.

51. Interview with Sócrates in Bellos, *Futebol,* 361.
52. Ibid.
53. Carmen Rial, "Women's Soccer in Brazil: Invisible but Under Pressure," Re-Vista: Harvard Review of Latin America (Spring 2012), http://revista .drclas.harvard.edu/publications/revistaonline/spring-2012/womens-soccer -brazil.
54. Jason Margolis, "The Struggle for Female Soccer Equality in Brazil," radio interview with transcript, Public Radio International, May 27, 2013, http://pri.org/stories/2013-05-27/struggle-female-soccer-equality-brazil.
55. Rial, "Women's Soccer in Brazil."
56. Ibid.
57. Ibid.
58. Galeano, *Soccer in Sun and Shadow,* 6.
59. FIFA website, "Marta Vieira da Silva," 2014, www.fifa.com/worldcup /organisation/ambassador/marta.html.
60. Bellos, *Futebol,* 126.
61. Ibid., 141.
62. CNN.com, "Another Black Eye for Brazil Ahead of World Cup as Foot-ballers Protest," November 15, 2013, http://edition.cnn.com/2013/11/15 /sport/football/brazil-football-crossing-arms-protests.
63. Ibid.
64. Bellos, *Futebol,* 21.
65. Quoted in Bellos, *Futebol,* 21.
66. Bellos, *Futebol,* 340.
67. Ilan Stavans, *Fútbol* (Westport, CT: Greenwood Press, 2011), 78.
68. Quoted in Eduardo Galeano, "The Finest Liars in the World," *Tom Dis-patch,* August 14, 2003, www.tomdispatch.com/blog/886/tomgram%3A __eduardo_galeano_on_champion_liars/print.

Chapter 5

1. Douglas Hartmann, *Race, Culture, and the Revolt of the Black Athlete: The 1968 Olympic Protests and Their Aftermath* (Chicago: University of Chicago Press, 2004), 171. Some material in this chapter is drawn from Dave Zirin, "The Ghosts of Olympics Past," in *China's Great Leap: The Beijing Games and Olympian Human Rights,* edited by Minky Worden (Boston: Seven Stories Press, 2008), 73–84.

2. Simon Kuper and Stefan Szymanski, *Soccernomics* (New York: Nation Books, 2009), 287.

3. Associated Press, "Sepp Blatter: Brazil Protesters Shouldn't 'Use Football,'" June 19, 2013, http://sportsillustrated.cnn.com/soccer/news/20130619 /brazil-protests-confederations-cup-sepp-blatter.ap.

4. Jules Boykoff, "What Is the Real Price of the London Olympics?" *Guardian*, April 4, 2012, www.theguardian.com/commentisfree/2012/apr /04/price-of-london-olympics.

5. Ibid.

6. Quoted in Howard Zinn, *A People's History of the United States: 1492–Present* (New York: Harper Perennial, 2005), 292.

7. Quoted in Thierry Terret and J. A. Mangan, *Sport, Militarism and the Great War* (New York: Routledge, 2010), 95.

8. Avery Brundage archive, University of Illinois, Box 250, Reel 144.

9. Allen Guttmann, *The Olympics: A History of the Modern Games* (Champaign: University of Illinois Press, 2002), 56.

10. Jeremy Schaap, *Triumph: The Untold Story of Jesse Owens and Hitler's Olympics* (New York: Houghton Mifflin, 2008), 72.

11. Quoted in Schaap, *Triumph,* 124.

12. Brett Popplewell, "Torch Run: Peace or Propaganda?" *Toronto Star*, April 12, 2008, www.thestar.com/news/world/2008/04/12/torch_run_peace_or _propaganda.html.

13. Chris Bowlby, "The Olympic Torch's Shadowy Past," BBC News, April 5, 2008, http://news.bbc.co.uk/2/hi/7330949.stm.

14. Ibid.

15. Schaap, *Triumph,* 76.

16. Quoted in Schaap, *Triumph,* 161.

17. Ibid., 153.

18. George Orwell, "The Sporting Spirit," 1945, available at http://orwell.ru /library/articles/spirit/english/e_spirit.

19. John Carlos and Dave Zirin, *The John Carlos Story: The Sports Moment that Changed the World* (Chicago: Haymarket Books, 2011), 83.

20. Jan Stradling, *More than a Game: When Sport and History Collide* (St. Leonards, NSW, Australia: Pier 9, 2009), 71.

21. Christopher A. Shaw, *Five-Ring Circus: Myths and Realities of the Olympic Games* (Gabriola Island, BC: New Society Publishers, 2008), 65.

22. Dave Zirin, *Welcome to the Terrordome: The Pain, Politics, and Promise of Sports* (Chicago: Haymarket Books, 2007), 129.

23. Ibid., 129.

24. For a full treatment, read Andrew Jennings, *Foul! The Secret World of FIFA* (New York: HarperSport, 2006).

25. Kurt Badenhausen, "Mayweather Tops List of the World's 100 Highest-Paid Athletes," *Forbes*, June 18, 2012, www.forbes.com/sites/kurtbadenhausen /2012/06/18/mayweather-tops-list-of-the-worlds-100-highest-paid -athletes.

26. Galeano, *Soccer in Sun and Shadow*, 37.

27. Ibid.

28. Ibid., 95.

29. Ibid., 145.

30. Christopher R. Hill, *Olympic Politics* (Manchester, UK: Manchester University Press, 1992), 64.

31. Ali Abunimah, "Sepp Blatter Feeling Heat over UEFA Under 21 in Israel," *Electronic Intifada*, December 23, 2012, http://electronicintifada.net/blogs /ali-abunimah/fifa-boss-sepp-blatter-feeling-heat-over-uefa-u21-israel -promises-rebuild-bombed.

32. Jonathan Liew, "England at the World Cup: Dirt, Drama and Defeat in 1950," *Telegraph*, October 19, 2013, http://www.telegraph.co.uk/sport /football/teams/england/10390871/England-at-the-World-Cup-Dirt -drama-and-defeat-in-1950.html.

33. Marco Impiglia, "Mussolini and the 1934 FIFA World Cup: England v. Italy," presentation at the Relevance and Impact of World Cups 1930– 2010 Conference, Zurich, April 25, 2013.

34. Robert S. C. Gordon and John London, "Italy 1934: Football and Fascism," in *National Identity and Global Sports Events: Culture, Politics, and Spectacle*, edited by Alan Tomlinson and Christopher Young (Binghamton, NY: SUNY Press, 2006), 50; Associated Press, "Did Dictators Fix World Cup Title for Italy, Argentina?" *NDTV Sports Football* (blog), April 25, 2010, http://sports.ndtv.com/football/news/206855-did-dictators-fix-world-cup -title-for-italy-argentina.

35. Impilia, "Mussolini and the 1934 FIFA World Cup."

36. Robin Hackett, "First XI: World Cup Quotes," *ESPN Soccernet*, May 20, 2010, http://espnfc.com/world-cup/columns/story?id=785678&cc=5901 &ver=us.

37. Galeano, *Soccer in Sun and Shadow*, 153.

38. David Winner, "But Was This the Beautiful Game's Ugliest Moment?" *Financial Times*, June 21, 2008, www.ft.com/cms/s/0/e6347c16-3f2a-11dd -8fd9-0000779fd2ac.html#axzz2sCmeCuF4.

39. Martin Rogers, "Argentina's 1978 World Cup Win against Peru Was Fixed

in a Brutal Political Deal, Former Senator Says," Yahoo Sports, February 11, 2012, http://ca.sports.yahoo.com/soccer/news?slug=ro-rogers_argentina _peru_fixing_scandal_world_cup_021012.

40. Associated Press, "Dictators Said to Fix Italy, Argentina WCup Titles," April 25, 2013, http://sports.espn.go.com/espn/wire?section=soccer&id=9210733; Rogers, "Argentina's 1978 World Cup Win."

41. Associated Press, "Dictators Said to Fix Italy, Argentina WCup Titles."

Chapter 6

1. Galeano, *Open Veins of Latin America*, 2.

2. Much of this section is based on my article "Olympic-Sized Horror in Greece," originally published in *Common Dreams*, August 16, 2004, http://www.commondreams.org/views04/0816-12.htm.

3. Ibid.

4. Ibid.

5. Mark Golden, *Greek Sport and Social Status* (Austin: University of Texas Press, 2008), 135.

6. Ibid., 135.

7. *Democracy Now!*, "Crackdown on Homeless, Refugees and Prisoners in Athens," August 10, 2004, http://www.democracynow.org/2004/8/10 /headlines#8107.

8. BBC News, "Greek Group 'Behind Athens Bombs,'" May 13, 2004, http:// news.bbc.co.uk/2/hi/europe/3710371.stm.

9. Ibid.

10. John Clarke, "Olympics... The Other Greek Tragedy," *Forbes*, February 15, 2012, www.forbes.com/sites/johnclarke/2012/02/15/olympics-the-other -greek-tragedy.

11. Some material in this section is drawn from Zirin, "The Ghosts of Olympics Past."

12. Xinhua News, "IOC Chief: Beijing Olympics 'Glorious Days' to 'Cherish Forever,'" August 24, 2008, http://news.xinhuanet.com/english/2008-08 /24/content_9691378.htm.

13. Thomas Boswell, "They Made the Buses Run on Time," *Washington Post*, August 25, 2008, www.washingtonpost.com/wp-dyn/content/article/2008 /08/24/AR2008082400603.html.

14. Mark Magnier, "Many Eyes Will Watch Visitors," *Los Angeles Times*, August 7, 2008, http://articles.latimes.com/2008/aug/07/world/fg-snoop7.

15. Human Rights Watch, "China: Hosting Olympics a Catalyst for Human

Rights Abuses," August 23, 2008, www.hrw.org/news/2008/08/21/china
-hosting-olympics-catalyst-human-rights-abuses.

16. Ibid.

17. Some material in this section is drawn from Dave Zirin, "As Olympics
    Near, People in Vancouver Are Dreading Games," *Sports Illustrated*, blog
    post, January 25, 2010, http://sportsillustrated.cnn.com/2010/writers
    /dave_zirin/01/25/vancouver/index.html#ixzz2r4woHBJX; Dave Zirin, "The
    Vancouver Olympic Blues," *Edge of Sports*, January 27, 2010, www
    .edgeofsports.com/2010-01-27-494; and Dave Zirin, "When Snow Melts:
    Vancouver's Olympic Crackdown," *Nation*, February 9, 2010, www.thenation
    .com/blog/when-snow-melts-vancouver%E2%80%99s-olympic-crackdown#.

18. Greg Bishop, "Vancouver's Former Mayor Remains Face of the Games,"
    New York Times, January 1, 2010, www.nytimes.com/2010/01/31/sports
    /olympics/31sullivan.html?pagewanted=all.

19. Doug Ward, "Support for Olympics on the Decline in B.C.: Poll," *Van-
    couver Sun*, January 21, 2010.

20. CBC News, "U.S. Journalist Grilled at Canada Border Crossing," Novem-
    ber 26, 2009, http://www.cbc.ca/news/canada/british-columbia/u-s-jour-
    nalist-grilled-at-canada-border-crossing-1.801755. See also Amy
    Goodman and Denis Moynihan's book *The Silenced Majority* (Chicago:
    Haymarket Books, 2012), 272–73.

21. Some material in this section is drawn from Dave Zirin, "'At Least Under
    Apartheid': South Africa on the Eve of the World Cup," *Huffington Post*,
    June 10, 2010, www.huffingtonpost.com/dave-zirin/at-least-under-
    apartheid_b_607823.html, and Dave Zirin, "The South Africa World
    Cup: Invictus in Reverse," *Huffington Post*, March 10, 2010, www
    .huffingtonpost.com/dave-zirin/the-south-africa-world-cu_b_493802.html.

22. Simon Kuper, "The World Cup Is No Economic Boon for South Africa,"
    Financial Times, November 28, 2009, www.ft.com/intl/cms/s/0
    /2911d7f6-dbbd-11de-9424-00144feabdc0.html#axzz1x7TYE4gb.

23. Oliver Harvey, "Homeless and Away," *Sun* (London), April 19, 2010,
    www.thesun.co.uk/sol/homepage/features/2936217/Tin-Can-Town
    -next-to-South-Africa-World-Cup-stadium.html.

24. David Smith, "Life in 'Tin Can Town' for the South Africans Evicted
    Ahead of World Cup," *Guardian*, April 1, 2010, www.guardian.co.uk
    /world/2010/apr/01/south-africa-world-cup-blikkiesdorp.

25. Sapa, "Mpumalanga ANC Distances Itself from Hit List," *Politics Web*, Feb-
    ruary 10, 2010, http://www.politicsweb.co.za/politicsweb/view/politicsweb
    /en/page71619?oid=159819&sn=Detail.

26. Government of South Africa, "National Flag," government website, March 16, 2009, www.info.gov.za/aboutgovt/symbols/flag.htm.

27. Daniel Bloom and Dave Zirin, "World Cup Hangover Hits South Africa," *Nation*, September 14, 2010, www.thenation.com/article/154706/world -cup-hangover-hits-south-africa#.

28. Barry Bearak, "Cost of Stadium Reveals Tensions in South Africa," *New York Times*, March 12, 2010.

29. Wikiquote, "Leymah Gbowee," Junne 29, 2013, http://en.wikiquote.org /wiki/Leymah_Gbowee.

30. Kate Griffiths, "1.3 Million Public Workers Strike to Confront South Africa's Inequalities," *Labor Notes*, September 8, 2010, http://labornotes.org/2010 /09/13-million-public-workers-strike-confront-south -africas-inequalities.

31. William Ernest Henley, "Invictus," 1875. Available at the Poetry Foundation website: www.poetryfoundation.org/poem/182194.

32. Some material in this section is drawn from Jules Boykoff and Dave Zirin, "Protest Is Coming to the London Olympics," *Nation*, May 21, 2012, www.thenation.com/blog/167979/protest-coming-london-olympics, and Dave Zirin, "'Drones, Missiles and Gunships, Oh My!' Welcome to the 2012 London Olympics," *Nation*, May 14, 2012, www.thenation.com /blog/167874/drones-missiles-and-gunships-oh-my-welcome-2012 -london-olympics.

33. Ed Howker, "London 2012 Olympics: The Five Questions We Really Need Answered," *Guardian*, May 7, 2012, www.theguardian.com /commentisfree/2012/may/07/london-2012-olympics-five-questions ?cat=commentisfree&type=article&view=mobile.

34. Stephen Graham, "Olympics 2012 Security: Welcome to Lockdown London," *Guardian*, March 12, 2012, www.theguardian.com/sport/2012/mar /12/london-olympics-security-lockdown-london.

35. Ibid.

36. Ibid.

37. Greg McNeal, "London Olympics Security Focuses On Deterrence: Use Of Drones, Electric Fences, Missiles And More," *Forbes*, July 23, 2012, www.forbes.com/sites/gregorymcneal/2012/07/23/london-olympics-security -focuses-on-deterrence-use-of-drones-electric-fences-missiles-and-more.

38. Graham, "Olympics 2012 Security."

39. Michael Joseph Gross, "Jumping through Hoops," *Vanity Fair*, June 2012, www.vanityfair.com/culture/2012/06/international-olympic-committee -london-summer-olympics.

40. Sandra Laville, "Olympics Welcome Does Not Extend to All in London

as Police Flex Muscles," *Guardian*, May 4, 2012, www.theguardian.com /uk/2012/may/04/olympics-welcome-london-police.

41. Reuters, "Final Cost of London 2012 Games Revealed," October 23, 2012, http://uk.eurosport.yahoo.com/news/london-2012-final-cost-london-2012 -games-revealed-135956051.html.

42. Some material in this section is drawn from Dave Zirin, "Boycott Sochi?" *Grantland*, August 1, 2013, http://grantland.com/features/gay-rights -sochi-boycott-movement.

43. ESPN.com, "Putin Camp: Kraft's Story 'Weird,'" June 17, 2013, http://espn.go.com/boston/nfl/story/_/id/9392090/vladimir-putin-denies -stealing-new-england-patriots-owner-robert-kraft-super-bowl-ring.

44. Ibid.

45. Elizabeth Shockman, Denis Dyomkin, and Alissa de Carbonnel, "Olympic-Sized Corruption Plagues Sochi Winter Games, Report Claims," Reuters, http://worldnews.nbcnews.com/_news/2013/05/30 /18631119-olympic-sized-corruption-plagues-sochi-winter-games-report -claims?lite.

46. Simon Shuster, "Fortress Sochi: Russia's Security Plan Risks Killing the Olympic Spirit," *TIME*, January 7, 2014, http://world.time.com/2014/01 /07/fortress-sochi-russias-security-plan-risks-the-killing-olympic-spirit /#ixzz2qd0a9y4A.

47. Joshua Yaffa, "The Waste and Corruption of Vladimir Putin's 2014 Winter Olympics," *Businessweek*, January 2, 2014, www.businessweek.com /articles/2014-01-02/the-2014-winter-olympics-in-sochi-cost-51-billion.

48. Timothy Hopkins and Maxim Shemtov, "High Stakes for Putin as His Olympic Dream Nears," Reuters, October 9, 2013, www.reuters.com /article/2013/10/09/us-olympics-russia-idUSBRE9980EC20131009.

49. Associated Press, "Sochi Games Run-Up a Hotbed of Corruption: Kremlin Critic," May 30, 2013, www.cbc.ca/sports/olympics/sochi-games-run -up-a-hotbed-of-corruption-kremlin-critic-1.1368218.

50. Katie McDonough, "First Tourists Arrested under Russia's Ban on 'Gay Propaganda,'" *Salon*, July 22, 2013, www.salon.com/2013/07/22/first_tourists _arrested_under_russias_ban_on_gay_propaganda; Cavan Sieczkowski, "Dutch Tourists Jailed under Russia's 'Gay Propaganda' Law," *Huffington Post*, July 24, 2013, www.huffingtonpost.com/2013/07/22/dutch-tourists -jailed-russia-gay_n_3635803.html.

51. BBC News, "Arrests over 'Anti-Gay' Murder in Volgograd Russia," May 13, 2013, www.bbc.co.uk/news/world-europe-22509019.

52. Thomas Grove and Steve Gutterman, "Russia's Gays Fear More Violence

234 **Dave Zirin**

after Brutal Murder," *Reuters*, May 13, 2013, www.reuters.com/article/2013/05/13/us-russia-gay-idUSBRE94C0AX20130513.

53. Russia Today, "Nobody Will Face Discrimination at Sochi Olympics, Putin Pledges," January 16, 2014, http://rt.com/news/putin-sochi-olympics-discrimination-709.

54. Harvey Fierstein, "Russia's Anti-Gay Crackdown," *New York Times*, July 21, 2013, www.nytimes.com/2013/07/22/opinion/russias-anti-gay-crackdown.html.

55. Pete Pattisson, "Revealed: Qatar's World Cup 'Slaves,'" *Guardian*, September 25, 2013, www.theguardian.com/world/2013/sep/25/revealed-qatars-world-cup-slaves.

56. Ibid.

57. Robert Booth, "Qatar World Cup Construction 'Will Leave 4,000 Migrant Workers Dead,'" *Guardian*, September 26, 2013, www.theguardian.com/global-development/2013/sep/26/qatar-world-cup-migrant-workers-dead.

58. Rachel Czyszczewski, "Squatter's Rights: The Basics," *Rio on Watch*, October 7, 2011, http://rioonwatch.org/?p=1987.

Chapter 7

1. Galeano, *Open Veins of Latin America*, 64.

2. Czyszczewski, "Squatter's Rights."

3. Fiona Hurrell, "Rio Favela Population Largest in Brazil," *Rio Times*, December 23, 2011, http://riotimesonline.com/brazil-news/rio-politics/rios-favela-population-largest-in-brazil/#.

4. McCann, *Hard Times in the Marvelous City*, 35.

5. Tom Phillips, "Rio World Cup Demolitions Leave Favela Families Trapped in Ghost Town," *Guardian*, April 26, 2011, www.theguardian.com/world/2011/apr/26/favela-ghost-town-rio-world-cup.

6. Ibid.

7. Ibid.

8. Matthew Elliot, "Vila Autódromo Community Avoids Eviction," *Rio Times*, August 13, 2013, http://riotimesonline.com/brazil-news/rio-politics/vila-autodromo-community-avoids-eviction.

9. Malte Warburg Sørensen, "Mega Events in Rio de Janeiro—The Case of Vila Autódromo: Community Planning as Resistance to Forced Evictions," master's thesis, Roskilde University (Roskilde, Denmark), 2013, www.academia.edu/3005429/Mega_Events_in_Rio_de_Janeiro_-_The_Case_of_Vila_Autodromo_Community_Planning_as_Resistance_to_Forced_Evictions.

10. See also Erica Tapley, "The Story of Dona Rita," *Rio on Watch*, September 24, 2012, http://rioonwatch.org/?p=5199.

Conclusion

1. Dave Zirin, "Eduardo Galeano Speaks Out on Brazil's World Cup Protests," *Nation*, June 26, 2013, www.thenation.com/blog/174999 /eduardo-galeano-speaks-out-brazils-world-cup-protests.

2. Wright Thompson, "Generation June," *ESPN: The Magazine*, December 5, 2013, http://espn.go.com/espn/feature/story/_/id/10079392 /generation-june.

3. Samantha Pearson, "Brazil: Can a Marketing Strategy Be Too Successful?" *Financial Times*, September 23, 2013, www.ft.com/intl/cms/s/0/439afd42 -1b96-11e3-b678-00144feab7de.html#axzz2qzYKavfi.

4. Jonathan Watts, "Brazil Protests Erupt over Public Services and World Cup Costs," *Guardian*, June 18, 2013, www.theguardian.com/world/2013 /jun/18/brazil-protests-erupt-huge-scale.

5. Yuseph Katiya and Simon Benoit-Guyod, "Transport Fee Hikes and Police Repression Inspire Protests across Brazil," *Media Co-Op*, June 17, 2013, www.mediacoop.ca/story/transport-fee-hikes-and-police-repression-inspire /18018.

6. Shasta Darlington, "Protesters, Police Clash in Demonstration against Bus Fare Increases in Brazil," CNN.com, June 14, 2013, www.cnn.com/2013 /06/14/world/americas/brazil-fare-protests.

7. Vanessa Barbara, "Brazil's Vinegar Uprising," *New York Times*, June 21, 2013, www.nytimes.com/2013/06/22/opinion/brazils-vinegar-uprising.html.

8. Chris Gaffney, private email communication, June 17, 2013, quoted with permission.

9. Paul Szoldra, "Protests Spreading across Brazil Are Getting Ugly," *Business Insider*, June 17, 2013, www.businessinsider.com/protests-are-spreading-across -brazil-and-theyre-getting-ugly-2013-6; Todd Benson and Asher Levine, "Protests Build in Brazil as Discontent Spreads," Reuters, June 17, 2013, www .reuters.com/article/2013/06/17/us-brazil-protests-idUSBRE95G15S20130617.

10. Yuseph Katiya, private communication, June 2013.

11. Dave Zirin, "Mass World Cup Protests Rock Brazil," *Nation*, June 18, 2013, www.thenation.com/blog/174844/we-want-health-and-education -world-cup-out-mass-protests-rock-brazil.

12. David Kent, "Brazil President Rousseff Defends Public Spending on World Cup as Protests Continue," *Daily Mail*, June 22, 2013; FoxSports.com, "FIFA

shows Support in Brazil WC Plans," June 22, 2013, http://msn.foxsports
.com/foxsoccer/worldcup/story/fifa-has-confidence-that-brazil-can-host
-world-cup-2014-despite-protests-062213.

13. Associated Press, "Sepp Blatter."

14. Associated Press, "Romário, Ronaldo at Odds over Brazil World Cup,"
     July 11, 2013, http://bigstory.ap.org/article/romario-ronaldo-odds-over
     -brazil-world-cup.

15. Tom Etherton, "Brazil-Mexico: Neymar Voices Support for Protests,"
     Sambafoot, June 19, 2013, www.sambafoot.com/en/news/48748_brazil
     -mexico__neymar_voices_support_for_protests.html

16. Reuters, "Neymar Stars as Brazil Triumphs at Confederations Cup," *New
     York Times*, June 20, 2013, www.nytimes.com/2013/06/20/sports/soccer
     /neymar-stars-as-brazil-triumphs-at-confederations-cup.html.

17. Luiz Inácio Lula da Silva, "The Message of Brazil's Youth," *New York
     Times*, July 16, 2013, www.nytimes.com/2013/07/17/opinion/global/lula
     -da-silva-the-message-of-brazils-youth.html.

18. Tariq Panja, "World Cup Organizers Tell Brazil Protestors Event Creates
     Jobs," *Businessweek*, June 24, 2013, http://www.businessweek.com/news
     /2013-06-24/world-cup-organizers-tell-brazil-protestors-event-creates-jobs.

19. John Lyons and Paul Kiernan, "Middle-Class Brazil Finds Its Voice in
     Protests," *Wall Street Journal*, June 19, 2013, http://online.wsj.com/news
     /articles/SB10001424127887324021104578553491848777544?mg=reno64-
     wsj&url=http%3A%2F%2Fonline.wsj.com%2Farticle%2FSB1000142412788
     7324021104578553491848777544.html.

20. Associated Press, "Brazilian Leaders Reverse Bus and Subway Fare Hikes,"
     USA Today, June 19, 2013, www.usatoday.com/story/news/world/2013
     /06/19/brazil-protests-bus-subway-fare/2440287.

21. Gibson and Watts, "Brazil Plans 'World Cup Courts.'"

22. Luca Persico, "Romário: 'There's No Good Schools, There's No Good Hos-
     pitals—How Can There Be a World Cup?'" Reuters, in *Sambafoot*, Octo-
     ber 17, 2013, www.sambafoot.com/en/news/53063_romario_____there
     ___s_no_good_schools__there___s_no_good_hospitals_____
     how_can_there_be_a_world_cup_____.html.

23. Quoted in Ivone Gebara, *Longing for Running Water: Ecofeminism and
     Liberation* (Minneapolis: Fortress Press, 1999), 25.

Index

About the Author

© Michele Bollinger

Dave Zirin is the author of five books, including *Game Over, Bad Sports, A People's History of Sports in the United States, Welcome to the Terrordome,* and *What's My Name, Fool?* and is the coauthor, with John Carlos, of *The John Carlos Story.* He writes the popular weekly sports blog *Edge of Sports* and is a regular contributor to *SportsIllustrated.com, SLAM,* the *Los Angeles Times,* and the *Nation,* where he is the publication's first sports editor.